U.S. STAMP YEARBOOK 1990

A comprehensive record of technical data, design development and stories behind all of the stamps, stamped envelopes, postal cards and souvenir cards issued by the United States Postal Service in 1990.

By
George Amick

Published by *Linn's Stamp News,* the largest and most informative stamp newspaper in the world. *Linn's* is owned by Amos Press, 911 Vandemark Road, Sidney, Ohio 45365. Amos Press also publishes *Scott Stamp Monthly* and the Scott line of catalogs.
Copyright 1991 by Linn's Stamp News.

033024

ISSN 0748-996X

With Gratitude . . .

As always, we have depended on the generous assistance of many people in assembling the facts and figures in this *Yearbook*. My associates at *Linn's* and I extend to them our thanks.

For the many concept sketches and other art-in-progress developed by the U.S. Postal Service in the creation of stamp and stationery designs, and for many hours of recollections as to how the stamps themselves and the designs came to be, we are indebted to Donald M. McDowell, director, Office of Stamp and Philatelic Marketing; Joe Brockert and Jack Williams, program managers, philatelic design, and Howard Paine, Dick Sheaff and Derry Noyes, design coordinators for the Citizens' Stamp Advisory Committee.

Invaluable production information was furnished by Joseph Y. Peng, general manager, USPS Stamp Manufacturing Division; Frank Thomas, Jim Murphy, Kim Parks, Bill Paine, John Spiehs, Mike O'Hara, Mike Doyle, Peter Papadopoulos and Gerald Griffin of USPS; Leonard Buckley, Peter Cocci, Ira Polikoff and Cecilia Hatfield of the Bureau of Engraving and Printing; George Whitman and Paul Martien of the Government Printing Office; Richard Sennett and Sandra Lane of Sennett Enterprises; Alan Green and Bob Birnbaum of Avery International; Marty Goodman of the Postal Buddy Corporation, and John Schmidt and Barry Levenson of Westvaco-USEnvelope Division.

Time, artwork and information were also generously shared by CSAC members Jack Rosenthal, Belmont Faries and Mary Ann Owens; stamp designers Tom Blackshear, Christopher Calle, John Dawson, Harry Devlin, Bart Forbes, Lunda Hoyle Gill, Michael Hagel, Jim Hautman, Howard Koslow, Jim M'Guinness, Pierre Mion, Chuck Ripper, M. Gregory Rudd and Libby Thiel; Norma Opgrand of the U.S. Fish and Wildlife Service, and Jim Bruns of the Smithsonian Institution's National Philatelic Collection.

For answering a multitude of questions and filling in a multitude of details, we thank Bruce Mosher of the Bureau Issues Association; Sandi Risser of Stanford University; Evelyn Meine and Susan Wade Dewey of the Chicago Symphony; Mrs. Eldred Martin Yochim, president general, Daughters of the American Revolution; Dr. Mardges Bacon of Northeastern University and the Society of Architectural Historians; Jay B. Griffin, curator, Isaac Royall House; Priscilla Goodwin, assistant curator, U.S. Supreme Court; Lydia Tederick of the White House curator's office; Leslie Morris of the Rosenbach Museum, Philadelphia; William M. Smith Jr. of the University of Arkansas; Tim Frystak of the Palos Heights, Illinois, Regional News; William Victor Kriebel of Philadelphia, and the stamp auction houses of Jacques C. Schiff Jr., William A. Fox and Aubrey Bartlett.

Thanks also to stamp writer Ken Lawrence for reading the manuscript and offering corrections and valuable suggestions.

Last but not least, thanks to my wife, Donna, whose computer expertise made the writing and editing of this book far simpler than it would have been if I had been obliged to solve the mysteries of word processing by myself.

George Amick

CONTENTS

Introduction —5

Commemoratives —7
25¢ Idaho Statehood, January 6 —8
25¢ Ida B. Wells, February 1 —16
25¢ U.S. Supreme Court, February 2 —21
25¢ Wyoming Statehood, February 23 —30
25¢ Classic Films block of four, March 23 —37
25¢ Marianne Moore, April 18 —49
$5 Lighthouses booklet, April 26 —56
25¢ Rhode Island Statehood, May 29 —66
25¢ Olympians strip of five, July 6 —75
$5 Indian Headdresses booklet, August 17 —91
25¢ Micronesia/Marshall Islands Compact, September 28 —101
25¢ Creatures of the Sea block of four, October 3 —112
25¢ Grand Canyon, Americas series, October 12 —123
25¢ Dwight D. Eisenhower Birth Centennial, October 13 —128

Special Stamps —137
25¢ Love sheet stamp, January 18 —138
$5 Love booklet, January 18 —146
25¢ Christmas Madonna and Child sheet stamp, October 18 —149
25¢ Christmas Madonna and Child booklet, October 18 —154
25¢ Christmas Greetings sheet stamp, October 18 —158
25¢ Christmas Greetings booklet, October 18 —162

Definitives —165
$3 Beach Umbrella booklet, February 3 —166
5¢ Luis Munoz Marin, February 18 —172
$1 Seaplane coil, April 20 —183
25¢ Flag ATM-vended sheetlet, May 18 —188
$2 Bobcat, June 1 —201
5¢ Circus Wagon coil, August 31 —206
40¢ Claire Lee Chennault, September 6 —210

Airmail Stamp —219
45¢ Caribbean Coastal Scene, Americas series —219

Migratory Bird Hunting —222
$12.50 Black-Bellied Whistling duck stamp, June 30 —222

Stamped Envelopes _228
45¢ Official Mail, March 17_229
65¢ Official Mail, March 17_232
45¢ Official Mail, self-sealing, August 10_233
65¢ Official Mail, self-sealing, August 10_236
25¢ Football hologram, September 9_238

Postal Cards_245
15¢ American Papermaking, March 13_246
15¢ Literacy, March 22_251
15¢ George Caleb Bingham, May 4_257
15¢ Isaac Royall House, June 16_264
15¢ Postal Buddy, July 5_271
15¢ Quad at Stanford, September 30_279
15¢ Constitution Hall-Memorial Continental Hall, October 11_286
15¢ Chicago Orchestra Hall, October 19_295

Souvenir Cards_301
Aripex 90, April 20_301
Stamp World London 90, May 3_304
Stampshow 90, August 23_307
Migratory Bird, June 30_310

Appendix_312
The Year in Review_312
Varieties_321
Plate numbers_331
Items withdrawn from sale in 1990_333
1989 first-day cover totals_334
Errata_335

INTRODUCTION

In 1990, two continuing and interrelated trends of great significance to collectors of U.S. stamps became more obvious than ever.

One is the determination of the U.S. Postal Service, in developing stamp products, to modernize and innovate, with greater efficiency and customer convenience as its goals. Donald M. McDowell's claim that USPS is taking the lead in "re-inventing the postage stamp" after 150 years is no idle boast.

The second trend is the growing reliance of USPS on cooperative efforts with private industry to generate stamp products. USPS justifies this move on several grounds, citing in particular lower costs, greater flexibility, and access to wider resources of research and development.

The two trends have already resulted in a variety of new items for stamp collectors to collect. Many more are just over the horizon.

These new items have raised, and will raise, novel questions to challenge the hobby. What constitutes a collectible unit of these stamps or cards or "what-is-its"? In what form should they be saved? How should they be stored and displayed? Collectors and dealers and catalog makers will ponder and debate such questions — but no one can say that USPS isn't making their lives interesting.

Here are some of the events of 1990 that will have long-term effects on stamp collecting:

- USPS and the Bureau of Engraving and Printing signed a five-year agreement setting forth the terms under which BEP will continue to supply postage stamps. Over this period, BEP will fill a decreasing percentage of Postal Service stamp needs.
- USPS "opened a dialogue with the private sector" by hosting a conference on stamp production attended by representatives of 44 different printers and paper suppliers, including some from overseas. Solicitations for stamp printing contracts covering all current stamp printing methods, including intaglio, were distributed.
- Several private companies made their debut as manufacturers and/or vendors of postal items for USPS. Two remarkable innovations were among the results of these arrangements.

One was a sheetlet of stamps made of "plastic" (actually, a polyester film), produced by a maker of pressure-sensitive labels for test-marketing through automatic teller machines by a Seattle bank. The other was a postal card printed on demand by a laser printer, created (under USPS supervision) by an entrepreneur who saw financial opportunity in a nomadic American population's need to notify people of changed addresses.

For all of that, USPS in 1990 also issued its share of conventional postal items and items that, if not exactly conventional, at least followed previously established precedents.

The year saw 60 new collectible varieties of stamps and stationery, not counting the Interior Department's annual duck stamp. That was the lowest total since the 55 that appeared in 1984.

The 1990 crop included old familiar types (statehood commemorative stamps, Transportation coils) and examples of genres still in their infancy (picture postal cards, a hologram envelope). Minor novelties included USPS' first self-adhesive stamped envelopes and the first Love stamp to appear in booklet form.

The only other significant new stamp developments in 1990 had to do with design policy. Designers and platemakers, on orders of Postmaster General Anthony M. Frank, began providing stamp users with some basic information on the often-unfamiliar deceased Americans whose faces look out at them from between the perforations. There was a feeling shared by many that this helpful new practice was long overdue.

And USPS introduced a new method of expressing denominations on low-value stamps. Rather than restore the "¢" sign or the "c" for cents, USPS began placing a zero in front of the single digit: 01 through 09 would henceforth represent 1¢ through 9¢.

In this, the eighth annual *Linn's U.S. Stamp Yearbook,* we offer the full story of each of the postal issues of 1990. There's also information on the 1990 duck stamp, on souvenir cards and on varieties discovered, plus a review of the highlights of the year in U.S. philately. We hope — as we always do — that you'll find the book useful and interesting. We at *Linn's* — as we always do — found it fascinating to put together.

COMMEMORATIVES

More than half of the 1990 postal items were commemorative stamps, not counting the single commemorative airmail that was also issued. But the trend in this category in the last three years has been one of relative restraint. There were 33 commemoratives in 1990, 37 in 1989 and 31 in 1988; for the five years preceding 1988, the annual average had been nearly 50.

A high proportion of 1990's commemoratives came in se-tenant multiples. There were two blocks of four, Classic Films and Creatures of the Sea. The latter was a joint issue with the Soviet Union. There were two different topical booklet panes of five different designs each, showing lighthouses and Indian headdresses, and one unprecedented sheet-stamp configuration, a horizontal strip of five, honoring U.S. Olympic champions.

There was also a horizontal se-tenant pair honoring the Republic of the Marshall Islands and the Federated States of Micronesia, produced as a joint issue with those two former trust territories.

The Constitution Bicentennial observance continued, but at a diminished level, with two stamps. There were single-stamp additions to the Black Heritage and Literary Arts series. The America series, part of an omnibus issue with other members of the Postal Union of the Americas and Spain, continued with a single first-class rate stamp, plus the aforementioned airmail. Finally, a long tradition of statehood anniversary stamps was continued with commemoratives for the centennials of Idaho and Wyoming. Dwight D. Eisenhower, like several other presidents before him, was honored on a major anniversary of his birth.

25¢ IDAHO STATEHOOD CENTENNIAL

Date of Issue: January 6, 1990

Catalog Number: Scott 2439

Colors: yellow, magenta, cyan, black and line red

First-Day Cancel: Boise, Idaho (Idaho Statehouse)

FDCs Canceled: 252,493

Format: Panes of 50, vertical, 10 across, 5 down. Gravure printing cylinders of 200 (10 across, 20 around) manufactured by Armotek Industries Inc., Palmyra, New Jersey

Perf: 10.9 (L perforator)

Selvage Markings: ©United States Postal Service 1990, Use Correct ZIP Code®

Designer: John Dawson of Sun Valley, Idaho

Art Director and Typographer: Howard Paine (CSAC)

Project Manager: Jack Williams (USPS)

Modeler: Richard Sennett (Sennett Enterprises) for American Bank Note Company

Printing: Stamps printed and sheeted out by American Bank Note Company on a leased Champlain gravure press (J.W. Fergusson and Sons, Richmond, Virginia) under the supervision of Sennett Enterprises (Fairfax, Virginia). Perforated, processed and shipped by ABNC (Chicago, Illinois).

Quantity Ordered: 173,000,000
Quantity Distributed: 173,000,000

Cylinder Number Detail: One group of five cylinder numbers preceded by the letter "A" over/under corner stamps.

Tagging: overall

The Stamp

In 1990, Idaho and Wyoming each was honored on the centennial of its statehood with a 25¢ commemorative stamp. It was the second round for them; back in 1940, each had received a 3¢ stamp for its 50th anniversary.

This 3¢ stamp depicting the Idaho state capitol was issued July 3, 1940, to mark the 50th anniversary of Idaho statehood. It was designed by BEP's William K. Schrage.

This "second helping" phenomenon promises to become increasingly common, as states that have been honored previously reach new milestones. It began in 1977, when Colorado, which had gotten a stamp for its 75th anniversary in 1951, got another one for its centennial (albeit a year late). Second-time statehood stamps were issued in 1986 for Arkansas and in 1987 for Michigan. Then, in 1989, four stamps were produced for the centennials of Montana, Washington, North Dakota and South Dakota. On their 50th anniversaries, back in 1939, the four states had been collectively honored with a single commemorative.

Idaho's centennial stamp was the first commemorative issue of 1990. It was printed for USPS by the American Bank Note Company and was dedicated January 6 in Boise, the state capital.

Idaho's peculiar shape, with its narrow northern panhandle, is the result of an almost random act of map-drawing. As historian F. Ross Peterson put it, "When Congress during the Civil War completed its geographical carving in the northern Rocky Mountains, it had no idea what it had done." From the old Oregon Country and the Territory of Washington, the lawmakers created the Idaho Territory, a tract larger than Texas.

After organizing and naming the territory in 1863 (the name Idaho, originally suggested for Colorado, is of unknown derivation), they chopped away at the eastern boundary until, by 1868, Wyoming and Montana were separate entities. For Idaho's eastern border, Congress created a rambling line that included a straight northward extension of the Utah border, a 200-mile swing along the Continental Divide, a veer to the northwest along the crest of the Bitterroot Mountains and then another straight line to Canada.

The Idaho that remained, wrote Peterson, "was an eccentrically shaped entity whose boundaries resembled a side view of a rustic, hand-carved church pew, or, as one humorist called it, 'a pregnant capital L.' John Corlett of Boise called it a crazy patchwork and postulated that geographically Idaho is a state that should not have been. Bordered by six other states and Canada, Idaho's unique geographical boundaries are another ramification of diversity."

Two major groups constituted most of the territory's early population: Mormons moving north from Brigham Young's Utah, and prospectors. In 1889 Idaho voters approved a proposed state constitution and forwarded it to Washington with a request for statehood. Republicans, who held a narrow majority in Congress, were more than willing to admit new states that would elect Republican representatives. According to historian Peterson, Speaker Thomas "Czar" Reed used underhanded maneuvers to get the Idaho admission act passed by the House, including declaring a quorum present even though Democrats refused to answer the roll call. The Senate also approved the bill, and on July 3, 1890, President Benjamin Harrison signed it into law, making Idaho the 43rd state.

The 50th anniversary stamp back in 1940 (Scott 896), depicting the state capitol in Boise, was issued on the actual anniversary date of July 3. Other than this commemorative, Idaho's representation on stamps has been slight. With the other 49 states, it was honored on the 1976 pane of 50 State Flags and the 1982 pane that pictured

Dawson's original four concept sketches in pencil showed a Nez Perce warrior on horseback beside a lake in central Idaho, an 1890s homestead with log cabin near the Salmon River, horse-drawn ore wagons passing in front of Devil's Bedstead Mountain in the Pioneer range, and a mill built for smelting operations in the Bayhorse district.

state birds and flowers. The 12th Boy Scout World Jamboree, held at Farragut State Park in August 1967, was marked by a 6¢ airmail postal card (Scott UXC7).

The Design

Howard Paine, the design coordinator for the Citizens' Stamp Advisory Committee who served as art director for the Idaho stamp, asked an Idaho artist, John Dawson of Sun Valley, to submit concept sketches. Dawson prepared four pencil drawings.

Two horizontals depicted an 1890s homestead with log cabin near the Salmon River and horse-drawn ore wagons passing in front of Devil's Bedstead Mountain in the Pioneer range. Two verticals showed a Nez Perce Indian warrior on horseback beside a lake with a mountain in the background — this was Dawson's own favorite — and mill buildings at an old silver mine.

The CSAC members preferred the mining camp scene, and Dawson did a finished painting in late 1988. Howard Paine designed a

Dawson based his sketch of the mining mill on this cover photograph from an issue of Idaho Yesterdays.

11

typographical frame for it, with the word IDAHO in bright red poster-type capitals across the top and USA 25 1890 across the bottom. Dawson's design source was a photograph on the cover of the Summer 1983 issue of *Idaho Yesterdays,* the quarterly journal of the Idaho Historical Society. It showed the 1880s-vintage mill buildings on a steep hillside in the Bayhorse district of central Idaho, on the eastern front of the Salmon River Mountains, as they appeared in 1972. Using artistic license, Dawson added some beehive-shaped charcoal kilns of the kind used in 19th-century smelting operations. In a further afterthought, he placed blossoms of syringa, the Idaho state flower, in the foreground.

However, Bureau officials said the picture contained too much detail for effective reproduction on their combination offset-intaglio D press. Dawson tried to simplify the painting, particularly in the background, but couldn't fix what BEP saw as the basic problem.

Meanwhile, the Postal Service was coming under heavy criticism from officials of another state whose centennial had just been postally commemorated. North Dakotans, including the governor and lieutenant governor, disliked the design USPS had chosen for the North Dakota stamp. Officials of the state hadn't been consulted about the design — a grain elevator on a prairie — and were further offended that the painting was by a New York City artist. Because of this adverse reaction, Postmaster General Anthony M. Frank decreed that future statehood stamp designs must be approved in advance by the governor of the state involved.

This sketch illustrated the Idaho Centennial Commission's idea for a se-tenant block of four statehood commemorative stamps.

In that spirit, Postal Service officials took another look at a proposal they had received in April 1987 from the Idaho Statehood Centennial Commission for a se-tenant block of four Idaho stamps. The proposal, accompanied by sketches, had called for stamps showing white-water rafting, a skier, a scene in Idaho's National Birds of Prey Refuge and a mountain bluebird, the state bird of Idaho, superimposed on an outline map of the state. A block of four stamps was out of the question, but Paine showed John Dawson the sketches and asked him to see what he could make of these or similar ideas as subjects for a single. Dawson made four quick, rough paintings, at about 2½ times stamp size rather than the normal "five times up." One of these was of the Centennial Commission's mountain bluebird, seated on a fencepost, against a backdrop of the state's Sawtooth Mountains at sunset.

John Dawson prepared these quick paint sketches after his original finished painting was turned down because BEP concluded it wouldn't print satisfactorily. As Dawson labeled them, they are "skiers," "late evening fisherman," "fields of wildflowers in a mountain meadow" and "Idaho bluebird at sunset."

By now, it was midsummer of 1989, and the lead time for preparing the stamp had mostly evaporated. The committee approved the bluebird as what one member termed "the safest way to go." Howard Paine suggested some changes in Dawson's bluebird sketch, however. His concern, he told the artist, was that the background, which Paine called a "Gauguin mix" of green, yellow, red and black, with strong shapes of light and dark, would be confusing to the viewer at stamp size unless the bird could be separated clearly from the scene. He liked the sunset idea, Paine said, but only if the whole scene was pink or gold or yellow.

Eventually, Dawson abandoned the sunset and put the scene in broad daylight, which allowed use of a light background that contrasted strongly with the dark blue of the bird's plumage. The background consisted of a section of the snowy Sawtooth range above Stanley Lake, which he adapted from a photograph he found

Dawson turned his mill sketch into this finished painting after it was approved by the Citizens' Stamp Advisory Committee, placing charcoal kilns in the mid-ground and, later, adding syringa, the Idaho state flower, to the foreground. The design was eventually rejected, however, because of potential printing difficulties.

in a book of pictures entitled *Rocky Mountains* by David Muench. The Sawtooths were familiar ground to Dawson, who had frequently backpacked there. The artist also accepted another Paine suggestion, that he make the bird larger and add some "weatherbeaten detail" to the fencepost. The finished painting was done in acrylic on a heavy pasteboard with the trade name of Bainbridge board.

Dawson happened to be a specialist in animal and bird art — he had designed the se-tenant block of four Cats stamps for USPS in 1988, and had done many paintings for the Audubon Society — and he had numerous photographs of mountain bluebirds from which to work. The principal photo he relied on, showing a bird in the same profile view that appeared on the stamp, was one he had taken in Idaho's Salmon River valley.

"I thought I was going to get a lot of criticism about this design," Dawson said. "I thought people would say that, since I'm a bird painter, I was the one who pushed the bluebird as the subject. But after the stamp came out, I heard nothing but praise.

"Our condo in Sun Valley was at about 5,000 feet altitude, and you don't find mountain bluebirds as a rule below around 6,500 feet, so we didn't have any right at the house. I could take a hike of about half a mile and find them, though."

Jack Williams of USPS, project manager for the stamp, flew to Boise to show the painting to Idaho's governor, Cecil Andrus, a former secretary of the Interior. "We were ready to go to press — the stamp was ready to be printed — and we really had no option, but I was elected to go out and discuss it with the governor and his staff," Williams laughed. Fortunately, Andrus liked the design.

No one seemed to mind the fact that the mountain bluebird had been featured only eight years earlier on the Idaho stamp of the 50 State Birds and Flowers pane (Scott 1964). The late Arthur Singer's painting for that stamp showed the bird coming in for a landing, wings elevated and outstretched. "We didn't think that the repetition factor was important, because this was a different aspect," Jack Williams said. "The committee thought it was a striking design, and well done, and done by an Idaho artist."

Ironically, by the time the stamp was issued, the "Idaho artist" who had designed it was a resident of Hawaii, a state he and his wife Kathleen had frequently visited. In October 1989, after Dawson had completed the Idaho stamp artwork, the couple bought a home near Hilo. "We had lived in Idaho for 12 years and, frankly, we were tired of the cold winters," Dawson explained.

First-Day Facts

The first-day ceremony was held in the capitol. Governor Andrus delivered the welcome, Martin L. Peterson of the Idaho Centennial Commission gave the principal address and Kenneth J. Hunter, associate postmaster general, dedicated the stamp. Guests included

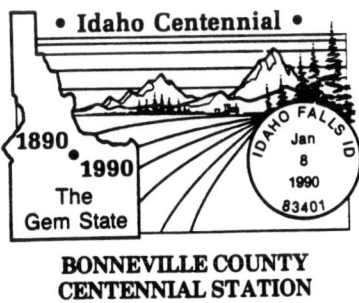

This second-day cancellation was used in 25 Idaho counties on January 8.

Lieutenant Governor C.L. "Butch" Otter and other state officials.

USPS authorized a pictorial cancellation commemorating Idaho's centennial for use January 8 at a post office in each of the state's 25 counties. The cancellations depicted the outline of Idaho, mountains, pine trees and a field.

25¢ IDA B. WELLS
BLACK HERITAGE SERIES

Date of Issue: February 1, 1990

Catalog Number: Scott 2442

Colors: magenta, yellow, cyan, black and purple

First-Day Cancel: Chicago, Illinois

FDCs Canceled: 229,226

Format: Panes of 50, vertical, 10 across, 5 down. Gravure printing cylinders of 200 subjects (10 across, 20 around) manufactured by Armotek Industries Inc., Palmyra, New Jersey.

Perf: 10.9 (L perforator)

Selvage Markings: ©United States Postal Service 1989, Use Correct ZIP Code®

Designer: Thomas Blackshear of Novato, California

Art Director and Project Manager: Jack Williams (USPS)

Modeler: Richard Sennett (Sennett Enterprises) for American Bank Note Company

Typographer: Bradbury Thompson (CSAC)

Printing: Stamps printed and sheeted out by American Bank Note Company on a leased Champlain gravure press (J.W. Fergusson and Sons, Richmond, Virginia) under the supervision of Sennett Enterprises (Fairfax, Virginia). Perforated, processed and shipped by ABNC (Chicago, Illinois).

Quantity Ordered: 153,125,000
Quantity Distributed: 153,125,000

Cylinder Number Detail: One group of five cylinder numbers preceded by the letter "A" over/under corner stamps.

Tagging: overall

The Stamp

The 13th stamp in the annual Black Heritage series was issued February 1 in Chicago. It honored Ida Bell Wells, who was born in slavery in 1862 and became a leader in the fight against lynching and racial discrimination. As with the other stamps in the series, this one's issuance was timed to coincide with the beginning of Black History Month. Its design was unveiled December 19, 1989, by Assistant Postmaster General Elwood A. Mosley during the National Association for the Advancement of Colored People's Image Awards Ceremony in Los Angeles.

Ida B. Wells was born July 16, 1862, in Holly Springs, Mississippi. The end of the Civil War three years later brought emancipation to her and her family. She was educated at a freedmen's school in Holly Springs and at 14 became a country schoolteacher.

In 1884 she moved to Memphis and continued teaching, but the school board fired her in 1891 after she had refused to give up a seat in a whites-only railroad car and sued the railroad for damages, finally losing the suit in the Tennessee Supreme Court. She bought an interest in the *Memphis Free Speech,* and in 1892, after three friends were killed by a lynch mob, she began a newspaper campaign against lynching and called for a boycott of white businesses as a protest measure. It wasn't surprising, in that time and that section of the country, that hoodlums retaliated by destroying her newspaper office and threatening her life.

She moved to New York City, where she continued her anti-lynching crusade, first as a staff writer for a publication called the *New York Age* and then as a lecturer and organizer of anti-lynching societies. Lynching was then a common crime in the South, claiming 226 victims in 1892 alone. Wells spoke in several cities and twice visited Great Britain on lecture tours. She attracted widespread attention with a pamphlet, *A Red Record,* in which she vividly described the mob murder of a mentally retarded black man in Paris, Texas, a crime witnessed by thousands of men, women and children. In 1898 she headed a delegation that met with President William McKinley to urge federal action against lynching.

She married Ferdinand Barnett, a Chicago lawyer and editor, in 1895 and contributed articles to his newspaper, the *Conservator.* From 1898 to 1902 she served as secretary of the National Afro-American Council, and in 1910 she founded and became first president of the Negro Fellowship League, which aided newly arrived migrants from the South. She established what may have been the first black women's suffrage group, Chicago's Alpha Suffrage Club.

From 1913 to 1916 Wells served as a probation officer for the Chicago municipal court. She was militant in her demand for justice for black Americans and in her insistence that it must be won by their own efforts. She died in Chicago March 25, 1931.

In her autobiography, *Crusade for Justice,* published posthumously in 1970, Ida Wells explained that she wrote to record "the gallant fight and marvelous bravery of the black men of the South, fighting and dying to exercise and maintain their newborn rights as freemen and citizens."

The Design

Thomas Blackshear, a Novato, California, artist and illustrator who had designed the previous three Black Heritage stamps, also designed the Ida B. Wells stamp.

The Postal Service furnished Blackshear with photocopies of portraits that it in turn had received from the Regenstein Library at the

In painting Ida Wells' portrait for the stamp, designer Tom Blackshear worked with these photocopies of photographs from the University of Chicago library. The portrait on which the finished stamp design was based bore the penciled notation "circa 1915"; the other, on the back of a postcard, was dated "circa 1910." The family portrait shows Ida Wells with her daughters Ida and Alfreda in 1914.

University of Chicago, where Ida Wells' papers are kept. Blackshear made pencil sketches based on two of these portraits. The library could give no information on the original photographs other than that one had the note penciled on the back "circa 1915," when Wells would have been 53 years old, and the other was on the front of a postcard bearing the notation "circa 1910." The artist also had for reference a photograph of Wells with her daughters Ida and Alfreda, dated September 1914. The portrait the Citizens' Stamp Advisory Committee preferred, and on which the finished stamp was based, was the one that was dated 1915.

Blackshear works with acrylic, which he applies with an airbrush, and colored pencil. The most difficult part of the Wells stamp assignment, the artist said, was choosing the small vignette that is customarily added to the design of a Black Heritage stamp to symbolize the career of the person being honored. A hangman's noose would have evoked Ida Wells' anti-lynching crusade, he said, "but, of course, I couldn't use that."

"It took me a while before it finally clicked in," Blackshear said. "Just use protesters in the background with picket signs and so forth to symbolize her efforts. I asked myself, why couldn't I have thought of that in the beginning?"

The men and women that Blackshear painted in the background were dressed in 19th-century garb. Similar sign-carrying figures, representing 1960s civil rights marchers, had been shown on the second stamp of the Black Heritage series, honoring Dr. Martin Luther King Jr. and designed by Jerry Pinkney (Scott 1771, issued in 1979). The artist said he placed the figures behind Wells' portrait rather than in the foreground so that nothing would obscure the elaborate lace collar she was wearing or detract from the words "Black Heritage" across the bottom of the stamp.

Another consistent feature of Black Heritage stamps is a background of a solid color, usually a pastel. For Ida Wells, Blackshear

These three sketches by Thomas Blackshear are part of the evolution of the finished Ida Wells stamp design.

19

chose a purple hue that hadn't been used before in the series, and for it the American Bank Note Company used a separate purple ink in addition to the standard four process colors in which the stamp was printed. The purple blended rather abruptly into orange just behind the picketing figures. In retrospect, Blackshear said, he wished he had made a "softer blend."

He also expressed mild disappointment at the "hard edge" that showed around the subject's head on the printed stamp. "She looks kind of like a cutout," Blackshear said. He was almost certain he had provided a softer outline on his painting, he added, "because as an illustrator I'm always aware of that kind of thing."

First-Day Facts

The first-day ceremony was held at the Museum of Science and Industry in Chicago. The stamp was dedicated by Assistant Postmaster General Mosley, who had presided at the design unveiling.

Principal speakers were author Paula Giddings and Donald L. Duster, a grandson of Ida B. Wells. Two other Wells grandsons, Benjamin C. Duster and Charles E. Duster, were among the honored guests. Introductions were made by Syd Finley, executive secretary of the NAACP's Chicago Southside Branch.

25¢ U.S. SUPREME COURT CONSTITUTION BICENTENNIAL SERIES

Date of Issue: February 2, 1990

Catalog Number: Scott 2415

Colors: yellow, red, blue-black (offset); olive (intaglio)

First-Day Cancel: Washington, D.C. (Lower Great Hall, Supreme Court Building)

FDCs Canceled: 233,056

Format: Pane of 50, vertical, 10 across, 5 down. Offset printing plates of 200 subjects (10 across, 20 around); intaglio printing sleeve of 400 subjects (10 across, 40 around).

Perf: 11.2 (Eureka off-line perforator)

Selvage Markings: John Marshall (1755-1835) "The Great Chief Justice." Legislator, Diplomat, Secretary of State; Fourth Chief Justice, U.S. Supreme Court (1801-1835); ©United States Postal Service 1989, Use Correct ZIP Code ®

Designer: Howard Koslow of East Norwich, New York

Art Director and Typographer: Howard Paine (CSAC)

Project Manager: Joe Brockert (USPS)

Engravers: Thomas Hipschen, vignette (BEP)
Michael J. Ryan, lettering and numerals (BEP)

Modeler: Peter Cocci (BEP)

Printing: BEP 6-color offset, 3-color intaglio D press (902)

Quantity Ordered: 150,600,000
Quantity Distributed: 150,545,000

Plate/Sleeve Number Detail: One group of three offset plate numbers on large selvage each pane, single-digit intaglio sleeve number on selvage of adjacent stamp.

Tagging: overall

The Stamp

The 200th anniversary of the judicial branch of the federal government was commemorated with a 25¢ stamp that depicted the nation's fourth and most famous chief justice, John Marshall. It was issued in Washington February 2.

The stamp was the last in a mini-series begun in 1989 to mark the bicentennials of the three branches of government. It was preceded by two stamps for the Legislative Branch (one each for the Senate and House of Representatives) and one for the Executive Branch. It was also part of a larger set celebrating the 200th anniversary of the U.S. Constitution. That series, consisting of stamps and postal cards, began in 1987 and was scheduled to end in 1991 with a card marking the ratification of the Bill of Rights.

The Judicial Branch stamp was issued on the anniversary of the date in 1790 that the Supreme Court of the United States met in New York City, the temporary national capital, to hold its first session. The session had been scheduled for the day before, February 1, 1790, but only three justices — not a quorum — were present.

The court met in the Royal Exchange building, a two-story commercial structure across the street from the Fulton Fish Market. The ground floor was a farmers' market and the court's hearing room above echoed with the cries of farmers hawking their produce and the bleating of animals. The justices admitted lawyers to the bar and appointed a "cryer" and a clerk but heard no cases.

These organizational steps were taken by authority of the Judiciary Act of September 24, 1789, which was passed by the First Congress and signed into law by President George Washington. The Judiciary Act, among other things, created the position of chief justice of the United States and provided for five associate justices. It implemented Article III, Section 1, of the Constitution, which provided that "(t)he judicial Power of the United States, shall be vested in one supreme Court, and in such inferior Courts as the Congress may from time to time ordain and establish."

The judicial arm of government now comprises the Supreme Court, consisting of the chief justice and eight associate justices, plus the lower federal district courts and 11 circuit courts of appeals. Power to nominate all federal judges is vested in the president, and appointments are made with the advice and consent of the Senate.

The first chief justice was John Jay, who served from 1789 to 1795. Little has been known until recently of the first decade of the court's history, but in 1977 a group of legal historians, working on what was called the Documentary History Project, began painstakingly reconstructing the period. They eventually collected more than 20,000 documents, including justices' letters, lawyers' notes and contemporary newspaper accounts, which Columbia University planned to publish in eight volumes.

These papers showed that the life of an early Supreme Court justice could be rugged. The justices spent most of their time "riding circuit," serving as trial judges of the Federal Circuit Courts created by Congress to settle criminal or civil cases. This job took them on horseback or coach trips of 1,000 miles or more each spring and fall through the sparsely settled back country of the young nation.

In 1801 President John Adams, as he prepared to leave office, appointed John Marshall, his secretary of state, to be the fourth chief justice. Marshall dominated the court for 35 years and did more than any other member to establish its role as a co-equal force with Congress and the president.

His most significant contribution was the opinion he wrote in Marbury versus Madison in 1803, in which the court asserted its power to declare laws unconstitutional. This authority was implied in the Constitution, but was not specifically asserted until Marbury.

Marshall had previously appeared on five U.S. stamps: the first four $5-denomination definitives (Scott 263, 278, 313 and 480) and the 40¢ stamp of the Liberty series in 1954 (Scott 1050).

Chief Justice Jay was shown on the 15¢ stamp of the Liberty series in 1958 (Scott 1046). Other chief justices to be depicted on stamps were William Howard Taft, who served in that office after leaving the presidency (Scott 685, 831, 2218h), Charles Evans Hughes (Scott 1195) and Harlan F. Stone (Scott 965). Associate Justices Oliver Wendell Holmes (Scott 1288) and Hugo Black (Scott 2172) have also been postally honored. Chief Justices Roger B. Taney and Salmon P. Chase were both former secretaries of the treasury, and as such appeared on various U.S. documentary, stock transfer and silver tax stamps of 1940-41.

The Cass Gilbert-designed Supreme Court building was shown on a 3¢ stamp of 1950 marking the National Capital sesquicentennial (Scott 991) and on 20¢ definitives of 1981 (Scott 1894 and 1895). One of the Marshall court's most significant decisions, handed down in the Dartmouth College case of 1819, was commemorated with a 6¢ stamp in 1969 (Scott 1380).

The Supreme Court Historical Society marked the bicentennial of the Judiciary Act of September 24, 1789, with a special pictorial cancellation on September 22, 1989.

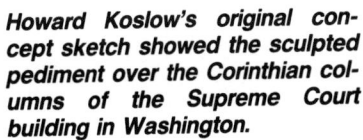

Howard Koslow's original concept sketch showed the sculpted pediment over the Corinthian columns of the Supreme Court building in Washington.

23

The Design

The stamp follows the format and style of the first three stamps in the series, and was credited to the same team that created those stamps. Howard Koslow was the designer; Howard Paine, a design coordinator for the Citizens' Stamp Advisory Committee, was art director; Joe Brockert, program manager, philatelic design, USPS, was project manager; Thomas Hipschen and Michael J. Ryan of the Bureau of Engraving and Printing were the engravers, and Peter Cocci of BEP was the modeler.

Like the other stamps, this one was printed by a combination of offset and intaglio on BEP's D press. It was vertically arranged and showed its subject in intaglio olive and offset yellow against an offset blue-black background. On red and yellow bands across the top were the words "Bicentennial/U.S. Supreme Court."

In the early stages of planning the series, Koslow had sketched horizontal designs showing buildings and artifacts associated with the different branches of government. For the House and Senate he used the Capitol and, respectively, the speaker's mace and a carved eagle from the old Senate chamber. For the Supreme Court he depicted Robert Aitken's sculptured pediment above the columns on the front of the Supreme Court building.

Later, CSAC decided that the stamps should be of a uniform basic design, arranged vertically, and that each should show a sculptured object appropriate to the branch of government being honored. Finding suitable pieces of sculpture for the House, Senate and Executive Branch was relatively easy. But that wasn't the case with the Supreme Court. Settling on a subject that satisfied everyone involved in the decision proved to be difficult and time-consuming.

This plaster relief in the old Supreme Court chamber on the ground floor of the Capitol provided elements for three different design concept sketches that Howard Koslow prepared — none of which was finally used.

Koslow based one concept sketch on this statue of a seated Marshall. Sculpted by William Wetmore Story, the statue was located for many years outside the West front of the Capitol and is now in the Supreme Court building.

Howard Koslow and Joe Brockert began by visiting the Capitol and the Supreme Court building in search of likely images. While making their rounds they looked in on the original Supreme Court chamber, located on the ground floor of the Capitol, where the court had sat before moving to the old Senate chamber directly overhead in 1860. The room is known, among other things, as the place where Samuel F.B. Morse first demonstrated the telegraph in 1844, tapping out the message "What hath God wrought?"

What caught their eye here was a lunette on the wall containing a plaster relief created in 1817 by Carlo Franzoni, the Italian-born craftsman who had also made the "Car of History" sculpture that was shown on the House of Representatives stamp of 1989. The relief consists of three figures against a light blue background, with accents of gold. In the center, Justice is seated, her left hand holding the scales and her right hand resting on a sword. At the right, an eagle guards the laws. At the left, a youthful winged figure, presumably typifying the young nation, crowned by the rising sun, is pointing to the Constitution of the United States.

Koslow prepared two sketches in the prescribed format. One showed the winged figure, the other the figure of Justice. The former seemed preferable for at least two reasons, Brockert said. First, it was the only sculpture they had found in their research for the series that specifically referred to the Constitution, the *raison d'etre* for the whole project. Second, they wanted to avoid cliches, and the other image, Justice holding scales, plainly fell in that category.

The committee, and subsequently Postmaster General Anthony M. Frank, agreed that the winged figure was the better choice. The four designs for the three branches of government were then shown to former Chief Justice Warren Burger, chairman of the Commission on the Bicentennial of the United States Constitution. Burger was "non-committal" about the proposed Supreme Court design, Brockert recalled: "He was neither thrilled nor opposed to it, but he thought it would be a good idea for us to go to the current chief justice and get his opinion on it."

As it turned out, Chief Justice William Rehnquist had a definite opinion. When Postmaster General Frank showed him the winged figure, Rehnquist said he didn't like it. He was willing to consider other allegorical sculptures, the jurist told Frank, but he would also like to see design proposals incorporating the likenesses of the early chief justices, John Jay and John Marshall.

(Koslow later admitted that he had been "a bit apprehensive" himself about taking the winged figure "out of context." "It just didn't 'read' right without the other figures in the group," he said.)

Back at USPS, the design process recommenced. The figure of Justice was back in contention, and Koslow also tried a design incorporating the third of the three relief figures in the old Supreme Court chamber, the eagle guarding the books of law. But, in deference to the chief justice's request, the busy artist also prepared two essays showing sculptured busts of Jay and Marshall.

None of these satisfied the design team. The head of Jay was copied from a bust by Giuseppe Ceracchi, on display on the ground floor of the Supreme Court building, that shows the first chief justice in a Roman toga, a fashionable affectation of sculptors in the early 19th century. The Marshall head came from William Wetmore Story's large bronze seated statue, which graced the West Front of the Capitol from 1883 until 1980 and is now also on the ground floor of the Supreme Court building. "It's a wonderfully imposing sculpture," Brockert said, "but the effect comes from the whole thing; the face is not really all that interesting, or all that well rendered."

Nevertheless, the four essays were sent to the chief justice, and in time word came back that the allegorical figures were unsatisfactory: They seemed more representative of justice in general than of the Supreme Court as an institution. As for the two busts, Rehnquist wanted to see a better rendering of John Marshall, and suggested that a likely source would be a circa-1828 portrait done by John B. Martin that hangs in the Supreme Court justices' conference room.

Koslow tried again. Using the painting for reference, he produced a bustlike head of Marshall. Though the design team still wasn't

These designs were prepared by Howard Koslow during the long effort to find a suitable sculpture for the Supreme Court stamp. (1) The winged figure, representative of the young nation, which USPS originally chose as the design but which was rejected by Chief Justice Rehnquist. (2) The figure of Justice, which USPS considered but turned down as being trite. (3) The eagle guarding the books of law, which Koslow tried as a possible design subject. (4) A bust of John Jay in a Roman toga. (5) The first attempt at a bust of John Marshall, copied from the statue of a seated Marshall in the Supreme Court building. (6) An adaptation in sculptural form of a painting of Marshall in the Supreme Court justices' room. The final version resembled this last portrait, with modifications adapted from other sources, including the seated statue.

27

wholly satisfied — the eyes and hair needed work, they thought — the essay was shown to Rehnquist, who pronounced it an improvement. The job now was to improve the image still more, and to this end other portraits of Marshall were found and used for reference.

In Koslow's final composite painting, influences from several sources could be identified. In overall appearance it was similar to the Martin painting. The facial features, hairline, and coat lapels were reminiscent of those on the statue. The mouth resembled that on an engraving by Charles Schlecht, after a painting by Henry Inman. (This engraving was the source of the design for Scott 313.)

This portrait of John Marshall by John B. Martin, which hangs in the justices' conference room, was suggested by Chief Justice Rehnquist as a reference for the Supreme Court stamp design.

The resulting image met — at last — with everyone's approval. But Postmaster General Frank ordered one final detail added. He had become convinced that many stamps weren't giving the user enough information about the subject (for a fuller discussion of this point, see the chapter on the 5¢ Luis Munoz Marin stamp) and he wanted Marshall's name included in the design of this one. The USPS staff had independently come to a similar conclusion; after all, John Marshall had a face that was recognizable to very few Americans (unlike George Washington, whose portrait was used without identification on the Executive Branch stamp of 1989). Therefore, this stamp was unique among the four of the mini-series in that it had a line of dropout white type on the bottom tablet which read: "Chief Justice John Marshall."

Then, although Frank hadn't ordered it, the staff went one step further. As it had done with the Postal People set of 1973 (Scott 1489-1498), USPS provided additional information about the stamp subject in the selvage. This came as a surprise to collectors, because

28

the official USPS announcement of the stamp had mentioned only the standard marginal markings (sleeve and plate numbers, copyright and ZIP code inscriptions). The wide selvage next to the fifth and sixth stamps in the top or bottom row of each pane contained these messages, respectively: "John Marshall/1755-1835)/'The Great Chief Justice.'/Legislator, Diplomat,/Secretary of State" and "Fourth Chief Justice,/U.S. Supreme Court/(1801-1835)."

"We decided to add the additional explanatory text in the selvage as a way of trying to make the connection between John Marshall the individual and the Supreme Court," Brockert said. "The stamp focuses on the Supreme Court, and we wanted to give more explanation as to why Marshall was an appropriate design subject."

Addition of the biographical information to the selvage meant that, on each pane, six out of the 10 stamps with wide selvage adjacent to them had collectible marginal markings.

First-Day Facts

Chief Justice Rehnquist joined Postmaster General Frank for the public dedication ceremony February 2 in the Lower Great Hall of the Supreme Court building. Associate Justice William Brennan and former Associate Justice Lewis Powell also attended. Former Chief Justice Burger, who was listed on the program as an honored guest, wasn't there, however.

The present chief justice, describing himself as "both an amateur stamp collector and an American history buff," observed that "United States postage stamps have not been particularly generous in their depiction of members of the Supreme Court." He listed for his audience all the stamps that had honored Supreme Court justices and said: "When we come to members of the court who were not John Marshall, and who were not also president of the United States (a reference to William Howard Taft), the pickings are slim." Responded Postmaster General Frank: "I get lobbied for stamps all the time but I have never been lobbied more graciously."

In his prepared remarks, the postmaster general referred to the search for a design subject, but didn't mention the chief justice's role in that search. "Several design elements were researched and considered," he said. "It was suggested that the scales of justice would be an appropriate illustration, or the Supreme Court building itself. Or even the first chief justice, John Jay. But it was decided that John Marshall, the man who did the most to shape the destiny of the court, would best represent the Supreme Court on this commemorative stamp." That made the process sound considerably simpler than in fact it had been.

25¢ WYOMING STATEHOOD CENTENNIAL

Date of Issue: February 23, 1990

Catalog Number: Scott 2444

Colors: magenta, yellow, cyan and black (offset); black (intaglio)

First-Day Cancel: Cheyenne, Wyoming (Cheyenne Civic Center)

FDCs Canceled: 317,654

Format: Panes of 50, horizontal, 5 across, 10 down. Offset printing plates of 200 (10 across, 20 around); intaglio printing sleeve of 400 subjects (10 across, 40 around).

Perf: 11.2 (Eureka off-line perforator)

Selvage Markings: ©United States Postal Service 1989, Use Correct ZIP Code®

Designer: Jack Rosenthal of Casper, Wyoming (CSAC)

Modeler: Peter Cocci (BEP)

Engravers: Gary Chaconas, vignette (BEP)
Dennis Brown, lettering (BEP)

Art Director and Typographer: Bradbury Thompson (CSAC)

Project Manager: Jack Williams (USPS)

Printing: BEP's 6-color offset, 3-color intaglio D press (902)

Quantity Ordered: 169,500,000
Quantity Distributed: 169,495,000

Plate/Sleeve Number Detail: One group of four offset plate numbers on the large margin of each pane, a single-digit intaglio sleeve number on the selvage of the adjacent stamp.

Tagging: block

The Stamp

The second of two statehood centennial stamps issued in 1990 honored Wyoming and was dedicated at a joint centennial session of the Wyoming legislature in Cheyenne February 23.

The stamp design was unveiled at a press conference January 16 in the office of Governor Mike Sullivan. Among those present were Jack Rosenthal of Casper, Wyoming, the stamp's designer and a member of the Citizens' Stamp Advisory Committee, and Leno Menghini, superintendent of the Wyoming Highway Department. The ceremony also marked the first distribution of the Highway Department's 1990 centennial road map, which incorporated the Wyoming stamp in its design.

Congress created the Wyoming Territory in 1868 and named it for the Wyoming Valley in Pennsylvania, the home state of one of the bill's sponsors. Its name came from the Delaware Indian language and means "on the great plain"; among its attractions was the fact that it was euphonious and easy to spell. A proposal to name the territory "Lincoln" for the recently martyred president was rejected.

Wyoming today is nicknamed "The Equality State" because of a remarkable action taken early in its history. In 1869 the territory's first legislature, with little debate, granted Wyoming's one thousand or so adult women the right to vote, hold office and serve on juries. It was the first government in the world to grant these rights in full to its female citizens.

Although some of the lawmakers were motivated by considerations of justice, the majority approved the bill because of its public-relations value. They thought it would advertise the territory and attract settlers to its sparsely populated plains and river basins. It turned out, though, that suffrage probably didn't do much to increase the population. And although most of the territory's women did vote — contradicting skeptics who predicted that they wouldn't exercise this new right that they hadn't even asked for — few took advantage of the corollary right to run for office. None ever served in the territorial legislature, although a handful were elected county superintendents of schools.

Wyoming survived one threat to its existence when Congress ignored President Ulysses S. Grant's suggestion that the territory, being small and with dubious prospects for growth, be abolished and divided among surrounding territories. But its future status was still uncertain a decade later when Wyoming was only one of several western territories seeking admission to the union as states.

Five other territories — the two Dakotas, Montana, Washington and Idaho — all had more people than Wyoming, and a better claim to statehood. And female suffrage, which had earned Wyoming so much attention, now loomed as a threat. Since no existing state allowed women to vote, it was assumed that strong objections would be raised in Congress. In Wyoming's constitutional convention in September 1889, a Cheyenne lawyer proposed that the issue of the female vote be submitted to the electors as a separate article. He and others were afraid that either the voters of the territory would turn down a constitution with woman suffrage in it, or Congress would. The convention rejected the idea, though, and when the constitution with the woman suffrage clause intact went to referendum, it was approved by a ratio of 3 to 1.

As feared, there was considerable opposition to Wyoming statehood in the U.S. House of Representatives. Most of the debate centered on woman suffrage, although questions were also raised about the small number of inhabitants. Finally the statehood bill squeaked by, 139-127, with 63 members abstaining, and then passed the Senate 29-18. Fortunately for Wyoming, the Republicans had gained control of both houses of Congress in the 1888 elections, and were inclined to look with favor on the territory, which had also voted Republican that year.

At 5:30 p.m. on July 10, 1890, the Republican president, Benjamin Harrison, signed the bill into law, making Wyoming the 44th state. "Proclaim to the people that Wyoming is a member of the indestructible union of American States," Joseph M. Carey, Wyoming Territory's delegate to Congress, telegraphed to Acting Governor John W. Meldrum. "To them extend hearty congratulations."

This 3¢ brown-violet stamp showing elements of the Wyoming state seal was issued July 10, 1940, to mark the 50th anniversary of Wyoming statehood. It was designed by A.R. Meissner of the Bureau of Engraving and Printing.

Wyoming had been postally honored on several previous occasions. Its 50th anniversary of statehood was commemorated in 1940 by a 3¢ stamp (Scott 897) depicting a portion of the state seal, on which a female figure bearing the banner "equal rights" was flanked by a rancher and a miner. This stamp, unlike the 1990 centennial stamp, was issued on the actual anniversary date of July 10.

Yellowstone National Park, the state's greatest tourist attraction, founded in 1872 as the first national park in the nation, has been recognized with two stamps, in 1934 (Scott 744) and in its centennial year of 1972 (Scott 1453). Both depict the park's best-known attraction, Old Faithful geyser. Devil's Tower in the Black Hills, a landmark made widely known by the movie *Close Encounters of the Third Kind*, was shown on a 1956 3¢ stamp (Scott 1084) issued for the 50th anniversary of its establishment as the country's first national monument. Buffalo Bill Cody, who founded the town of Cody, Wyoming, where a museum featuring his memorabilia is now located, was portrayed on a 15¢ definitive in 1988 (Scott 2178).

The Design

Like 1989's Montana commemorative, the Wyoming stamp reproduced a painting of an indigenous scene by an artist who was closely identified with the state, and was printed by offset and intaglio on the Bureau of Engraving and Printing's D press.

CSAC member Jack Rosenthal, a broadcasting executive from Casper, Wyoming, came to the committee in 1985 as an advocate of and authority on Western themes. When the time came shortly thereafter to pick a subject for Wyoming's centennial stamp, the committee looked at some ideas put together by a researcher who worked for USPS under contract, including sketches of the state capitol, Old Faithful, Devil's Tower and a cowboy on a bucking bronco. But it gave its most serious consideration to Rosenthal's ideas for a stamp to honor his home state.

What he wanted, Rosenthal recalled, was a "summer scene with flowers" that would help dispel the widespread perception that Wyoming was an "icebox" — a perception which he said was

This is the complete painting of **High Mountain Meadows.** *A portion of the foreground was cropped to convert the work to postage-stamp proportions.*

nurtured by regular reports of sub-zero wintertime temperatures from high-altitude weather stations such as Big Piney.

"I looked around for paintings that were in public collectons, and I just didn't see anything that I thought was appropriate," Rosenthal said. In his own collection, however, he found just the right picture: an oil painting *High Mountain Meadows* done around 1970 by an old friend and Wyoming resident, the late Conrad Schwiering.

The painting, measuring 24 inches across by 30 inches deep, was a view of the Cathedral Group of the Grand Teton range in Grand Teton National Park, near Schwiering's home of Jackson Hole. In the foreground is Pilgrim Creek Meadow, covered with yellow buckwheat, purple penstemon (whose color repeats the purple of the mountains) and Indian paintbrush.

Wyoming's then-governor, Ed Herschler, its two senators, Alan K. Simpson and Malcolm Wallop, and then Representative-at-large Dick Cheney all endorsed Rosenthal's design proposal in letters to CSAC, and the committee quickly approved it.

There was a problem, however. USPS declines to use privately owned art on stamps because of the likelihood that the publicity would enhance its value. To make it possible to reproduce his friend's painting, Rosenthal arranged to donate the canvas to the Nicolaysen Art Museum in Casper. The formal transfer of title was later done as part of the first-day ceremony.

To guide typographer Bradbury Thompson in placing the lettering, Rosenthal made a Polaroid photograph of the painting, cropped

Three stages of development of the Wyoming stamp design. (A) is Jack Rosenthal's original conceptual paste-up, using a Polaroid print and white press type. (B) is an essay by Bradbury Thompson, using a different style of type and positioning the dates at upper left. (C) is another essay by Thompson, using the Clarendon typeface that was used on the finished stamp but placing the dates at upper right.

it at the bottom to give it the proportions of a horizontal commemorative stamp, and pasted white press-on type on it. Later, when it was necessary to furnish BEP with color separations from which to make the offset plates, Rosenthal took the painting to the Unicover Corporation, the well-known cachetmaker and philatelic agent in Cheyenne, where photographer Tom Engel did the photo work. Because of USPS' secrecy policy on new stamps, nobody at Unicover knew that the pictures were being made for a stamp design.

At BEP, Gary Chaconas engraved the row of evergreen trees that stands between the mountains and the meadow; this constituted the intaglio portion of the stamp. The rest of the design was printed in four-color offset, although the typography — done in dropout white outlined in black — was engraved beforehand by Dennis Brown to provide crisp definition. The typeface chosen by Thompson was called Clarendon and had been popular in the West a century ago.

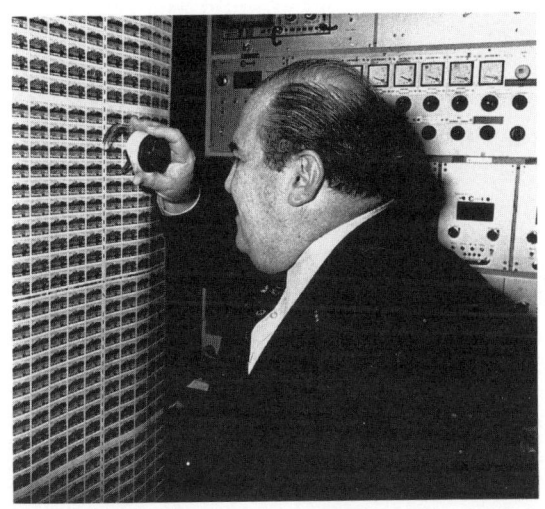

Jack Rosenthal examines a printed web of Wyoming stamps on the Bureau of Engraving and Printing's D press.

The preliminary essays for the stamp all bore the double dates that traditionally had been used on anniversary stamps — in this case, "1890" and "1990." The committee eventually decided to use only the "1890," in keeping with a feeling on the part of its members that designs should be as simple as possible. The Montana statehood stamp of 1989, which was designed after the Wyoming stamp, was actually the first anniversary stamp to be issued bearing only a single date, however.

Oscar Conrad Schwiering called himself an impressionist, an artist who tried to translate the effect of light onto a canvas. Born in Boulder, Colorado, in 1916, he grew up in Wyoming. He graduated

35

from the University of Wyoming with a degree in business and law, studied art in New York City, saw military service in World War II, then returned to Wyoming with his wife Mary Ethel to settle in Jackson Hole, in sight of the magnificent Tetons. For some 35 years he painted those mountains and other scenes of the American West, working outdoors in summer heat and the sub-zero cold of winter to capture the ever-changing look of the landscape created by light, shadow and weather. "This is really what a mountain painter does," Schwiering once said. "He catches, if he can, the essence of the moods as they come across the mountains, hoping he can pass them on to others." Later he painted seascapes and also the people and architecture of Mexico. He died January 27, 1986, at the age of 69.

Jack Rosenthal previously had received design credit for the 15¢ Buffalo Bill Cody definitive of 1988. He is well-known to philately as a collector of U.S. classic stamps with a special interest in proofs and essays and the 1898 Trans-Mississippi series.

First-Day Facts

More than 1,000 people attended the stamp dedication ceremony and joint session of the Wyoming Legislature at the Cheyenne Civic Center. It was the first time the state's Senate and House of Representatives had convened outside the state capitol.

Governor Mike Sullivan gave the welcome, and speeches were made by U.S. Senator Alan Simpson and John Turner, director of the U.S. Fish and Wildlife Service. Kenneth J. Hunter, associate postmaster general, dedicated the stamp.

The legislature approved a joint resolution expressing its "profound sense of gratitude to the United States postmaster general, Anthony M. Frank, on behalf of the citizens of Wyoming." The statehood stamp had been "rendered in an extraordinarily skillful artistic fashion," the resolution stated, reflecting "the unspoiled beauty of our state in a manner so exemplary as to generate great pride in Wyoming." USPS officials found this reaction to be especially gratifying after the criticism they had encountered the year before from the North Dakota governor, lieutenant governor and others over the design of their state's centennial stamp.

25¢ CLASSIC FILMS (BLOCK OF FOUR)

Date of Issue: March 23, 1990

Catalog Numbers: Scott 2445-48 (stamps); Scott 2448a (block of four)

Colors: magenta, yellow, cyan and black, plus red

First-Day Cancel: Hollywood, California (Academy of Motion Picture Arts and Sciences, Beverly Hills)

FDCs Canceled: 863,079

Format: Panes of 40, vertical, 8 across, 5 down. Gravure printing cylinders of 160 (10 across, 16 around) manufactured by Armotek Industries Inc., Palmyra, New Jersey.

Perf: 10.9 (L perforator)

Selvage Markings: ©United States Postal Service 1990, Use Correct ZIP Code®

Designer: Thomas Blackshear of Novato, California

Art Director and Typographer: Derry Noyes (CSAC)

Project Manager: Joe Brockert (USPS)

Modeler: Richard Sennett of Sennett Enterprises for American Bank Note Company

Printing: Stamps printed and sheeted out by American Bank Note Company on a leased Champlain gravure press (J.W. Fergusson and Sons, Richmond, Virginia) under the supervision of Sennett Enterprises (Fairfax, Virginia). Perforated, processed and shipped by ABNC (Chicago, Illinois).

Quantity Ordered: 176,808,000
Quantity Distributed: 176,808,000

Cylinder Number Detail: One group of five gravure cylinder numbers preceded by the letter "A" over/under corner stamps.

Tagging: overall

The Stamps

The U.S. Postal Service saluted the motion picture industry on the eve of the 1990 Academy Awards ceremony with a se-tenant block of four stamps, designed in movie-poster style, honoring four famous American films. The block was issued March 23 in Hollywood, three days before the Academy Awards, or "Oscars," were presented for the 62nd time.

The films were all from 1939, which *Time* magazine has called "that year of genius and glitter . . . the most memorable 12 months in the history of the American cinema" because it produced so many pictures that are now regarded as classics.

As the 50th anniversary year approached, USPS staff members saw the opportunity to respond to continuing requests from the public for stamps honoring specific films, actors and actresses. But because the project was late in getting under way, and obtaining the necessary clearances from copyright holders and estates turned out to be a complicated process, USPS decided to hold the issue until 1990. Resourceful Postal Service publicists pointed out that 1990 was a 50th anniversary year too — the anniversary of the Academy Awards program at which three of the four honored films received awards and a fourth was nominated.

In its first announcement of its 1990 stamp program June 1, 1989, USPS said: "Next year, fans of Americana can look forward to one or more commemoratives shouting 'Bravo!' to the entertainment arts." Not until February 15, 1990, did USPS disclose that the

"Bravo!" would be in the form of a Classic Films block of four. The designs were unveiled March 7.

Each stamp depicted a star or stars from its movie and a background scene evocative of the film, together with the title. Though the stars weren't named on the stamps, their faces were familiar to anyone having the slightest acquaintance with U.S. films of the past. The pictures and people were *The Wizard of Oz* (Judy Garland as Dorothy and her dog Toto, played by a female cairn terrier named Terry), *Gone With the Wind* (Clark Gable and Vivien Leigh as Rhett Butler and Scarlett O'Hara), *Beau Geste* (Gary Cooper in the title role) and *Stagecoach* (John Wayne as the Ringo Kid).

It was the first U.S. stamp appearance for any of these charismatic actors and actresses, although each had been shown on the stamps of one or more foreign countries, including Great Britain, Montserrat, Dominica, Tonga and Antigua and Barbuda. All five stars had been dead for more than 10 years, as USPS guidelines require: Wayne's death, in 1979, was the most recent.

Cinema personalities previously shown on U.S. stamps included D.W. Griffith, the director (Scott 1555), Walt Disney, the animated-cartoon pioneer (Scott 1355) and actors Will Rogers (Scott 975 and 1801), W.C. Fields (Scott 1803), John, Ethel and Lionel Barrymore (Scott 2012) and Douglas Fairbanks (Scott 2088). Stamps were issued in 1944 for the 50th anniversary of motion pictures (Scott 926) and in 1977 for the 50th anniversary of talkies (Scott 1727).

Comedian Jay Leno, on NBC-TV's *Tonight* show, kidded USPS for its choice of films for the 1990 block of four. "They should have come out with movie stamps that really reflect the Postal Service," he said, "such as . . . Around the World in 80 Days . . . From Here to Eternity . . ." Others were quick to note with amusement that the Gone With the Wind stamp had been issued just in time to use for mailing income tax returns.

A more serious, if belated, criticism came from consumer activist Ralph Nader. On November 13, almost eight months after the stamps were issued, Nader wrote a letter to Postmaster General Anthony M. Frank — copies of which he released to the press — criticizing the issue on two grounds.

First, Nader wrote, "The distribution of 176 million stamps bearing the names and characters of these films amounts to a huge advertising campaign for the four movies." He called on Frank to stop the spread of "creeping commercialism" and pledge to prohibit advertising on all USPS products.

"What is most troubling," Nader went on, "is that the Postal Service actually paid the owners of these films in order to depict the movies — still being shown in cinemas — on the stamps." These expenditures, Nader noted, came at the same time the Postal Service was asking for higher rates, including a 30¢ first-class rate.

In a reply dated December 6, Frank told Nader he had made "several erroneous conclusions" about the Classic Films stamps. "The United States Postal Service paid no fees whatsoever to secure permission to depict" the four movies on stamps, Frank wrote. And he rejected Nader's "suggestion that the Classic Films stamps somehow represent an attempt by the Postal Service to exploit commercialism at the cost of providing quality mail service."

"On the contrary," Frank wrote, "the overwhelming acceptance of the Classic Films stamps clearly demonstrate an extremely satisfied group of mailers and stamp collectors. As you indicated, we distributed nearly 177 million of these stamps nationwide, a quantity which historically meets demand for 60 days. But the Classic Films stamps were so popular that nearly all were sold within 25 days! Moreover, nearly $7 million was generated from the sale of those stamps to individuals who saved them for their stamp collections. All of that revenue went to offset our costs for doing business, which, as you know, ultimately benefits the American ratepayer."

Frank agreed "that the American stamp program must never be allowed to become an advertising vehicle for private company interests." "But I hope you understand that the stamp program and the American public are best served when the subjects depicted are popular with mailers and collectors alike," he told Nader.

Among the additional movies released in 1939 that are still highly regarded today are *Babes in Arms, Dark Victory, Destry Rides Again, Drums Along the Mohawk, Goodbye, Mr. Chips, Gunga Din, The Hunchback of Notre Dame, Idiot's Delight, Intermezzo, Mr. Smith Goes to Washington, Ninotchka, Of Mice and Men, Union Pacific, The Women, Wuthering Heights, You Can't Cheat an Honest Man* and *Young Mr. Lincoln.* Nevertheless, choosing the four for the block turned out to be relatively easy.

As Joe Brockert, USPS project manager for the stamps, pointed out, several of the great 1939 movies were automatically eliminated because their stars were still alive when the issue was being planned, such as Jimmy Stewart, Bette Davis and Henry Fonda, or, as foreigners, were inappropriate for a series with "an American thrust," such as Robert Donat and Greer Garson. (British-born Vivien Leigh was an unavoidable choice; besides, she would be paired on her stamp with that exemplary American, Clark Gable.)

"The staff told the committee that these were four of the best-known films of the year, with the best-recognized people, best design potential and best balance," Brockert said. "We said, if you can suggest a better movie and tell us which of these four you would replace, we'll be glad to consider it. They had no better suggestions."

Some outsiders assumed that CSAC's newest member, George Stevens Jr., was the moving force behind the issue. Stevens, a well-known motion picture producer and director and founder and co-chairman of The American Film Institute, was named to the committee in April 1988 by Postmaster General Frank. However, Stevens' principal contribution was to help USPS obtain background material, such as original posters, to help in the design process.

THE WIZARD OF OZ. Producer Mervyn LeRoy's MGM technicolor musical, based on L. Frank Baum's 1900 children's book, has become such a part of American popular culture, thanks to annual screenings on network television, that it's surprising to find that it wasn't universally loved from the first. It got a number of favorable reviews, but some were negative ("No imagination, good taste or ingenuity," groused *The New Yorker*. "A real stinkeroo.") When at the end of 1939 *New York Times* film critic Frank S. Nugent listed 18 films he considered outstanding that year, *The Wizard* wasn't one of them. It won no New York Film Critics awards or major Oscars, although it did receive three minor ones, for best song (the Harold Arlen-E.Y. Harburg *Over the Rainbow*), best musical scoring, and a special award to Judy Garland for the outstanding performance as a "screen juvenile."

In retrospect the picture's merits can be seen even more clearly: in particular, the innocent charm of the 16-year-old Garland, the slapstick-and-sentiment of her co-stars, Ray Bolger (the Scarecrow), Bert Lahr (the Cowardly Lion) and Jack Haley (the Tin Woodman), and the special effects, quite ingenious for their time.

GONE WITH THE WIND. From the time Margaret Mitchell's 1936 novel of passion set in a gallant but doomed Confederacy became a huge best-seller and Pulitzer Prize winner, Americans played the game of casting the movie. Gable seemed a natural for Rhett Butler, but producer David O. Selznick's selection of British actress Vivien Leigh to play the self-centered and headstrong Scarlett was a surprise. She turned out to be perfect, however, and the film, too, was an overwhelming critical and financial success.

"Is it the greatest motion picture ever made?" asked *New York Times* critic Frank Nugent the day after it opened at two Times Square movie houses December 19, 1939. "Probably not, although it is the greatest motion mural we have seen and the most ambitious film-making venture in Hollywood's spectacular history . . . To have treated so long a book with such astonishing fidelity required courage — the courage of a producer's convictions and of his pocketbook." (In an aside that seems quaint 50 years later, Nugent added: "We still feel that color is hard on the eyes for so long a picture.")

At the 1940 Academy Awards ceremony, *Gone With the Wind* won nine Oscars, including best picture, best actress (Leigh), best supporting actress (Hattie McDaniel) and best director (Victor Fleming). It had been nominated for five others, including best actor (Gable) and best supporting actress (Olivia de Havilland, the only major member of the cast to still be alive 50 years later).

Margaret Mitchell, author of Gone with the Wind, *was pictured on this Great Americans stamp of 1986.*

Margaret Mitchell, author of the novel, was honored with a 1¢ stamp in the Great Americans series in 1986 (Scott 2168).

BEAU GESTE. This prototype of French Foreign Legion pictures, filmed in black and white by Paramount, told of the three Geste brothers and their ill-starred encounters with desert tribes and villainous legionnaires, bandits and informers in North Africa. Its outstanding cast, in addition to Cooper, included Ray Milland and Robert Preston as the other Gestes, Brian Donlevy, J. Carrol Naish, Broderick Crawford and Susan Hayward. It was based on a novel by Percival Christopher Wren that was first filmed as a silent movie with Ronald Colman in 1926. "Beau is now Gary Cooper, with unimpaired Texas accent," noted *New York Times* reviewer B.R. Crisler. The film was the only one of the four in the block of stamps that won no Academy Awards, although it received two nominations. Cooper, who left Paramount after this movie, won a best-actor Oscar three years later for *Sergeant York*.

STAGECOACH. *Stagecoach,* shot on location in Arizona in an era when directors rarely worked outside greater Los Angeles, was John Ford's "greatest epic of the frontier," said Jay Robert Nash and Stanley Ralph Ross in their multi-volume *Motion Picture Guide.* "This western eclipsed all films in the genre that had gone before it," they continued, "and so vastly influenced those that followed that its stamp can be found in most superior westerns made since Ford stepped into Monument Valley for the first time. (John) Wayne . . . had been languishing on the tiny back lots of Poverty Row studios, riding nondescriptly through a host of forgettable B westerns, until being summoned to fame, fortune and stardom by Ford in this film." Producer Walter Wanger wanted Gary Cooper for the part of the Ringo Kid, but Ford held out for Wayne.

The film was touted as "a powerful story of nine strange people" traveling to separate fates in a perilous stagecoach journey across the Southwest. Other stars included John Carradine, Thomas Mitchell, Claire Trevor, Andy Devine and Donald Meek. Mitchell won a best supporting actor Oscar for his role as the drunken doctor, Josiah Boone. The movie also won the best musical score award and was nominated for five others, including best picture and best director.

For cachetmakers, the issue created problems of access even more complicated than those that had accompanied the W.C. Fields, Girl Scouts and Lou Gehrig commemoratives of recent years. The subject was discussed by Frank Thomas, acting manager of the Stamp Product Development Branch, in a letter sent out to first-day cover manufacturers before the stamps were issued. It read in part:

"The most difficult element of this issue . . . has been in regards to the rights for the use of the names of the films and the rights of publicity for the use of the names and images of the actors and actresses portrayed on the stamps.

"There have not been any concerns among the three companies owning the film rights and the three agents representing the heirs of the performers regarding the Postal Service use of the 'properties' on stamps, annual and subscription service philatelic products, and the promotion or advertising thereof.

"However, negotiations pertaining to the use of the properties by commercial organizations on first-day covers and/or other philatelic, or even non-philatelic, products are what have caused most of the problems in finalizing agreements with the film companies and agents. The following points serve to illustrate the problems encountered and the questions which have arisen in this regard:

"Turner Entertainment claims that the license they grant for the use of *Gone With the Wind* and *The Wizard of Oz* allows the licensee to use the images of Vivien Leigh, Clark Gable, Judy Garland and Toto, if they are depicted specifically as the characters they portrayed in the movie. As you might expect, the agents representing the heirs of these performers dispute this claim, and both parties admit that the courts still are in the process of deciding this same issue for similar situations, with neither knowing for sure what the outcome will be.

"Turner Entertainment will not allow its two properties, as noted above, to be used on a product which also features the other, less significant, properties.

"Some of the companies and agents have agreed, if all concerned parties do so, to a 'most favored nation' clause, whereby each company and/or agent would evenly split the usual royalty so that licensees would not have to pay multiple royalties when more than one party claims a right to the elements of the stamp(s). However, not all parties will agree to this, with some believing that the property or properties they represent are more significant and, therefore, the royalty should not be shared evenly, if at all.

"The agent for Mrs. Gary Cooper has indicated that she is completely against any commercial use of her late husband's name and/ or image, specifically citing such items as T-shirts and coffee mugs, and, therefore, most likely will not grant such licenses under any circumstances, regardless of the royalty involved. The following wording has been provided:

" '. . . The Gary Cooper Estate has agreed (that) the Postal Service may issue the commemorative stamp bearing the likeness of Gary Cooper only for philatelic activity. Therefore, if any broader license is sought whereby the stamp would be reproduced in connection with the advertising of any product or service or in connection with any item of merchandise such as T-shirts, coffee mugs, china dishes, etc., you must first obtain the written consent of the Cooper Estate. If such a consent is not obtained, you may not make use of the stamp except for philatelic activity.'

"These are just some of the concerns with which we have had to deal and, thus, which have made it impossible to develop a single agreement with all parties, especially one in which Postal Service stamp design licensees as well as first-day cover manufacturers are fairly represented, as we have attempted to do. Negotiating six separate agreements has been time-consuming and, as of this writing, is not yet complete.

"Therefore, we suggest that those manufacturers needing or wishing to use either the exact design of one or more of the stamps, or original art incorporating the names of the films and/or the names and images of the performers (rather than just a 'generic' design representing films, such as was done by some companies for the Gehrig issue using a baseball-related image) should contact directly the individuals noted on the attached.

"Some of these parties may very well grant royalty-free licenses, especially for first-day covers, in light of our ongoing discussions with them in which we have advised them that cachet covers are a basic element of philately. However, since we cannot be certain which, if any, will do so, it is advisable for each to be contacted in the appropriate instances."

Several major cachetmakers, including Artcraft, Artmaster and House of Farnam, did in fact choose to avoid the licensing problem and go generic. For example, Washington Stamp Exchange, manufacturer of Artcraft envelopes, offered a composite design that included a theater marquee, motion picture equipment, a director's chair and an Academy Award statuette.

The Designs

To launch the project, the USPS staff took a promotional photograph made for each of the four films, added type and created a concept design for a block of four. But this approach presented a problem, said project manager Brockert.

Gone With the Wind and *The Wizard of Oz* were filmed in color; the other two pictures weren't. The Citizens' Stamp Advisory Committee decided that printing two of the stamps in color and two in black and white wouldn't do (although, in fact, the public might

These are Thomas Blackshear's pencil sketches for the Classic Films stamps. On the finished stamps, Judy Garland has been given a shoulder; the black bar at the bottom of Gone With the Wind has been removed, and some of the titles have been slightly altered.

have considered it a novel and interesting combination). On the other hand, the committee believed that to reproduce what looked like actual photographs from *Stagecoach* and *Beau Geste* in color would have smacked of Ted Turner's controversial practice of "colorizing" black and white films.

Movie posters, on the other hand, are always in color, and this led CSAC to opt for designs that would be reminiscent of (but different from) the original posters made to advertise the four films. Thomas Blackshear of Novato, California, the illustrator who had designed the four most recent stamps in the Black Heritage series, was chosen for the design assignment. One of Blackshear's recent jobs, as it happened, had been to paint 18 limited-edition *Wizard of Oz* plates for The Hamilton Collection, nine of them showing scenes from the movie and nine bearing portraits of its stars.

USPS supplied Blackshear with photocopies of old movie posters, plus the photographs it had used to create the original concept design for a block of four, along with other pictures. In addition, the artist visited movie-memorabilia shops and consulted a number of books in search of reference material.

Of the film stars to be painted, Judy Garland and "Toto" were the only ones Blackshear had portrayed before. "I've been doing so much *Wizard of Oz* stuff that it was probably the easiest design to come up with," he said. Even so, good, clear photographs of Toto were hard to come by, and in order to make the dog's face distinct, Blackshear had to lighten the brown color of its hair.

On his original sketch of *Gone With the Wind,* Blackshear placed a black bar at the bottom to provide a background for the red lettering. The committee thought this made the stamp look inconsistent with the other three, and that too much detail was lost with the bar covering Leigh's hair and Gable's suit. So they asked Blackshear to remove the bar and carry the outlines of the figures downward, and add a bit of green background in the area. "I personally didn't like it as much," said Blackshear, "because you don't see the lettering as well, but I guess they wanted it to look a little more natural than the way I had done it."

For *Beau Geste,* Blackshear referred to a photograph of Gary Cooper without the Foreign Legion headgear, and copied in the cap from another source. The desert fort in the background came from

Movie publicity photographs were used to make this prototype of the Classic Films block. The Judy Garland and John Wayne portraits on the finished stamps were based on these pictures.

an actual *Beau Geste* movie poster, and the artist added palm trees at the left. The landscape was done in bright yellows that evoked the desert heat. "The stamp worked well, color, design, lettering," Blackshear said. "After *Gone With the Wind*, it was my favorite."

His "least favorite," he admitted, was *Stagecoach*. He was unable to find a satisfactory photograph of John Wayne as the Ringo Kid until USPS sent him a photocopy of the portrait it had used in creating its original concept design of the block. Although the face had a lot of shadows in it, it was "better than nothing," Blackshear said. The composition of the design also raised problems; putting a horizontal vignette such as a stagecoach and team of horses behind a large portrait wouldn't work, so he had to place the stagecoach in the foreground, whereas on the other three stamps the representative illustrations were all behind the portraits. "We were afraid we'd lose all the detail on that one when it was printed, and all those horses would turn into brown mush," confessed Derry Noyes, the CSAC design coordinator who served as art director for the block. That didn't happen, and the end result was a well-balanced design, one that included such graceful touches as the curve of the driver's whip that duplicated the curve of Wayne's suspender strap.

Blackshear also drew the lettering for the film titles, which he based on the original posters, including the distinctive antebellum-period style of *Gone With the Wind*. Lettering wasn't a skill he had used often, and USPS hadn't originally planned to have him do it.

"We tried to standardize the titles and go with typography out of books," said Derry Noyes, who in private life heads a Washington-area graphics firm. "We decided it lost the poster 'feeling' when we did that. So we went back to Tom Blackshear. He had done sketches with hand lettering for *Beau Geste* and *Stagecoach,* and I just had him carry on with hand lettering for the other two to be consistent. And I arranged them so the typography would work with 'USA 25,' which I had chosen the typeface for.

"So we made each one an individual poster-like stamp rather than providing the consistency of a block of four which you normally see, with the 'USA 25' always in the same place and the typography standardized. The 'USA 25' jumps around. It couldn't go in the same position on each stamp; as soon as we tried to do that, they lost a little of their pizazz. So we let each one be an individual. It wasn't quite clear that that was going to work on a whole sheet — to see this type bouncing all over the place — but in its own way that's probably what gives it its poster quality. As long as the 'USA 25' was readable, and was always black and was always the same typeface, the fact that it jumped around didn't hurt it."

The stamps were printed by gravure by the American Bank Note Company and issued in the large, 40-to-a-pane format last used for the Prehistoric Animals block of four in 1989. Derry Noyes said her only disappointment was that Blackshear's original lettering for *Beau Geste* was "much finer, much more chiseled" than what appeared on the finished stamp. "The yellow came out a little too strong," she said. "It wasn't that strong or that thick in the original. But that's what happens in printing. Things always come out a little different from the original artwork. They must have had to beef up the yellow to make it print."

The fact that the faces appeared on the stamps without identification was unusual, although not unprecedented. In the 19th century, portraits consistently appeared without names on U.S. stamps, and the annual Christmas stamps depicting Mary and the infant Jesus obviously have no need of identifying labels.

"We considered identifying the actors and actresses on the stamps," Joe Brockert said. "But we realized that the inscriptions could easily get too long. 'Judy Garland as Dorothy in *The Wizard of Oz*,' for instance, or, even worse, 'Clark Gable and Vivien Leigh as Rhett Butler and Scarlett O'Hara in *Gone With the Wind*.' You'd almost have to give birth-and-death dates, too, to be really complete. So we said, 'No, let's keep this very simple. If people don't know who the people on the stamps are they will appreciate the designs just as the movie posters that they are, and if they do know who they are we don't need to identify them.' We felt this was the cleanest and easiest way to proceed."

First-Day Facts

The first-day postmark was Hollywood, but the first-day ceremony was held in nearby Beverly Hills, in the auditorium of the Academy of Motion Picture Arts and Sciences. Actor Karl Malden, president of the Academy, was on hand to help Postmaster General Frank dedicate the stamps. William J. Good, general manager and postmaster of the Long Beach Division of USPS, presided.

On the following day, March 24, USPS joined with the Pinnacle Stamp Club of Little Rock, Arkansas, to hold a second-day cere-

North Little Rock, Arkansas, used this pictorial cancellation for its second-day covers of the Gone With the Wind stamp.

mony for the *Gone With the Wind* stamp at the Old Mill, a city park in North Little Rock. The Old Mill was shown in the 1939 film in a montage of scenes that ran behind the opening credits.

The original deadline for collectors to obtain first-day covers with the March 23 Hollywood postmark was April 22, but USPS later extended the time period by 30 days, to May 22.

25¢ MARIANNE MOORE
LITERARY ARTS SERIES

Date of Issue: April 18, 1990

Catalog Number: Scott 2449

Colors: magenta, yellow and blue

First-Day Cancel: Brooklyn, New York

FDCs Canceled: 390,535

Format: Panes of 50, vertical, 10 across, 5 down. Gravure printing cylinders of 200 subjects (10 across, 20 around) manufactured by Armotek Industries Inc., Palmyra, New Jersey.

Perf: 10.9 (L perforator)

Selvage Markings: ©United States Postal Service, Use Correct ZIP Code®

Designer: M. Gregory Rudd of Trumbull, Connecticut

Art Director and Project Manager: Jack Williams (USPS)

Modeler: Richard Sennett of Sennett Enterprises for American Bank Note Company

Typograhper: Bradbury Thompson (CSAC)

Printing: Stamps printed and sheeted out by American Bank Note Company on a leased Champlain gravure press (J.W. Fergusson and Sons, Richmond, Virginia) under the supervision of Sennett Enterprises (Fairfax, Virginia). Perforated, processed and shipped by ABNC (Chicago, Illinois).

Quantity Ordered: 150,000,000
Quantity Distributed: 150,000,000

Cylinder Number Detail: One group of three cylinder numbers preceded by the letter "A" over/under corner stamps.

Tagging: overall

The Stamp

On April 18, USPS issued what it described as the eighth in its Literary Arts series of stamps to honor Marianne Moore, a modern American poet. The stamp had its first-day sale in Brooklyn, New York, where Moore made her home in later years.

The Literary Arts series is a rather arbitrary grouping of commemorative stamps depicting writers of prose and poetry. Those previously honored in the series, which began in 1979, were John Steinbeck, Edith Wharton, Nathaniel Hawthorne, Herman Melville, T.S. Eliot, William Faulkner and Ernest Hemingway. What those stamps had in common was a vertical format and a simple design that included no identification of the subject other than his or her name — for Hawthorne and Hemingway, only the last name.

But in 1989 Postmaster General Anthony M. Frank decided that stamps ought to be more self-explanatory. (See chapters on the 25¢ Supreme Court and 5¢ Luis Munoz Marin stamps.) Consequently, the Marianne Moore design contained more information than its predecessors in the series. It not only included the inscription "American Poet" — words that had previously been used on several stamps that USPS doesn't consider part of the Literary Arts series — but also the years of Moore's birth and death, 1887-1972.

Marianne Craig Moore was one of the country's most highly honored poets. Her "Collected Poems" (1951) brought her the Bollingen Prize, the National Book Award and the Pulitzer Prize for Poetry. In 1953 she received the gold medal of the National Institute of Arts and Letters, and France gave her the Croix de Chevalier des Arts et Lettres for her translation of the 241 fables of La Fontaine, a task that took her eight years. T.S. Eliot said that "her poems form part of the small body of durable poetry written in our time; of that small body of writings in which an original sensibility and alert intelligence and deep feeling have been engaged in maintaining the life of the English language."

"She was a painstaking craftsman whose verse, which she composed in a spidery hand, was notable for its rhythms and its use of homely speech," wrote *The New York Times*' Alden Whitman. "Her poems utilized rhythms to create moods as well as to convey her admiration of such no-nonsense virtues as patience, firmness, courage, loyalty, modesty and independence. Much of her writing in this vein was a wry but gentle criticism of human conduct, literature and art, sometimes presented in unusual or baffling typographical arrangements. She made her point obliquely, for animals and plants rather than people were usually the formal subjects of her verse."

Miss Moore's compact poetry wasn't always easy to read or comprehend, even though she professed to have "a burning desire to be explicit," but for those who might have preferred the obvious, she had this answer: "It ought to be work to read something that was work to write." The critic Thomas Lask, who called her the century's most original and singular poet writing in English, concluded that "she is one poet who can stand much rereading. The very hardness of her verse makes it resistant to wear."

A slight woman with luminous blue-gray eyes, Marianne Moore was immediately recognizable by her attire — a cape and a tricorn hat, of which she had dozens. "I like the tricorn shape," she explained, "because it conceals the defects of the head." She became a well-known personality; the public was charmed by, among other things, her belated discovery and embrace of baseball. A friend took her to Brooklyn's Ebbets Field in 1949, and thereafter she was a fervent fan of the game and of the Brooklyn Dodgers. Her 1961 poem, "Baseball and Writing," began this way:

Fanaticism? No, writing is exciting
and baseball is like writing.
You can never tell with either
how it will go
or what you will do;
generating excitement —
a fever in the victim —
pitcher, catcher, fielder, batter.
Victim in what category?
Owlman watching from the press box?
To whom does it apply?
Who is excited? Might it be I?

In 1955 the Ford Motor Company enlisted her gift for evocative words in a quest for a name for a new automobile it was developing. Among the exotic appellations she offered were Resilient Bullet, Silver Sword, Impeccable, Mongoose Civique, Andante Con Moto, Varsity Stroke and Utopian Turtletop — what one historian called "quite the most original and refreshing selection of names ever suggested for an American motorcar." In the end, however, the company opted for a more prosaic title borrowed from the Ford family itself: Edsel.

Marianne Moore was born November 15, 1887, in the St. Louis suburb of Kirkwood, Missouri. While at Bryn Mawr College she had several poems published in the campus literary magazine. She later taught at Carlisle Indian Academy, where one of her pupils was the athlete Jim Thorpe. T.S. Eliot helped bring her to public attention when, in 1915, he printed several of her poems in the *Egoist*, a London journal of Imagism, the literary movement dedicated to poetry of naturalness, directness and precision. In the 1920s she was editor of the *Dial*, the foremost U.S. literary journal of its day.

Moore lived in a Brooklyn apartment for 37 years. In 1966 she moved across the East River to Greenwich Village. She died in her

The committee decided that this painting of an older Marianne Moore in her characteristic tricorn hat, done by another artist, was too unflattering.

sleep at her home February 5, 1972, at the age of 84. She had been a semi-invalid for nearly two years following a series of strokes.

The Design

The Rosenbach Museum and Library in Philadelphia, which holds the Marianne Moore papers, supplied USPS with a selection of photographs of the poet, including some that showed her in later years, wearing her characteristic tricorn hat. Using these photos, two artists prepared design concepts for the Citizens' Stamp Advisory Committee's consideration.

This portrait of a stern-looking, younger Marianne Moore was done by M. Gregory Rudd.

The committee members examined one artist's sketch of an older Moore but decided it was too unflattering. They chose instead a presentation by M. Gregory Rudd of Trumbull, Connecticut, who had previously designed the 25¢ Francis Ouimet stamp of 1988 and the 25¢ Ernest Hemingway stamp of 1989.

Rudd worked with at least two different younger portraits of Moore, but the one he preferred was a photograph made by George Platt Lynes in 1935 when the poet was 47. It showed her in a pensive pose, with her left hand against her cheek, her face strongly lit from the right side. "It was a very romantic, very beautiful kind of 1930s-1940s genre picture that looked as if someone had taken it in a Hollywood studio, with great black and white contrast and wonderful shadows," Rudd said. "It seemed so unlike any of the others, so atypical, that I was attracted to it, and the committee also seemed to like it best."

The 1935 photograph by George Platt Lynes on which the stamp design was based. Artist Rudd had to create a right eye in his painting because the eye in the photograph was in deep shadow.

In the photograph, the left side of Moore's face (her own right) was in deep shadow, and in painting the portrait Rudd had to make that side much lighter so the features would come through clearly. "I had to take some liberties," he said. "I had to become a kind of painter-photographer and manipulate the shadows in a way that allowed the viewer to see more detail. It was more of a challenge. It was fun to go after it, to try to make it work."

A comparison of the stamp and the photograph shows that Rudd also changed the hairstyle. "In the photograph her hair is braided and wrapped around her head," observed Leslie Morris, curator of books at the Rosenbach Museum. "On the stamp it looks almost

A sketch by Rudd in which a smaller portrait, based on the Lynes photograph, fronted the large principal portrait.

like a 1950s hairstyle, sort of a soft curl." The artist also altered the angle at which Moore's left hand touches her cheek, making it come up from below rather than from the horizontal in order to better fit the vertical design format. Additional refining was done when the image was processed on the American Bank Note Company's electronic scanner to bring out the lifelike glints of light in the eyes.

At CSAC's request, Rudd first provided a light-colored background. He tried a light green and a light blue, but neither one satisfied the committee, so he finally changed it to "a deep kind of black-purple." "They wanted that image to really pop," Rudd said. "They wanted a lot more contrast, and I think they were right." He noted, however, that the color was revised on the scanner at ABNC and emerged as more of a dark blue. "It worked out well," the artist said.

Rudd's earlier essays were cropped less tightly than the final version, in which the portrait filled more of the design space. They also showed a portion of the poet's blouse through her open sweater. But the blouse descended into the lettering and so he painted it out, leaving visible only a wide collar with a flower at the throat.

At one point, M. Gregory Rudd provided a lighter background for the portrait and typography, and extended the blouse lines into the lettering at the bottom.

54

First-Day Facts

The first-day ceremony at The Brooklyn Museum included a poetry reading, "Moore of Brooklyn," by the Brooklyn Heights Players, in which Lois Look played the role of Marianne Moore.

Ann McK. Robinson, USPS consumer advocate, dedicated the stamp. Speakers included Marianne Craig Moore, niece of the poet, and James R. Tanis, director of libraries for the poet's alma mater, Bryn Mawr College. Another niece, Sarah E. Moore, was an honored guest.

$5 LIGHTHOUSES BOOKLET

Date of Issue: April 26, 1990

Catalog Numbers: Scott 2470-74 (stamps); Scott 2474a (booklet pane)

Colors: magenta, yellow, cyan and black (offset); opaque white (intaglio)

First-Day Cancel: Washington, D.C. (National Archives)

FDCs Canceled: 805,133

Format: Four panes of five different vertical stamps, arranged horizontally. Offset printing plates of 240 subjects (20 across, 12 around); intaglio printing sleeve of 480 subjects (20 across, 24 around).

Perf: 9.75 (Goebel booklet machine stroke perforator)

Selvage Markings: Single-digit sleeve number superimposed on a black registration rectangle on each pane binding stub.

Cover Markings: ©United States Postal Service 1990 inside front cover. Universal Product Code (UPC) on outside of back cover.

Designer: Howard Koslow of East Norwich, New York

Art Director and Typographer: Howard Paine (CSAC)

Project Manager: Jack Williams (USPS)

Engraver: Gary Slaght (BEP) (lettering)

Modeler: Peter Cocci (BEP)

Printing: Stamps printed on BEP's six-color offset, three-color intaglio D press (902). Covers printed and booklets formed on Goebel booklet-forming machine.

Quantity Ordered: 37,000,000 booklets
Quantity Distributed: 36,680,400 booklets

Sleeve Number Detail: Single intaglio sleeve number on each pane binding stub.

Tagging: block

The Stamps

Each year since 1986, USPS has issued a topical booklet featuring five different designs. Topics covered in the past were fish, locomotives, classic automobiles and steamboats. The first of two such booklets issued in 1990 depicted American lighthouses.

The stamps were dedicated April 26 at the National Archives in Washington, D.C. Their designs had been unveiled the previous August 4 during ceremonies held at the Customs House Maritime Museum in Newburyport, Massachusetts, to mark the 200th anniversary of the act of Congress that created the Revenue Marine, the predecessor agency of the U.S. Coast Guard. Assistant Postmaster General Deborah K. Bowker and the Coast Guard commandant, Admiral Paul A. Yost, officiated. USPS prepared an attractive souvenir folder for the occasion, containing full-color reproductions of the stamps offset-printed on bright-white stiff coated paper.

The 1790 act authorized the construction of 10 small armed vessels whose mission was to stop smuggling and piracy along the U.S. seacoasts. The name of the service was changed to the Revenue Cutter Service in 1863 and the agency was combined with the Lifesaving Service in 1915 to create the Coast Guard. In 1939 the Coast Guard absorbed the Lighthouse Service, which had been created in 1789 to administer the nation's lighthouses.

In peacetime, the Coast Guard is an agency of the Department of Transportation. In time of war, it becomes an active part of the U.S. Navy. A 1945 stamp honored the Coast Guard for the role it played in World War II (Scott 936), and a 1965 postal card marked the 175th anniversary of the service's creation (Scott UX52). Another postal card, in 1978, depicted the Coast Guard training barque *Eagle* under full sail (Scott UX76).

For thousands of years lighthouses have guided mariners, let them know the shore was near and warned them of dangerous rocks and reefs. The Pharos of Alexandria, Egypt, a massive 400-foot tower built around 280 B.C. as a platform for a perpetually burning wood fire, was one of the Seven Wonders of the Ancient World. The tallest lighthouse ever built, it stood for some 15 centuries.

This vertical design showed the Split Rock, Michigan, lighthouse, which sits on top of a high cliff. The design was replaced in the final group of five stamps by a new, vertical depiction of Admiralty Head.

The first American lighthouse was erected in 1716 on Little Brewster Island at the entrance to Boston Harbor and was illuminated by candles or an oil lamp. It was destroyed by the British during the Revolutionary War, but another one was built on the same site in 1783 and still stands.

Over the last half-century, lighthouses have declined in importance because of the development of advanced electronic navigation aids. The number of operating lighthouses in the United States has fallen from about 1,500 in the early 1900s to about 340 today.

The five structures depicted on the stamps in the booklet were the lighthouses at Admiralty Head, Washington; Cape Hatteras, North Carolina; West Quoddy Head, Maine; American Shoals, Florida, and Sandy Hook, New Jersey. The cover of the booklet showed a sixth lighthouse, Maine's Portland Head light, and also displayed the crossed-anchor insignia of the Coast Guard.

In selecting these lighthouses, the Citizens' Stamp Advisory Committee was guided by a list of 10 recommendations submitted early in 1987 by James W. Hyland III, chairman of the Lighthouse Preservation Society of Rockport, Massachusetts, who had consulted with Robert Scheina, Coast Guard historian, and Francis Ross Holland Jr. of the National Park Service.

CSAC had originally proposed the issuance of 10 different stamps in two panes of five each. But USPS officials decided that 10 stamps would overload the commemorative mint sets assembled and sold by the Philatelic Sales Division, and so the number was cut to five.

Hyland had compiled a balanced list, with two lights from each major coastal region: New England, the mid-coast Atlantic, the South, the Great Lakes and the West Coast. All the lighthouses that ended up in the booklet were on Hyland's list except for Sandy Hook and Portland Head. The others Hyland had recommended were: Boston Light; New Jersey's twin-towered Navesink Light,

An unused Koslow sketch of the twin-towered Navesink lighthouse, a few miles south of Sandy Hook lighthouse on New Jersey's Sandy Hook Bay.

which is only a few miles from Sandy Hook; Thomas Point Shoal Light, Maryland; Spectacle Reef Light, Michigan, at the entrance to the Straits of Mackinac; Split Rock Light, Minnesota, and Old Point Loma Light, California.

Two of the six lighthouses that made it to the booklet had been on previous U.S. stamps as well. The Cape Hatteras lighthouse appeared on a 2¢ commemorative of 1972 (Scott 1449), which was part of a block of four stamps that together made up a confluent design honoring the Cape Hatteras National Seashore. The Sandy Hook tower was depicted on the 29¢ stamp of the Americana series, issued in 1978 (Scott 1605) and bearing the slogan "Lonely Beacon Protecting Those Upon the Sea."

Another lighthouse that had been postally depicted was Maine's Two Lights lighthouse on the rocky point of Cape Elizabeth, the subject of a painting by Edward Hopper that appeared on the Maine statehood stamp of 1970 (Scott 1391). Also, generic lighthouses were shown on the 18¢ America the Beautiful ("From Sea to Shining Sea") coil stamp of 1981 (Scott 1891) and the 15¢ America the Beautiful: The Seashore postal card of 1988 (Scott UX132).

ADMIRALTY HEAD. "This splendid masonry structure is unique for its Spanish design and is a real architectural gem," wrote James Hyland. Located near Coupeville, Washington, on Whidbey

The lighthouse at Sandy Hook was previously shown on the 29¢ Americana stamp of 1978 (Scott 1605).

59

Island at the entrance to Puget Sound, it was built soon after the 1887 discovery of gold in Alaska, which led to a boom in Washington's economy. The lighthouse guided ships bearing returning prospectors through Puget Sound to Seattle. It now serves as a visitor center at Fort Casey State Park.

CAPE HATTERAS. America's tallest lighthouse, rising 191 feet above the water, this brick structure with the distinctive black and white candy-cane stripes has stood since 1871 over one of three long thin islands that form North Carolina's Barrier Beaches, a perilous area for mariners. It is threatened by encroachment from the sea, which has led the National Park Service to propose a controversial plan to move the tower more than a mile inland at an estimated cost of $8.8 million. A storm in late October of 1990 brought the Atlantic Ocean to about 100 yards of the tower's base.

WEST QUODDY HEAD. This lighthouse stands 83 feet above the water in Lubec, Maine, at the easternmost point of the United States. There has been a lighthouse here since 1808; the present tower was built in 1858. Its red and white horizontal stripes constitute a day marker, enabling mariners to distinguish it from other lighthouses during the daytime.

AMERICAN SHOALS. Located in the Florida Keys, this lighthouse is an example of an offshore signaling rig, designed to stay in place in the shifting sands of the Gulf of Mexico. Its metal stilts are screwed into the sea floor, and its metal skeletal tower can withstand winds of hurricane force. A modern Coast Guard cutter of the *Reliance* class is shown in the foreground of the stamp design.

SANDY HOOK. The Western Hemisphere's oldest existing lighthouse, this one was built in 1764 and its 85-foot octagonal masonry tower still stands guard at the entrance to New York Harbor. At different times during the American Revolution it was the object of efforts by both British and Americans to put it out of action.

This earlier sketch of the Sandy Hook lighthouse placed the tower to the left and showed more of the adjacent building than appears on the finished stamp.

PORTLAND HEAD LIGHT. This lighthouse, at Cape Elizabeth, Maine, was begun in 1787. It was completed in 1790, but when the federal inspectors found that a neighboring headland shut off the view of the light, the building was made taller and the light wasn't actually lit until 1791. It rises 101 feet above high water.

The date and place of issue of the booklet were announced March 21, 1990. In its news release, USPS inaugurated a new policy, worked out in cooperation with the Scott Publishing Company, of providing the appropriate Scott catalog number or numbers with each new-issue announcement.

In a related promotion, USPS offered an 11- by 14-inch color print of the Pemaquid Point Lighthouse in Maine, along with a pane of five Lighthouses stamps and a Commemorative Stamp Club album page with a protective stamp mount, for $3.95. "Become a Lighthouse Keeper," USPS urged in its advertisements.

The Designs

As designer Howard Koslow and art director Howard Paine planned it, the booklet would have contained 10 designs divided between two panes of five stamps each. One pane would have consisted of stamps with designs laid out horizontally, like those in the previous five-variety topical booklets. On the other pane, the designs would have been arranged vertically.

"This would have been a beautiful way to present them," Koslow said. "Some of the lighthouses lent themselves better to a horizontal format. These would have given me more of an opportunity to do the designs as landscape paintings."

Later, when USPS decided to limit the number of varieties to five, the vertical format was specified for all of them. "Once we got to the verticals," Koslow said, "we felt obligated to do big images, rather than little landscapes, and focus in strongly on the towers."

Koslow's five horizontal designs were of the Admiralty Head, Thomas Point Shoal, Boston, Old Point Loma and Spectacle Reef lighthouses. His verticals were of Split Rock, Cape Hatteras, West Quoddy Head, American Shoals and Navesink; the latter was later dropped in favor of the nearby Sandy Hook.

The decision to go with only verticals meant that all of Koslow's horizontally executed lighthouses were eliminated with the exception of Admiralty Head, which the artist repainted as a vertical to replace Split Rock. If this switch hadn't been made, there would have been no West Coast lighthouses in the booklet, which would have displeased residents of that area (and probably would have also been noticed by Postmaster General Anthony M. Frank, who came to USPS after heading a San Francisco-based thrift institution).

In making his paintings, Koslow used several sources. For Sandy Hook and Cape Hatteras, he relied on photographs he had taken himself. Pictures of West Quoddy Head were furnished by James

Koslow's unused horizontal landscape-type paintings. From top to bottom: Boston Light; Admiralty Head; Spectacle Reef, Michigan; Old Point Loma, California, and Thomas Point Shoal, Maryland.

Hyland and by the Coast Guard. For American Shoals, his reference material came from the Coast Guard; the ship in the foreground, however, was copied from a picture supplied by The National Geographic Society, although Koslow checked with the Coast Guard's Robert Scheina first to make sure the vessel was an appropriate one for that location.

His biggest problem was finding the right picture of Admiralty Head. "I finally got in touch with John Harris, a park ranger at the park where the lighthouse sits," Koslow said. "He had a photo that was perfect for what I needed. It showed the building at an angle instead of straight perspective, so I could concentrate on the tower."

Koslow's acrylic paintings contained some striking touches: the delicate glow of sunrise illuminating the red and white bands of West Quoddy Head; a line of seabirds flying past the Cape Hatteras lighthouse; the lacework limbs of a leafless tree reaching in front of the cream-colored tower at Sandy Hook.

The stamps were printed on BEP's offset-intaglio D press. The only intaglio element on the stamps was the "25 USA" on each one, which was printed in opaque white over the offset picture portion, a technique BEP had pioneered with the 1987 Lacemaking block of four (Scott 2351-2354). A single intaglio sleeve number appeared on

For the vertical layouts, artist Howard Koslow at first envisioned the lighthouse names as running up the left side of the designs.

the selvage tab of each booklet pane, but because it was white BEP printed it on a black offset-printed rectangle to make it visible. Unlike the sleeve numbers on previous topical booklets, such as Locomotives, Classic Cars and Steamboats, this one was located on the right side of the selvage rather than the left. The black rectangles also served as the Length Register Marks (LRMs) to guide proper booklet pane cutting and perforating; previously, BEP had used a long, narrow LRM form on all book-stamp cylinder sleeves whose products were destined for the Goebel booklet-forming machines.

Because the designs were vertical, the straight edges on the stamps were at the top and bottom. On the fifth stamp of the pane (Sandy Hook), of course, there was a straight edge at the right side as well.

For the cover of the booklet, Koslow made a two-color line

This proposed booklet cover design placed the Coast Guard emblem at an angle and contained an inscription different from the one finally used.

63

A pane of Lighthouse stamps with the white engraved denomination and "USA" missing. Note the absence of the sleeve number on the black square of the binding stub.

drawing of the Portland Head lighthouse. Unlike the lighthouses on the stamps, this one bears no identifying label.

After doing the stamp paintings, Koslow was commissioned by The Hamilton Collection to create the artwork for a series of eight collectors' plates depicting lighthouses. He was also signed by another art firm to create brand-new paintings of the six lighthouses featured in the stamp booklet, on which a series of limited-edition prints would be based. He also prepared a poster for the Lighthouse Preservation Society that featured a montage of the 11 lighthouses he had originally painted for the booklet project. To collect additional lighthouse photographs for his files, Koslow and his wife made a trip to the West Coast in June 1990, starting with a visit to Admiralty Head and its helpful park ranger, John Harris.

Before the stamp booklet assignment, Koslow had taken part in a project coordinated by the Society of Illustrators in New York to create a series of historical paintings for the Coast Guard. He began designing stamps for USPS in 1971, and his recent credits included the designs of the four stamps marking the bicentennial of the three U.S. branches of government, including the Supreme Court stamp that had been issued earlier in 1990.

Varieties

Less than two weeks after the stamps were issued, Lighthouse booklets without white intaglio ink were discovered. Each stamp was missing the denomination and "USA," and on the binding stubs the offset-printed black blocks lacked the white sleeve numbers.

Julie Walker of Washington, D.C., bought a booklet shortly after the first day of issue and affixed the five stamps from the first pane to envelopes before noticing the error. Since she had not mailed the envelopes, she remailed the contents in new envelopes and saved those with the error stamps. Three panes remained intact.

A second report of the error came from the Staten Island, New

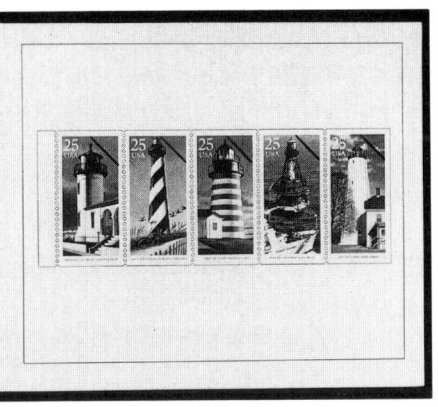

The inside pages of the Lighthouse souvenir folder, showing a full-color reproduction of the Lighthouse stamp designs. The folder was distributed at the design unveiling ceremony August 4, 1989, in Newburyport, Massachusetts.

York, area. Marilyn Green, a non-collector, purchased three booklets that were missing the intaglio ink and used two as postage before realizing they might be of value. She contacted the post office and was told that she could trade her remaining booklet for "good" stamps. After consulting with a *Linn's Stamp News* staff member, Green said she would try to recover some of the 40 error stamps that were mailed out, leaving them on cover if possible, and would keep the third booklet intact.

Jacques C. Schiff Jr., a New Jersey stamp dealer specializing in errors, reported selling one complete error booklet at auction in September 1990 for $528, including the 10-percent buyers' commission, and another in November 1990 for $374.

This Priority Mail cover, overfranked by 10¢, was returned for $2.40 postage, because the postage was "not legible." A handwritten notation reads, "no postage on stamps." The cover bears two panes of the intaglio-missing Lighthouse stamp error, which left stamps without a denomination. Cover courtesy of Jacques Schiff.

65

25¢ RHODE ISLAND STATEHOOD BICENTENNIAL CONSTITUTION BICENTENNIAL SERIES

Date of Issue: May 29, 1990

Catalog Number: Scott 2348

Colors: red, yellow, orange, green, black and blue (offset); black (intaglio)

First-Day Cancel: Pawtucket, Rhode Island (Slater Mill Historic Site)

FDCs Canceled: 305,566

Format: Panes of 50, vertical, 10 across, 5 down. Offset printing plates of 200 subjects (10 across, 20 around); intaglio printing sleeve of 400 subjects (10 across, 40 around).

Perf: 11.2 (Eureka off-line perforator)

Selvage Markings: ©United States Postage Service, Use Correct ZIP Code®

Designer: Robert Brangwynne of Boston, Massachusetts

Art Director: Richard Sheaff (CSAC)

Project Manager: Jack Williams (USPS)

Typographer: Bradbury Thompson (CSAC)

Engravers: Thomas Hipschen, vignette (BEP)
Michael Ryan, lettering (BEP)

Modeler: Ronald C. Sharpe (BEP)

Printing: 6-color offset, 3-color intaglio D press (902)

Quantity Ordered: 164,150,000
Quantity Distributed: 164,130,000

Plate/Sleeve Number Detail: One group of six offset plate numbers, a single-digit intaglio sleeve number in selvage of adjacent stamp.

Tagging: overall

The Stamp

More than six months before the Rhode Island statehood bicentennial stamp was issued, its design was made public in a unique way. It was one of scores of U.S. stamps whose images flashed across the multiple television screens of a video wall at the USPS-sponsored World Stamp Expo 89 that opened November 17, 1989. The 16-monitor video wall was used for repeated showings of *American Journey,* a 12-minute film that used U.S. stamps and archival footage to illustrate American history. Sharp-eyed collectors spotted, among the familiar stamp designs, six stamps that hadn't yet been issued or even formally unveiled: the Rhode Island commemorative and five stamps depicting Indian headdresses.

The Rhode Island stamp was part of the long-running series marking the bicentennial of the U.S. Constitution. It was the 13th and last of a sub-set that commemorated the anniversary of the ratification of the Constitution by each of the original 13 states. The act of ratification conferred "statehood" on these charter members of the Union, and Rhode Island held out the longest, finally giving its approval May 29, 1790.

The stamp was issued on the anniversary day, May 29, 1990, but not before the date of issue — and, even more so, the place — had become matters of controversy in Rhode Island.

Early in 1989, Jean McKenna, vice president of the Rhode Island Philatelic Society, had asked Governor Edward DiPrete to help obtain the first-day ceremony for the society's annual convention in Providence, the state capital, June 1, 1990. DiPrete endorsed the request in a February letter to USPS, and USPS agreed.

But after the public saw the design, which featured the historic Slater Mill in Pawtucket, other groups, including Pawtucket officials and the Rhode Island Bicentennial Foundation, called for a change of plans. They wanted the issue date to be May 29 and the place to be Pawtucket, both of which seemed more appropriate.

In March 1990, Governor DiPrete reversed himself and asked USPS to make the changes. Again, USPS was agreeable, and announced the new date and city April 2. "The governor is certainly cognizant of the fact that Old Slater Mill has historical significance," May Kernan, DiPrete's press secretary, told *The Providence Journal.* "We were not oblivious to the phone calls . . . and the governor saw the significance of issuing it on the exact day."

Patrick T. Conley, chairman of the Bicentennial Foundation, told the newspaper that Providence should never have been in the running in the first place. State law gave his foundation the task of coordinating and scheduling bicentennial events, he said, and he had been shocked in February 1990, when Providence Postmaster Wallace Kido told him the stamp would be issued in the capital.

"The stamp is dated May 29," Conley said. "To take it off that

Roger Williams, founder of Rhode Island, was shown on this 1936 stamp marking the event's 300th anniversary.

date is ill-advised. Besides, Slater Mill is on the stamp. And Slater Mill is in Pawtucket."

The philatelic society's Jean McKenna was understandably unhappy. The society's convention had been planned with the bicentennial stamp in mind, she told *The Journal,* and the first-day plans for June 1 in Providence had been widely publicized. Besides, Governor DiPrete had made a promise.

"I found the rules I had to play by, and I adhered to them by the letter of the law," she said. "I just feel a foul has been played."

After the change, there was speculation that USPS would find another first-day ceremony to give to the society as a consolation prize, but that didn't happen.

The issuance of the Rhode Island stamp made possible this philatelic trivia question: What is now the only state that has never had a stamp to mark an anniversary of its statehood? The answer is Utah, which missed its 50th anniversary in 1946 (probably because a stamp for the 100th anniversary of the area's settlement was scheduled to be issued the following year) and also missed its 75th anniversary in 1971. In 1996, Utah's centennial year, the Postal Service will no doubt correct that omission.

Several previous postal issues had had Rhode Island connections. The founding of the colony's first settlement, Providence, by Roger Williams in 1636 was marked by a 300th anniversary commemorative stamp in 1936 (Scott 777). The same event inspired a commemorative postal card on its 350th anniversary in 1986 (Scott UX112). The Touro Synagogue in Newport, first Jewish house of worship in America, was depicted on a stamp in 1982 (Scott 2017).

The Rhode Island Flag of 1775 was one of 10 historic American flags shown on a se-tenant strip in 1968 (Scott 1349), and a 1790 Rhode Island windmill was depicted in a 1980 stamp booklet (Scott 1739). The first automated post office in the United States, in Providence, was shown on a commemorative stamp of 1960 (Scott 1164). And, of course, Rhode Island, like the other 49 states, had a stamp in the 50-stamp pane of State Flags in 1976 (Scott 1645) and the 50-stamp pane of State Birds and Flowers of 1982 (Scott 1991).

Rhode Island natives portrayed on stamps include Gilbert Charles Stuart (Scott 884), Nathaniel Greene (Scott 785), Oliver Hazard Perry (Scott 261), his younger brother Matthew C. Perry (Scott 1021) and George M. Cohan (Scott 1756).

Rhode Island, fiercely independent, was the only one of the 13 states after the Revolutionary War not to send delegates to the Constitutional Convention in Philadelphia. Along with North Carolina, it withheld its ratification of the Constitution even after the other 11 states had elected a national Congress and a president and set up the new republic in business. Several things prompted Rhode Island to hold out. The state had created a paper-money program to pay off its war debt and ease the burden on its farmers and small property holders, and was fearful of jeopardizing this arrangement. It objected to the new Constitution's lack of a bill of rights and its failure to abolish slavery.

Most of all, Rhode Islanders believed in a weak central government like the one the Articles of Confederation had provided. They hadn't fought a revolution against British trade restrictions and import duties, they said, simply to hand that same power over to a federated Congress in which Rhode Island would have only a small voice. The legislature refused on 13 different occasions to support resolutions that would lead to ratification.

However, adoption of the Bill of Rights by the First Congress disposed of one of those objections. North Carolina's decision to ratify in December 1789, and increasing threats by the federal government to treat Rhode Island like the foreign state it in fact was, intensified Rhode Island's feeling of isolation. Creditors, who were eager to obtain the reimbursements Congress had promised for Continental war debts, pushed for Union.

Finally, on May 29, 1790, a convention ratified the Constitution by a 34-32 margin (three anti-federalist members, fortunately, were absent), and the "13 original states" were finally in place.

Almost simultaneously, Rhode Island was taking a significant step to transform itself — and the rest of New England — from an agrarian to an industrial economy, based at first on textile manufacturing. The key event was the establishment of the Slater Mill.

Samuel Slater was the man who, in the words of a descendant, historian Arnold Welles, "successfully transplanted the infant Industrial Revolution, which was in many ways an English monopoly, across an ocean to a new country." Late in his life Slater was visited by President Andrew Jackson, who said: "I understand you taught us how to spin, so as to rival Great Britain in her manufactures."

As a youth Slater worked for seven years in the cotton-spinning factories of Derbyshire, England. In New York City at the age of 21, he heard that a Rhode Island Quaker named Moses Brown had tried and failed to establish a water-driven cotton mill in Pawtucket.

These concept sketches by a Rhode Island artist showed various seashells, symbolic of the state's nickname, "The Ocean State"; a map of Narragansett Bay, circa 1800, and a 1786 10-shilling note issued by Rhode Island.

Slater told Brown he had emigrated in defiance of British law forbidding skilled mechanics to leave the country, and that he could reproduce from memory the blueprints for British state-of-the-art spinning machinery. All he needed was someone with enough faith in him and enough capital to build it in America.

Brown provided both, and Slater's machinery was installed in Brown's water mill on the Blackstone River in December 1790. Soon the mill was carding and spinning more thread and yarn than the hand weavers who processed it could possibly use on their home looms. In 1793 Slater built a large mill building (the one depicted on the stamp). He installed rows of looms adjoining the cotton-spinning machines, and told the weavers to come to the factory, where they worked under close supervision for wages for 60 to 70 hours a week. The factory system had arrived.

Wrote historian William G. McLoughlin: "The first workingmen's strike in American history occurred in Slater's mill in 1800, when the weavers walked out and left their looms idle in protest against Slater's hard-driving system. But protest was useless. Workers henceforth followed the relentless pace of the machines."

The Design

The design format was the same as that of the previous statehood bicentennial stamps: vertical, with a design representative of the state in an oblong frame above, and the state's name and date of ratification in red and black, respectively, at the bottom.

Two New England artists were commissioned by USPS to prepare concept sketches. One, a graphic designer, made several of these, showing, variously, a map of Narragansett Bay, circa 1800; a group

This concept sketch depicted the George Washington, a ship built in Providence in 1793 to be used for the India trade. The painting, by Thomas Chambers, is in the collection of the Rhode Island Historical Society.

of seashells, symbolic of Rhode Island's nickname, "The Ocean State," and a Rhode Island colonial 10-shilling note. The idea that this artist developed most fully was based on a painting of the *George Washington,* a ship built in Providence in 1793 for the firm of Brown & Francis and used in the India trade. The painting,

One artist sketched the anchor in several settings, including the bluffs of Block Island, the front of a Newport mansion and Easton Beach at Newport. His finished line drawing, showing the anchor on a dock, was approved by the Citizens' Stamp Advisory Committee but turned down by Postmaster General Frank.

71

owned by the Rhode Island Historical Society, was by Thomas Chambers (1845-circa 1866).

The other artist, who worked in a style reminiscent of wood engraving, did several pencil sketches of an old-fashioned anchor in various settings. The project's art director, Richard Sheaff, had suggested this approach because an anchor is featured on the state seal and represents Rhode Island's maritime tradition. The state seal itself, which also bears the one-word motto "Hope," had previously appeared on three stamps: the tercentenary commemorative of 1936 and the Rhode Island flag stamps in the Historic Flags block of 1968 and the State Flags pane of 1976.

May 29, 1790

Rhode Island

As a guide to the artist, art director Richard Sheaff combined typography with a portion of a pen-and-ink sketch by P.D. Malone that is distributed to visitors to Slater Mill.

The Citizens' Stamp Advisory Committee members liked the anchor concept. They selected a design that showed an anchor lying on a dock, and the artist made a finished work of it, which was then taken to Postmaster General Anthony M. Frank for his approval. But Frank turned it down. The anchor, shown out of context, would have no particular meaning for the people of Rhode Island, he said.

Art director Sheaff then went to Boston commercial artist Robert Brangwynne and asked him to do a sketch based on the 1793 Slater Mill, which still stands in Pawtucket. CSAC had received a number of requests over the years for a Slater Mill stamp, and this was "an opportunity to kill two birds with one stone," said Jack Williams of USPS, the project manager. To show Brangwynne what he wanted, Sheaff adapted a pen-and-ink drawing of the mill, done by one P.D. Malone, that is given to visitors to the Slater Mill Historic Site.

Brangwynne's painting of the cupolaed building, with the Blackstone River in the foreground and a small spillway just visible at the right, was approved by CSAC, which requested only minor touching-up changes, and shown to Postmaster General Frank. Fine, Frank said; if the governor likes it, you're in business. Williams carried the design to Providence, and Governor DiPrete's office telephoned the next day to announce that it had received gubernatorial approval.

There was one last-minute refinement added: a line of tiny white-dropout type at the bottom of the vignette with the words: "Slater Mill, 1793." None of the other 12 statehood bicentennial stamps had carried any design information. The wording was added in this case to make it clear that the other date on the stamp — the more prominently displayed May 29, 1790 — was the ratification date, not the date of the building.

This cautionary action, which was taken with Postmaster General Frank's blessing, was prompted at least in part by the criticism that USPS had received from a few literal-minded people in 1988 because the design of the New York stamp had showed Federal Hall in Manhattan in a setting that hadn't existed at the time of the ratification date printed beneath the picture, July 26, 1788.

The Rhode Island stamp was printed by BEP by offset and intaglio on the D press. The black portions of the picture, along with the black "May 29, 1790" and the red "Rhode Island," were printed by intaglio. However, other portions of Brangwynne's painting — sky, water, shadows — and the dropout lettering were also engraved before the offset plates were made, to provide sharp definition.

Art director Sheaff said he was satisfied with the result, but volunteered that "if we had done it my way — and on some of these things we're involved heavily in the production process, in others we aren't, and decisions get made elsewhere and nobody bothers to

The original Slater Mill stamp design didn't carry an inscription identifying its subject.

ask us — I would have used his artwork as the color plate for the offset basically, just as it was, and then strengthened whatever needed to be strengthened on the other (intaglio) plate. In the original it had a bit more softness to it . . .

"The Bureau people essentially redid the whole thing, trying their best to keep it close to the original, and, in fact, given that they did that, it's really quite close. The only thing I really dislike is the green trees in the background. They're sort of a bright, garish green, which they weren't intended to be and never were in the original."

The stamp was Robert Brangwynne's second. He had previously designed the 22¢ Social Security Act commemorative of 1985.

This pictorial first-day cancellation was similar to one used on previous stamps in the Statehood Bicentennial series.

First-Day Facts

Principal speakers at a rather extensive first-day ceremony at the Slater Mill Historic Site in Pawtucket were Governor DiPrete; Robert Macieski, curator of the Historic Site; Patrick T. Conley, chairman of the Rhode Island Bicentennial Foundation and the U.S. Constitution Council, and "Samuel Slater" himself, as played by Ed Shea of the Rhode Island Committee for the Humanities.

William R. Cummings, regional postmaster general, dedicated the stamp. Gary G. Gray, president of the Old Slater Mill Association's board of trustees, gave the welcome. Among several honored guests was William F. Turner, president of the Rhode Island Philatelic Society, the group that had learned that the expression "easy come, easy go" sometimes applies to stamp dedication ceremonies.

The pictorial first-day cancel featured a "We the People" scroll that had been used for the preceding stamps in the statehood bicentennial series.

25¢ OLYMPIANS (STRIP OF FIVE)

Date of Issue: July 6, 1990

Catalog Numbers: Scott 2496-2500 (stamps); Scott 2500a (strip of five)

Colors: red, yellow, blue and black

First-Day Cancel: Minneapolis, Minnesota

FDCs Canceled: 1,143,404

Format: Panes of 35, horizontal, 5 across, 7 down. Gravure printing cylinders of 140 (10 across, 14 around) manufactured by Armotek Industries, Inc., Palmyra, New Jersey.

Perf: 10.9 (L perforator)

Selvage Markings: ©United States Postal Service, Use Correct ZIP Code®; USPS logo above Olympic rings and the words "Official Olympic Sponsor." Jesse Owens won world acclaim by capturing four gold medals in track and field at Berlin in 1936. Three-time Olympian Ray Ewry won eight gold medals in the standing high jump and other jumping events. Donor of the trophy for the U.S.-Great Britain women's tennis series, Hazel Wightman won two gold medals in 1924. Boxer and bobsledder Eddie Eagan was the only U.S. gold medal winner in both the Summer and Winter Games. Swimmer Helene Madison won three Olympic gold medals in the Summer Games at Los Angeles in 1932.

Designer: Bart Forbes of Dallas, Texas

Art Director and Project Manager: Jack Williams (USPS)

Typographer: Howard Paine (CSAC)

Modeler: Richard Sennett of Sennett Enterprises for American Bank Note Company

Printing: Stamps printed and sheeted out by American Bank Note Company on a leased Champlain gravure press (J.W. Fergusson and Sons, Richmond, Virginia) under the supervision of Sennett Enterprises (Fairfax, Virginia). Perforated, processed and shipped by ABNC (Chicago, Illinois).

Quantity Ordered: 178,487,500
Quantity Distributed: 178,487,500

Cylinder Number Detail: One group of four gravure cylinder numbers preceded by the letter "A," forming horizontal plate block of 10 stamps (two stamps of each design).

Tagging: overall

The Stamps

The first stamps to be issued by USPS in its role as a sponsor of the 1992 Olympic Games and a marketer of Olympic-related products were five commemoratives in a se-tenant strip honoring American gold medal winners of past Olympics. The stamps were first sold July 6 in Minneapolis, Minnesota, which, with its sister city of St. Paul, was the site of the U.S. Olympic Festival 90.

The evolution of this issue was accompanied by a series of announcements and revisions that might well have made stamp collectors wonder what had happened to the U.S. Postal Service's planning procedures.

USPS originally contemplated issuing a single stamp honoring Jesse Owens, hero of the 1936 Olympics, as part of the American Sports series. The Citizens' Stamp Advisory Committee had recommended such a stamp on the basis of many requests from the public, and the Postal Service announced its intention to make it part of the 1990 stamp program when it released its first preview of that program on June 1, 1989.

But after the USPS officially became an Olympic Games sponsor in November 1989, officials decided to expand the issue into a booklet honoring not one but five U.S. Olympic athletes. The booklet plan was announced a few days before USPS celebrated Olympics Day on December 2 at World Stamp Expo 89, with Jesse Owens' wife Ruth and his daughter Gloria Hemphill among the honored guests.

On February 6, 1990, USPS unveiled the design of the Owens stamp during the 10th annual Jesse Owens International Trophy Award ceremony at the Hotel Waldorf-Astoria in New York City. Ruth Owens was again present, along with Olympic gold medalist Carl Lewis and Assistant Postmaster General Gordon C. Morison.

This is the photo Bart Forbes used as a source for the Jesse Owens picture on the stamp as issued. It was from a 1960 Olympic Guide distributed free by Kent Cigarettes.

At that time, collectors were still under the impression that the planned five stamps would be issued in booklet form.

However, when USPS issued a news release February 15 containing additional information on its 1990 first day program, the Olympians stamps were listed only as a "five-stamp issue," with no reference to a booklet. Finally, on April 2, USPS made a brief announcement that "because the issue was a late addition to the 1990 philatelic program, the Olympian stamps announced February 6 as a booklet will be a sheet stamp issue instead."

A major factor in all these revisions was the increasingly strained relationship between USPS and its long-time principal supplier of stamps, the Bureau of Engraving and Printing. The situation was made more difficult by a lack of a clear understanding of what each party expected of the other.

These unused concept sketches for the Jesse Owens stamp by Forbes showed Owens in a waist-up portrait, wearing Olympic medals, and executing a long jump.

77

After BEP officials learned of the Postal Service's decision to expand the Owens stamp into a booklet of five different varieties, they told USPS flatly that there was no way they could produce the Olympians booklet and another previously unscheduled booklet — one honoring American comedians — in fiscal 1990 because of commitments already made, including commitments to fill a growing demand for paper currency and to print large quantities of non-denominated F stamps in anticipation of 1991's rate change.

USPS, which as an Olympics sponsor considered it essential to issue the stamps as promised, quickly altered its plans. It decided to convert the Olympians stamps to sheet form and assigned the printing job to the American Bank Note Company, which had a standing contract with USPS for production of commemorative stamps in sheets. As for the Comedians booklet, USPS said, it would be postponed until at least 1991.

(Such misunderstandings between USPS and the Bureau are much less likely to occur in the future, as the result of a lengthy agreement that officials of both agencies signed June 11, 1990. The agreement, which resulted from 110 days of rather intensive negotiations, covered the quantities and types of stamps that BEP would print in the next five years and included a timetable for the exchange of specified information between the agencies during that period and a procedure for making late changes in agreed-upon stamp programs.)

Early in June, USPS announced further details of the Olympians stamps, including the identity of the four athletes who would be honored along with Owens: Ray Ewry, Hazel Wightman, Eddie Eagan and Helene Madison. The stamps would be distributed in an unprecedented format: se-tenant panes of 35, five across by seven deep, with each vertical strip of seven containing identical stamps.

In addition — in keeping with Postmaster General Anthony Frank's order that more information on stamp subjects be furnished to customers and postal clerks — a brief description of each Olympian's claim to fame would be printed in extra-wide selvage located at the top or bottom of the appropriate vertical row of stamps. This would create, for each stamp adjacent to the selvage, a tab similar to those on Israeli stamps. In effect, the markings would occupy space that normally would have been occupied by a horizontal row of stamps in a 40-stamp pane. Back when the issue was being thought of as a booklet, it had been USPS' intention to use the booklet cover for this informational purpose.

For collectors, the novel pane layout raised the question of just what quantity and arrangement of stamps to save. To get one stamp of each design, it was necessary to buy a horizontal strip of five stamps. A plate block, as recognized by the Scott catalog, consisted of a horizontal strip of five stamps by two stamps, which was the smallest grouping that would show all designs and constitute a block. In such a multiple, however, six of the 10 stamps were remote from the selvage, which was unique in plate block collecting. However, many collectors also wanted to have the large margin along the top or bottom row of the pane, which contained the information about the athletes along with a composite logo showing the USPS eagle and Olympic rings. Thus, the horizontal block of 10 with the inscription selvage constituted another collectible position.

A third possible collectible position was the vertical strip of 14, two stamps across by seven down, with the wide margin at the side containing the plate number, copyright and ZIP code markings, plus the USPS and Olympic symbols. The problem with this multiple was that it included only two of the five stamp designs.

An article in the July 12 *Postal Bulletin,* of USPS stated that the Olympians stamps could be sold in either of two ways: as a vertical strip of 14 (with marginal markings) or as a horizontal strip of 10 stamps (plate number or inscription blocks). No doubt some collectors avoided dealing with the question by saving the entire pane of 35 — the option calculated to please USPS most of all.

"As an official Olympic sponsor, we want Americans to know more about our own Olympians," Assistant Postmaster General Morison said in the news release giving details of the issue. "These five athletes were outstanding in their day and should be remembered for their contributions to our Olympic heritage."

The athletes who were honored were recommended to CSAC by USPS' Office of Olympic Marketing, headed at the time by W.L. (Pete) Davidson Jr., from a list of gold medalists that had been suggested to USPS by the U.S. Olympic Committee. To be eligible, of course, a candidate had to have been dead for at least 10 years. Two famous American Olympic champions were omitted from consideration because they had already been pictured on stamps: Babe Didrikson Zaharias (Scott 1932), who won the javelin and 80-meter hurdles in, coincidentally, 1932, and Jim Thorpe (Scott 2089), winner of the pentathlon and decathlon in 1912.

"We tried to identify unique or spectacular achievements" in choosing the other four athletes to join Jesse Owens, said Kim Parks of the Office of Olympic Marketing. "Each one we selected had done something that put their achievements just a little bit above what other athletes had done. We also tried to split the recognition between male athletes and female athletes."

These are the five who were chosen:

RAY EWRY

Few athletes in track and field history have dominated their specialty as Ray C. Ewry dominated his. The six-foot, three-inch "Deac" Ewry was a master of the long-lost art of the standing jump.

The second modern Olympic Games, held in Paris in 1900, in-

The stamp picture of Ray Ewry performing the standing high jump at the 1900 Olympics was based on this photo (Brown Brothers).

cluded three such events: the standing long jump, standing high jump and standing hop, step and jump. Ewry won all three. He accomplished the same feat in 1904, at the St. Louis games. In 1906 a special, unofficial Olympic Games was held in Athens, and Ewry won the standing high and long jumps. (The standing hop, step and jump had been dropped.) He won the same two events in the 1908 Games in London, then retired undefeated from Olympic competition. His tally: eight gold medals in official Olympic Games, plus two more in the off-year Games. No other Olympic track and field athlete has come close to that mark since.

"Ewry's performance is marvelous," wrote Malcolm Ford in the *New York Mail and Express* the day after his triple victories in Paris. "A man who can stand still before a bar five feet five inches high and lift himself over it not only must have wonderful spring, but also the ability to handle his legs very rapidly. The standing high jump is made by the athlete standing sideways to the bar. When the spring is made, the leg nearest the stick is put over first, and it begins descending on the other side again before the trailing leg is well up. The dropping of the forward leg over the bar after clearing it counterbalances the raising of the trailing leg. It is essentially a motion that only can be acquired with much practice."

The standing jump events were eliminated from the Olympics after 1912, and Ewry's five-foot, five-inch mark for the high jump set in 1900 and the 11-foot, 4⅞-inch distance for the long jump he achieved in 1904 remain Olympic records. He also won 15 Amateur Athletic Union titles, and held the amateur record for the backward standing long jump at nine feet, three inches.

As a boy in Lafayette, Indiana, Ewry contracted polio, but he recovered and built up his body through strenuous exercise. After graduation from Purdue University, he took a job as a hydraulic engineer for New York City. He lived in New York all his life, and died there in 1937 at the age of 62. The selvage opposite his stamp reads: "Three-time Olympian Ray Ewry won eight gold medals in the standing high jump and other jumping events."

HELENE MADISON

Like most world-class swimmers, Helene E. Madison accomplished her greatest triumphs at a very young age. In 1930, as a 17-year-old girl from Seattle, she held 26 freestyle world's records for distances from 50 yards to one mile. In the 1932 Olympic Games at Los Angeles, she won the 100-meter and 400-meter freestyle (setting an Olympic record of one minute, six and eight tenths seconds in the former) and was a member of the 400-meter relay team.

After the Olympics she taught swimming, had a brief fling at the movies, entertained in night clubs, sold sporting goods and studied nursing. She was one of those who advocated U.S. withdrawal from the 1936 Olympic Games in Nazi Germany, saying: "Fair competition for every eligible athlete in the world, regardless of color or creed or nationality, is what the Olympic Games stand for. I think America as a leading nation should refuse to compete where sportsmanship is threatened by prejudice." She contracted cancer and diabetes and died in 1970 at the age of 56. The selvage opposite her stamp reads: "Swimmer Helene Madison won three Olympic gold medals in the Summer Games at Los Angeles in 1932."

EDDIE EAGAN

Eddie Eagan was the only person to win gold medals in both the Summer and Winter Olympics. In 1920 at Antwerp, Belgium, he beat Sverre Sorsdal of Norway in the finals of the light-heavyweight boxing competition. Twelve years later he rode to victory as a member of the U.S. four-man bobsled team in the Winter Games at Lake Placid, New York.

Edward Patrick Francis Eagan learned to box in high school in Longmont, Colorado. After Army service in World War I, he worked his way through Yale University, where as a freshman he won the national amateur heavyweight title. After his Olympic victory and his 1921 graduation from Yale he attended Harvard Law School and was awarded a Rhodes Scholarship to Oxford. While at Oxford he fought world heavyweight champion Jack Dempsey in a series of three-round exhibitions. In the 1924 Olympics he competed as a heavyweight, but lost a decision in his first match.

Being a member of a bobsled crew requires no extraordinary skill — only weight and courage — and Eagan had never been on a bobsled before he went to Lake Placid in 1932 to join the U.S. four-

Forbes based his Eddie Eagan painting on this U.S. Olympic Committee photograph in The Complete Book of the Olympics, *by David Wallechinsky (Penguin).*

man team. "The first ride will always be vivid in my memory," he recalled afterward. "It took only two minutes to make that run, but to me it seemed like an eon . . . Speeding only a few inches from the ground without any sense of security, I hung on to the straps. My hands seemed to be slipping, but still I clung." A few weeks later,

This International Newsreel picture shows the 1932 U.S. four-man bobsled team, the gold medal winner at the Winter Olympics, rounding "Shady Corner" on the Lake Placid run. Eddie Eagan is the number 2 man, behind driver William L. Fiske. Bart Forbes modeled his bobsled image on the Eagan stamp on this photograph.

82

his technique (such as it was) polished by continuous practice, Eddie Eagan accepted his second gold medal in 12 years.

From 1945 to 1951 Eagan was chairman of the New York State Athletic Commission, which governed boxing in the Empire State. He died of a heart attack in 1967 at the age of 69. His stamp selvage reads: "Boxer and bobsledder Eddie Eagan was the only U.S. gold medal winner in both the Summer and Winter Games."

HAZEL WIGHTMAN

Tennis is no longer an Olympic event, but it was a recognized sport in the first seven Olympic Games, from 1896 to 1924. In the last of those Games, in Paris, 37-year-old Hazel Wightman won two gold medals. She teamed with her pupil, Helen Wills, who was nearly 20 years her junior, to win the ladies' doubles championship, then joined with Richard Norris Williams to win the mixed doubles.

After Wightman's death, her obituary in *The New York Times* didn't even mention the Olympic medals. She was much better known for her many national tennis titles — 45 in a span of 45 years, the last being the U.S. women's veterans doubles title in 1950, when she was 63 — and as the donor of the Wightman Cup as the trophy for an annual international tennis match between the best female amateurs of the United States and Great Britain. She played on the first U.S. Wightman Cup team in 1923 and was a member again in 1924, 1927, 1929 and 1931.

She was born Hazel Virginia Hotchkiss in California in 1886. Marriage in 1912 to George William Wightman, who was later

Bart Forbes used this U.S. Olympic Committee photograph of two players of the 1920s — neither of whom was Hazel Wightman — in developing his Wightman stamp design.

The artist made this pencil sketch in the process of "creating" a Hazel Wightman image for her stamp in the Olympians strip.

president of the U.S. Lawn Tennis Association, and rearing a family of five caused scarcely an interruption in her tennis career. She also played championship squash, ping-pong and badminton. She was the only one of the five Olympians in the stamp set to make it to age 70, and she continued to play tennis for several years after that. In 1973, on the 50th anniversary of the Wightman Cup, she was made an honorary commander of the British Empire by Queen Elizabeth II. She died in 1974 at the age of 87. Her stamp selvage reads: "Donor of the trophy for the U.S.-Great Britain women's tennis series, Hazel Wightman won two gold medals in 1924."

JESSE OWENS

The time was 1936; the place was Adolf Hitler's Berlin, site of the 11th Olympic Games and capital of an aggressive and totalitarian nation that had the whole world worried over its intentions.

Hitler was a prominent presence at the Games, noted William J. Baker in his biography, *Jesse Owens: An American Life.* "Confidently (Hitler) expected a stirring exhibition of Aryan athletic supremacy," Baker wrote. "He reckoned without the speed and stamina of a large contingent of black American athletes, who simply stole the show from their Aryan opponents during the first week of track and field competition.

"Jesse Owens led that coup, smashing records and claiming four gold medals in the premier events. First he tied the world record of 10.3 seconds in the 100-meter dash. Then he set new Olympic records of 26 feet, 5¼ inches in the long jump, and 20.7 seconds in the 200-meter sprint. Finally, he contributed a strong opening leg in the finals of the 400-meter relay, propelling his team toward a new world and Olympic mark of 39.8 seconds."

The story that Hitler snubbed Owens, refusing to shake his hand after his victories because he was black, was invented at the Games by American sportswriters and has persisted ever since. But Baker and others have pointed out that it was untrue. After Hitler had summoned two German gold medal winners to his box on the first day of the Games and congratulated them, he was advised by Olympic officials that as head of the host government he must be impartial and must congratulate all or none of the winners. He opted to greet none of the medalists thereafter, Baker wrote.

Even at Berlin, Jesse Owens didn't equal his own greatest sequence of performances on an athletic field, however. That had occurred May 25, 1935, at Ann Arbor, Michigan, where Owens, competing for Ohio State University in the Big Ten meet, broke three world records (220-yard dash, 220-yard low hurdles, long jump) and tied one (100-yard dash) in the span of a single hour. His times in the two 220-yard events were also recognized as world records for the slightly shorter 200-meter distance. The long jump record, 26 feet, 8¼ inches, would be unsurpassed for 25 years.

In later years Owens was a businessman and a popular public speaker and was a member of the U.S. Olympic Committee, serving as a goodwill ambassador for the Olympic Games. In 1950 the Associated Press selected him as the greatest track athlete of the past half-century; he received 291 votes to second-place Jim Thorpe's 74. He was awarded a Presidential Medal of Freedom in 1976. Lung cancer, probably caused by long years of heavy cigarette smoking after his athletic career ended, took his life in 1980 when he was only 66. His stamp selvage reads: "Jesse Owens won world acclaim by capturing four gold medals in track and field at Berlin in 1936."

The other medalists who were nominated by the U.S. Olympic Committee and considered by the USPS Office of Olympic Marketing were:

Margaret Abbott, the first female Olympic champion, who captured the women's singles title in golf in 1900; James B. Connolly, the first-ever gold medalist in the modern Olympics, who won the triple jump in 1896; Charles Meldrum Daniels, first American gold medalist in swimming, who won four golds in 1904 and 1908; William Fiske, a bobsled gold medalist in 1928 and 1932, who was killed in action with the Royal Air Force in 1941.

Also William DeHart Hubbard, 1924 long-jump champion, first black athlete to win an individual gold medal; Duke Paoa Kahanamoku, a Hawaiian sports hero, who won three swimming gold medals in 1912 and 1920; Alvin Kraenzlein, who won four track and field gold medals in 1900; Willie Lee, who won five gold medals in 1920 in individual and team shooting; Ralph Metcalfe, a member of the winning U.S. four- by 100-meter relay in 1936, later a U.S. congressman; Carl Townsend Osburn, another winner of five golds in shooting, in 1912 and 1920.

Also Charles Paddock, 100-meter winner in 1920 and first sprinter to be dubbed "the world's fastest human," who was killed while serving with the Marines in World War II; Melvin Winfield

Bart Forbes made pencil sketches for the Ewry, Eagan, Madison and Wightman stamps in the waist-up portrait format, but didn't do finished paintings of these.

Shepard, whose 1500-meter run victory in 1908 was the last in that event by an American (he also won two other gold medals that year); Martin Sheridan, who won three golds in the shot and discus in 1904 and 1908; John Baxter Taylor, who as a member of the winning U.S. 1600-meter medley relay team in 1908 was the first black athlete to win a gold medal, and Eddie Tolan, winner of the 100- and 200-meter dashes in 1932.

The Designs

The designer of the Olympians stamps was Bart Forbes of Dallas, Texas, whose previous assignments for USPS had included three stamps with sports themes: the Winter and Summer Olympics commemoratives of 1988 and the Lou Gehrig stamp of 1989.

Forbes was one of two artists commissioned by USPS to submit concept sketches, and each artist prepared a set of five. CSAC preferred Forbes' interpretations, and he received the design contract. There was no thought of mixing the two artists' designs, officials said: CSAC wanted a uniform style for the set.

For Owens, Forbes prepared three different design treatments, showing the subject (1) crouched at the starting line, the pose that was eventually used on the stamp; (2) in mid-air, performing the long jump, and (3) in a waist-up view in vertical format, in his track uniform with his Olympic medals around his neck. (The latter was done at the suggestion of USPS officials, who thought that the same pose might be used for all five Olympians, and Forbes went so far as to make matching pencil sketches of the other four.)

Forbes based his starting-line sketch of Owens on a photograph in a small brochure called the *1960 Olympic Guide,* listing a schedule of events and TV viewing times for the 1960 Games. The booklet, advertising Kent cigarettes, contained numerous photos of former Olympic athletes and was apparently printed as a magazine insert,

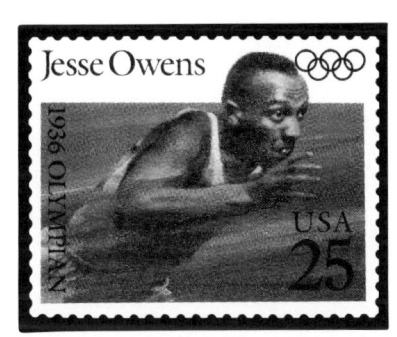

A second artist made these paintings for the set, but the Citizens' Stamp Advisory Committee preferred Bart Forbes' designs.

These are pencil sketches of the Bart Forbes designs that were given final approval for the Ewry, Eagan, Madison and Wightman stamps.

Forbes said. He based his picture of Owens performing the long jump on a photo in a book called *The Lincoln Library of Sports Champions*. The waist-up portrait came from another book, entitled Art Rust's *Illustrated History of the Black Athlete*.

The Hazel Wightman design "I pretty much had to make up," Forbes said, and for that reason it was the artist's least favorite of the five. "I didn't take it from a single photograph of her playing tennis," he said. "She was only in one Olympics and apparently was not photographed very much. She was by far the hardest to find good reference material on. I had a couple of shots of her, but they were both vertical and not very clear and they just didn't fit that format. I used a couple of other pictures of that era and incorporated a likeness of her as best I could."

Forbes, whose design credits also include the Abigail Adams stamp of 1985 and the America the Beautiful postal card series, feels strongly that artists should be given some kind of credit line in the stamp selvage, especially now that the selvage is being used increasingly to convey information to the stamp buyer.

"Artists are accustomed to getting credit lines in story illustrations, in book illustrations, in all sorts of things," he said. "Stamps are one of the very few instances where they are asked not to sign their art work. It would cost the Postal Service nothing to print the name on the stamp sheet and it would be a nice credit to the artist. And many people want to know who the designer was."

First-Day Facts

Associate Postmaster General Kenneth J. Hunter dedicated the stamps at the Wesley United Methodist Church, Marquette and Grant Streets, next to the Minneapolis Convention Center. Jack Kelly, president/executive director of U.S. Olympic Festival 90, was the principal speaker. The welcome was given by Marlene Johnson, lieutenant governor of Minnesota. Among the honored guests were the mayors of the Twin Cities, Donald M. Fraser of Minneapolis and James Scheibel of St. Paul.

This pane of Olympians stamps has been artistically "broken" with two solid lines and a line of dashes to show the three collectible position blocks.

89

This is Bart Forbes' sketch of a booklet cover made when the Postal Service planned to issue the five Olympians stamps in booklet form.

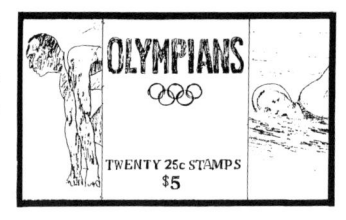

For first-day covers on which USPS affixed stamps, collectors were required to submit five self-addressed Number 6¾ envelopes and $1.25 for a set of five stamps, one per envelope. Requests for specific stamps from the set weren't honored.

$5 INDIAN HEADDRESSES BOOKLET

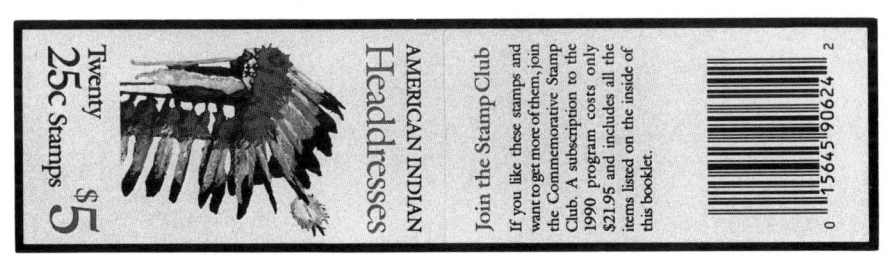

Date of Issue: August 17, 1990

Catalog Numbers: Scott 2501-05 (stamps); Scott 2505a (booklet pane)

Colors: magenta, yellow, cyan, black and olive (offset); black (intaglio)

First-Day Cancel: Cody, Wyoming (Buffalo Bill Historical Center)

FDCs Canceled: 979,580

Format: Two panes of 10 stamps each arranged horizontally 5 by 2. Five varieties on each pane. Offset printing plates of 200 subjects (10 across, 20 down) and intaglio printing sleeve of 400 subjects (10 across, 40 around).

Perf: 11.2 by 11.2 (Eureka off-line perforator)

Selvage Markings: Sleeve number on binding stub of each pane. Registration mark remnants on 17% of all binding stubs.

Cover Markings: ©United States Postal Service 1990 on inside of front cover. Universal Product Code (UPC) printed on outside of back cover.

Designer: Lunda Hoyle Gill of Riverside, California

Engravers: Thomas Hipschen, Kenneth Kipperman, Gary Chaconas, vignettes (BEP), Gary Slaght, lettering (BEP)

Art Director and Typographer: Howard Paine (CSAC)

Project Manager: Jack Williams (USPS)

Modeler: Peter Cocci (BEP)

Printing: BEP's 6-color offset, 3-color intaglio D press (902). Booklet covers printed on a 6-color Goebel Optiforma offset press (043) in magenta, yellow, cyan and black. Booklets formed on standard bookbinding equipment.

Quantity Ordered: 37,000,000 booklets
Quantity Distributed: 37,299,900 booklets

Plate/Sleeve Number Detail: One intaglio sleeve number on each pane binding stub

Tagging: overall

The Stamps

The elaborate feathered and beaded headdresses of Plains Indian tribes were the subjects of USPS' second topical booklet of 1990. The booklet, containing five varieties, was dedicated August 17 at the Buffalo Bill Historical Center in Cody, Wyoming, the location of the Plains Indian Museum.

The Indian Headdresses stamps had been unveiled to the public in an unprecedented way at World Stamp Expo 89, the USPS-sponsored stamp show that opened at the Washington, D.C., Convention Center November 17, 1989. Their images, along with that of the Rhode Island Statehood commemorative, were periodically flashed onto a 16-monitor video wall as part of *American Journey,* a 12-minute film that combined U.S. stamps and archival footage in a review of America's history.

The tribes honored on the stamps were the Assiniboine, Cheyenne, Comanche, Flathead and Shoshone. The booklet cover displayed a headdress of a sixth tribe, the Lakota Sioux, although it was not identified as such.

USPS considered the five stamps to be part of the Folk Art series, which began in 1977 with four Pueblo Indian pots shown on a se-tenant block (Scott 1706-1709) and has since depicted quilts, Pennsylvania toleware, Pacific Northwest Indian masks, duck decoys, Navajo Indian blankets, wood-carved figurines, lacework and carousel animals, all in blocks of four. The Indian Headdresses stamps were the first in the series to consist of more than four varieties and the first to be issued in booklet form.

They were also the first booklet stamps in recent years to be issued in the traditional commemorative size (1.56 inches wide by .99 inches deep, arranged horizontally) rather than with the elongated aspect ratio (1.75 by .88 inches) that had been used for the Classic Cars, Steamboats, Lighthouses and other topical booklets. The change was made for a practical reason. The original intention had been to issue these booklet stamps, too, in the extra-long size. Then the Office of Stamp and Philatelic Marketing learned that stamps of this length had been causing problems in mail processing. When people used the stamps on business reply envelopes that had facing identification marks (FIMs) imprinted at the top, they sometimes placed them over a portion of the vertical markings, thus interfering with the FIMs' purpose of identifying pre-bar-coded mail to automated postal equipment. For this reason, the stamp office agreed to issue no more of the extra-long stamps unless they had vertically arranged designs (like the Lighthouses) that would be less likely to intrude on the FIMs.

The revision in the Indian Headdresses stamps' dimensions necessitated a new kind of pane layout, however.

When a Headdresses pane is held sideways, so that the stamps are properly oriented, it consists of 10 stamps arranged in two horizontal strips of five varieties each, with matching pairs of each variety joined vertically. Thus each variety can be found with a straight edge at either the top or bottom. Each of the two Shoshone Headdress stamps (which by virtue of the alphabetical arrangement of the Indian tribes are the outermost stamps on the pane) also has a straight edge on its right side.

This layout resulted in an extra-long pane that had to be folded twice in order to fit inside normal-size booklet covers. The panes were folded between the second and third stamps from the stub, and again between the fifth and sixth. As with all recent booklets, however, USPS made unfolded panes with tabs available to collectors through the Philatelic Sales Division.

USPS also marketed a folder containing color illustrations of Indian-related scenes and a single 10-stamp pane of the Headdresses stamps, with a brief description of each headdress. The folder sold for $4.95.

The Indian Headdresses booklet was included in USPS' preliminary schedule of 1990 stamps and stationery that was released June 1, 1989. But it wasn't until more than a year later, on July 3, 1990, that USPS announced the first-day date and place. At about the same time, the July-August issue of the USPS *Philatelic Catalog* appeared, with the stamps illustrated in color on its back cover.

With two exceptions, which will be noted later, all the headdresses depicted on the stamps in the booklet were based on original specimens in the Plains Indian Museum.

ASSINIBOINE. The spelling of the tribe's name gave USPS some problems. The stamp design unveiled at World Stamp Expo carried the spelling "Assiniboine." Then USPS announced that this was in error and that there should be no "e" on the end of the word. Further research, however, satisfied the Postal Service that the spelling with the "e" was correct. The principal authority for this was

Lunda Hoyle Gill's original concept sketch of the Assiniboine bonnet, which she later made into a finished painting for use on the stamp. The painting had to be cropped just below the headband to make it fit the horizontal stamp format.

George P. Horse Capture, curator of the Plains Indian Museum, who wrote this letter to postal officials in January 1990:

"Most major publications utilize the 'e' at the end of Assiniboine and . . . the tribe that lives on the (Fort Belknap, Montana) reservation uses an 'e.' . . . If the tribe prefers the 'e,' who can disagree?" Rayna Green of the Smithsonian Institution's American Indian program also confirmed the correctness of the "e" spelling.

This Comanche bonnet, the property of the Panhandle Plains Historical Museum in Canyon, Texas, was made and worn by Chief Quanah Parker. Lunda Hoyle Gill made this concept sketch of the bonnet in a vertical stamp format. The Comanche bonnet that was actually shown on the stamp as issued is not this one, however, but one owned by a private collector in Santa Fe, New Mexico.

The Assiniboine war bonnet on the stamp, dating from about 1920, was handcrafted of felt and wool, with large ermine skins hanging from each side of the temple.

CHEYENNE. The bonnet on the stamp, dating from about 1890, was distinctive for its brass tack decorations across the brow, in addition to its golden eagle feathers, hair tassels and ribbons.

COMANCHE. The Comanche war bonnet on the stamp dated from the mid-1800s. It was made from golden eagle and dyed turkey feathers. The sides were trimmed in rabbit skin and fur. It is in the private collection of Alfred Aguilar of Santa Fe, New Mexico.

FLATHEAD. The bonnet on the stamp, dating from about 1905, was made from felt and large tail feathers of a golden eagle, with ermine skin spots and white cow tail hair at the end of each feather.

SHOSHONE. The Shoshone war bonnet on the stamp, dating from about 1900, was made from the tail feathers of a golden eagle. Uniquely, it had porcupine quills embroidered on the brow band.

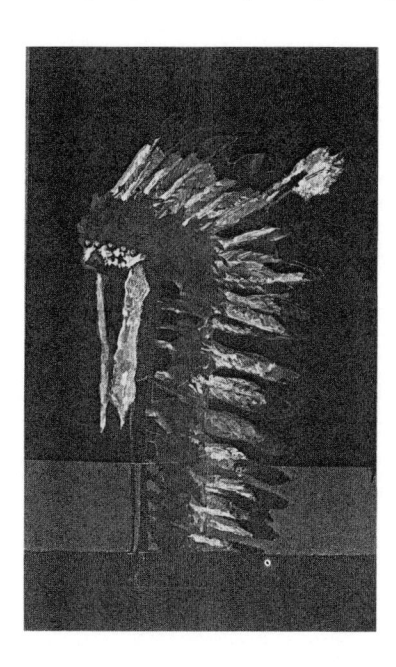

This concept sketch by Lunda Hoyle Gill of a Lakota Sioux bonnet in the Denver Art Museum wasn't used on a stamp, but was adapted for use on the booklet cover.

LAKOTA SIOUX. The 19th-century Lakota bonnet, pictured on the booklet cover, is in the Denver, Colorado, Art Museum.

The Designs

Indian Headdresses had been approved by the Citizens' Stamp Advisory Committee as a Folk Art subject, on the assumption that the stamps would be issued as a block of four. Later, the growing popularity of booklets led to the decision to issue the stamps in that form, with a fifth design added.

This sketch by Lunda Hoyle Gill shows an Oglala Sioux bonnet, the property of the Field Museum in Chicago. Note the American flag reproduced in beadwork on the headband. The bonnet wasn't chosen for the booklet.

Lunda Hoyle Gill of Riverside, California, was hired in 1987 to prepare concept sketches on the recommendation of Howard Paine, the CSAC design coordinator who had been named art director for the project. Gill is a world traveler who has painted native peoples, including American Indians, in many different environments.

In the early stages of the project, CSAC debated whether the headdresses should be pictured actually being worn, with faces beneath them. Paine's view prevailed: that these articles were folk art, like Navajo blankets and Pueblo pottery, and should stand alone.

Gill did a large amount of research, calling on the resources of such places as the Smithsonian Institution, New York City's Heye Museum and American Museum of Natural History, the Field Museum in Chicago, the Thomas Gilcrease Museum in Oklahoma (a state where she had lived for many years), the Denver Art Museum, the Panhandle Plains Historical Museum in Canyon, Texas, and, of course, the Plains Indian Museum in Cody. She then prepared and submitted about 10 painted sketches, or, as she called them, "research paintings," covering various parts of the country.

Some of the headgear she depicted was quite different from the typical feathered war bonnets that had become familiar to Americans through more than half a century of cowboy-and-Indian films. There were turban-like hats and cylindrical-shaped feather arrangements and single-feather bands and ornaments such as gourds and buffalo horns. "You couldn't 'read' some of them," recalled Howard Paine. "You couldn't recognize them for what they were; you had no point of reference. So we said, let's just do the feathered ones."

This decision basically limited the artist to Plains Indian headgear. She based the sketches that later became finished oil paintings on the four headdresses owned by the Plains Indian Museum, plus Alfred Aguilar's Comanche bonnet. Gill had painted the Aguilar bonnet previously, and to create the picture for the stamp she referred to that earlier painting, along with drawings and notes she had made at the time, and also discussed the project with Aguilar by telephone.

When she visited the museum in Cody, Gill said, Dr. Horse Capture "opened the vault and also the glass display cases to me and said, 'What do you want, Lunda?' He could not have been

These three concept sketches were among those turned down by the Citizens' Stamp Advisory Committee because the headgear didn't fit the popular concept of Indian headdresses and wasn't immediately recognizable as such. The traditional straight-up bonnet with the feathers arranged cylindrically is from the Blackfeet tribe; the headgear with the buffalo horns is a Hidatsa piece. Both of these are in the Plains Indian Museum. The third bonnet is a 19th-century Yankton Sioux piece and is in the Smithsonian Institution.

nicer." She stayed at the museum for two days, examining every bonnet in the collection. The quality of the four she chose to paint was "exceptional," she said. "All the feathers were there, all the beads were there. No parts of the bonnets were missing or damaged."

Gill prefers not to work from photographs. "It's important to me to have actually touched and looked at a bonnet all the way around," she said. "Some of the back pieces were so gorgeous that I almost wanted to paint the bonnets from the rear."

The finished paintings, once they were received by USPS, had to be cropped at the bottom to make them fit into the horizontal commemorative format that was originally envisioned for the stamps. This resulted in the deletion of the feathered trailer that hangs down from the back of each bonnet.

Then USPS decided to issue the stamps in booklets, which meant to Paine that the designs would have to be stretched into the longer horizontal aspect ratio. "But we didn't want to crop down on the paintings any more than we already had done," Paine said. "So I got the bright idea, 'Let's add a detail,' to fill that extra space on the side. The detail we chose was a strip of beadwork down the right side of each stamp, which duplicated the beadwork on the front of the headdress. The artist was delighted to provide that as a little decorative addition. And that brought us into the right aspect ratio for the long, skinny stamp."

Then, however, the word came down that "long, skinny stamps" with horizontal designs were no longer permitted. So Howard Paine,

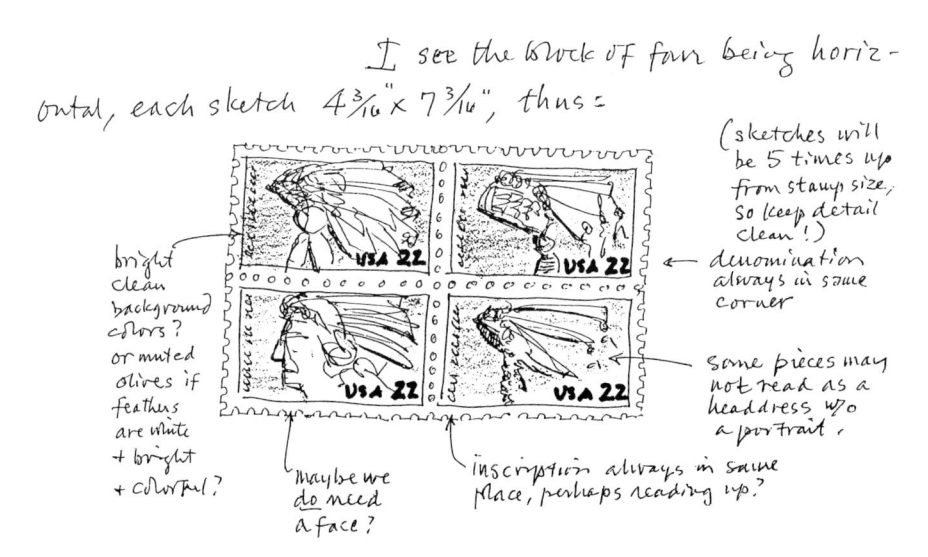

Art director Howard Paine sent this annotated rough sketch to artist Lunda Hoyle Gill early in the design process, when the stamps were planned as a block of four and many basic details remained to be resolved.

To "stretch" the Indian Headdresses designs into the extra-long format that had previously been used for booklet stamps, Lunda Hoyle Gill reproduced the beadwork headband of each bonnet down the right side of the stamp. Later, when it was decided to restore the stamps to commemorative size, the beadwork was removed.

together with project manager Jack Williams and Peter Cocci, the BEP artist who modeled the stamps, decided that the most logical course was to eliminate the beadwork in order to get the designs back to the shorter length-to-depth ratio they had started with.

The stamps were printed on the offset-intaglio D press. The background color on all five was a hue described by Howard Paine as "Army blanket." The detail work on the headdresses was printed in black, by intaglio. Four BEP engravers worked on the five stamps to expedite the project. Thomas Hipschen engraved the Comanche and Flathead designs; Kenneth Kipperman engraved the Shoshone and Assiniboine headdresses; Gary Chaconas engraved the Cheyenne headdress, and Gary Slaght engraved the lettering.

Gill was so delighted with BEP's translation of her paintings into finished stamps that she wrote letters to each of the engravers. "The bonnets are so sharply defined, so beautiful," she said. "I was truly grateful. One of the engravers wrote back and said he had worked on 66 stamps and nobody had ever thanked him before!"

The artwork of the Lakota Sioux headdress on the booklet cover was taken from one of Lunda Gill's concept sketches that wasn't developed as a stamp design.

Varieties

Late in 1990 Stan Goldfarb, a Potomac, Maryland, dealer who specializes in U.S. error stamps, informed *Linn's Stamp News* that two panes of Indian Headdresses stamps had been found with the black intaglio portion missing. In both cases the error pane was the second pane in the booklet.

First-Day Facts

For the little town of Cody, it was the second USPS first-day ceremony in a little more than two years. On June 6, 1988, the 15¢ Buffalo Bill Cody stamp in the Great Americans series had made its debut at Cody's Buffalo Bill Historical Center, which was also the site of the Indian Headdresses booklet dedication.

Regional Postmaster General Jerry K. Lee dedicated the stamps. Speakers were George P. Horse Capture, curator of the Plains Indian Museum, and Wyoming's senior U.S. senator, Alan K. Simpson. The welcome was given by Joseph Medicine Crow, historian of the Crow Indian tribe. Honored guests included Mrs. Henry H.R. Coe, chairman of the Buffalo Bill Memorial Association's board of trustees, and Peter Hassrick, director of the Historical Center. The musical prelude was by Indian drums, and the invocation was delivered by the Medicine Man of the Cheyenne tribe.

At the ceremony, Lunda Hoyle Gill dedicated her artwork on the stamps to the memory of an old friend from Norman, Oklahoma, Scott Tonamah of the Kiowa Indian tribe, who had died the preceding February. She brought Tonamah's 76-year-old widow, Doris, and the couple's niece to the first-day ceremony as her guests.

USPS affixed stamps to first-day covers upon request, as per its custom, but would service only sets of five (one stamp per cover). Collectors were required to submit five envelopes and $1.25 per request. Collectors who prepared their own covers found that a Number 10 envelope was needed for a full pane of 10 stamps, which measured 7.8 inches in length without the binding stub attached.

25¢ MICRONESIA/MARSHALL ISLANDS COMPACT OF FREE ASSOCIATION (JOINT ISSUES)

Date of Issue: September 28, 1990

Catalog Numbers: Scott 2506-07

Colors: magenta, yellow, cyan, blue and black (offset); black (intaglio)

First-Day Cancel: Washington, D.C. (U.S. Department of State's Dean Acheson Auditorium)

FDCs Canceled: 343,816

Format: Panes of 50, horizontal, 5 across, 10 down. Two varieties on each pane, arranged in alternating vertical rows. Offset printing plates of 200 subjects (10 across, 20 around); intaglio printing sleeve of 400 subjects (10 across, 40 around).

Perf: 11.2 (Eureka off-line perforator)

Selvage Markings: ©United States Postal Service 1990, Use Correct ZIP Code®

Designer: Herb Kawainui Kane of Captain Cook, Hawaii

Art Director and Typographer: Howard Paine (CSAC)

Project Manager: Jack Williams (USPS)

Engraver: Gary Slaght, lettering and denomination (BEP)

Modeler: Clarence Holbert (BEP)

Printing: BEP's 5-color offset, 1-color intaglio D press (902)

Quantity Ordered: 152,500,000
Quantity Distributed: 151,430,000

Plate/Sleeve Number Detail: One group of five offset plate numbers and a single-digit intaglio sleeve number appear on adjacent pieces of selvage.

Tagging: overall

The Stamps

On September 28, USPS issued a se-tenant pair of stamps to commemorate the Compact of Free Association that the United States had negotiated with the Republic of the Marshall Islands and the Federated States of Micronesia (FSM), two entities that were formerly part of the Trust Territory of the Pacific Islands.

Free association had been in effect since November 3, 1986. Under its terms, the FSM and the Marshall Islands became fully self-governing, with the United States assuming responsibility and authority for their defense for a minimum of 15 years and providing other services, plus economic aid, during that time.

The pair of U.S. stamps was part of a double joint issue. On the same day it appeared, the FSM dedicated a se-tenant strip of three commemorative stamps for the Compact of Free Association, and the Marshall Islands issued a single commemorative.

The joint issues were the result of agreements reached between the United States and the two island governments at the time the present postal arrangements were negotiated. Under these arrangements, which took effect in 1984, both Micronesia and the Marshall Islands manage their own postal operations and issue their own stamps, while USPS continues to provide international service.

In the early planning stages, USPS first intended to issue three stamps, and then switched to four stamps in a block. Each stamp would honor one of the governmental entities that had emerged from the old Trust Territory. Besides the Republic of the Marshall Islands and the FSM, these were Palau — which had also signed the Compact of Free Association — and the Northern Marianas, which had opted to become a commonwealth of the United States in lieu of independence.

But the four stamps were eventually whittled to two. One complication was the unexpected delay that developed in Palau's internal process of ratifying the Compact of Free Association. At the time the stamps were issued, Palau still had not completed ratification.

The six stamps of three nations that actually comprised the joint issues were designed by two artists and were printed in two different processes by three different printers. Nevertheless, they were very similar in appearance. Each was arranged horizontally, with its vignette set against a solid blue background, and featured a flag and

The single stamp for Free Association issued by the Republic of the Marshall Islands.

Micronesia's strip of three commemorative stamps issued to call attention to the Compact of Free Association with the United States.

a sailing vessel. Typefaces for lettering and numerals were identical. With their wording in English, and with each bearing a 25¢ denomination (the FSM and the Marshalls use the U.S. dollar as their currency), they were quite difficult to tell apart.

Furthermore, the three joint issues contained an unusual overlapping duplication of designs. The single stamp issued by the Marshall Islands depicted the republic's flag, a navigational stick chart and a canoe. The U.S. pair incorporated that design, plus a second design showing the FSM flag and a Micronesian canoe. And the FSM triptych contained both those designs, in addition to a third one that displayed the U.S. flag, the frigate *USS Constitution* and the national birds of both countries: the American eagle and the frigatebird of Micronesia.

Herb Kawainui Kane (pronounced Kay-nee) of Captain Cook, Hawaii, designed the two U.S. stamps, as well as the matching single from the Marshall Islands and the matching pair from Micronesia. Lloyd Birmingham of Putnam Valley, New York, created the design for the third FSM stamp, picturing the U.S. national symbols.

The U.S. stamps were printed by offset and intaglio on BEP's D press. The sheets were cut into 50-stamp panes for distribution. The House of Questa in London printed the three FSM stamps by multicolor offset-lithography in sheets of 12. The Marshall Islands stamp was produced by the Unicover Corporation of Cheyenne, Wyoming, by four-color process offset lithography in sheets of 50.

Unicover also manages philatelic affairs for the Republic of the Marshall Islands Postal Service and handles publicity and sales arrangements for all its stamps. The Inter-Governmental Philatelic Corporation of New York City is the official philatelic agent for the FSM. Both countries are prolific producers of postage stamps, especially the Marshalls, whose postal service has averaged 48 new issues a year since 1984.

After Herb Kane had finished work on the two U.S. stamp designs, representatives of the Marshall Islands asked USPS for permission to use on their own stamp Kane's design that honored their republic. USPS agreed, and even lent Unicover the color separations which BEP had made. At the same time, Howard Paine, art director and typographer for the pair of U.S. stamps, sent Unicover a set of the Raleigh Bold typeface letters and numerals he had used for the U.S. stamps, so that the Marshall Islands' stamp would match in this respect as well. (Paine was cited as the typographer in the selvage of the panes that Unicover printed.)

In 1947, after the defeat of Japan in World War II, the United Nations assigned to the United States trusteeship of a three million-square-mile area of atoll-dotted ocean in the western Pacific. This was the Trust Territory of the Pacific Islands (TTPI), and it consisted of the Marshall Islands; the Caroline Islands, which would eventually become the Federated States of Micronesia; the Northern Mariana Islands, and Palau.

In 1969 Washington offered the status of U.S. territory to the people of the TTPI, but their elected representatives favored a different relationship that involved greater local autonomy while retaining strong ties with the United States. To attain this, the areas making up the TTPI followed different routes.

Early in the planning stage, when the set was conceived of as three se-tenant square stamps, Herb Kane provided these designs showing outrigger canoes indigenous to the three island groups. Howard Paine provided the type overlays.

The Northern Marianas chose to integrate permanently into the United States as a commonwealth, with U.S. citizenship for the people. That agreement was reached in 1975, was ratified by a plebiscite in the islands and approved by Congress, and took effect November 3, 1986, when the trusteeship agreement was terminated for all portions of the TTPI except Palau. As a commonwealth, like Puerto Rico, the Northern Marianas use U.S. postage stamps.

Meanwhile, negotiations between Washington and the remaining portions of the TTPI continued. The United States and the U.N. Trusteeship Council had urged that these areas remain politically unified, but the people chose instead to create three separate political jurisdictions. The Marshall Islands and the FSM (made up of the former TTPI districts of Kosrae, Yap, Pohnpei and Truk) installed constitutional governments in May 1979, and Palau followed suit in January 1981. Consequently, the United States had to negotiate a free-association relationship with each jurisdiction.

By 1983, the United States and all three island governments had signed the Compact of Free Association. An additional agreement with the Marshall Islands provided for the settlement of all claims arising out of the U.S. nuclear testing program at Bikini and Eniwetok atolls from 1946 to 1958, as well as providing certain services for the people affected by the testing program.

The governments of the Marshall Islands and FSM approved the compact, and the voters ratified it by margins of 79 percent and 58 percent, respectively. Congress gave its approval as well, and on January 14, 1986, President Ronald Reagan signed it into law.

Palau was another story. Although its voters in seven separate referendums favored the compact by large majorities, the "yes" vote never reached the 75 percent mark required by the Palau Constitution as interpreted by the Palau Supreme Court. An attempt to amend the Palau Constitution to allow ratification by a simple majority was also rejected by the court on technical grounds. As of this writing, Palau was still part of the Trust Territory of the Pacific Islands — was, in fact, all of it that was left.

USPS issues se-tenant pairs of stamps such as the Marshall Islands-Micronesia pair only infrequently. Usually they appear only when the object being commemorated is of a dual nature, such as the Disabled American Veterans and U.S. servicemen (1970, Scott 1421-1422), the Apollo Soyuz joint space effort with the Soviets (1975, Scott 1569-1570), U.S. banking and commerce (1975, Scott 1577-1578), energy conservation and development (1977, Scott 1723-1724), Captain James Cook's voyages to Alaska and Hawaii (1978, Scott 1732-1733) and, on the most recent of these pairs, the battles of Yorktown and the Virginia Capes (1981, Scott 1937-1938).

Herb Kane drew this "wa lap" canoe for a National Geographic Society map supplement of the Pacific Ocean. He drew the same type vessel in his design for the U.S. Marshall Islands stamp.

This drawing of a "popo" canoe, which Herb Kane also created for the National Geographic Society map, was adapted by the artist for his U.S. Federated States of Micronesia stamp.

The Designs

Herb Kane, who was chosen to design the U.S. se-tenant pair, had previously designed another U.S. stamp with a Pacific theme: the 20¢ commemorative of 1984 marking the 25th anniversary of Hawaii statehood.

Under the original plan, USPS was to issue three square stamps, for FSM, the Marshall Islands and Palau. Kane prepared designs in this format featuring outrigger canoes of those areas: a "popo," "wa lap" and "kaep," respectively. He previously had researched these vessels when he illustrated a National Geographic Society map supplement of the Pacific Ocean, in 1974, and he used those drawings as reference.

The artist also offered alternative sketches in which each country's flag was featured as a unifying element, along with additional design elements such as breadfruit or a woman in native headdress (FSM), fish and a seashell (Palau) and canoes and a stick chart (Marshall Islands).

Then, late in 1986, the plan changed. Now USPS wanted four stamps, including one for the Northern Marianas, in standard commemorative size, arranged in a block of four. Art director Howard Paine sent Kane a layout showing the proposed positioning of the type, which was to be in the same location for each stamp. "I've positioned the elements clear to the edge, as if on a white background," Paine wrote in an accompanying letter. "If you want an overall color background, you'll have to move elements in from the edge. And don't forget, if type reverses out of a color, it can't be but a single color" — as opposed to a process-color background, where registration would have been a problem.

"The four flags were not the same size or aspect ratio," Paine recalled later, "and the names of the countries were as short as Palau and as long as the Commonwealth of the Northern Mariana Islands. So I developed a format that was a grid system in which the

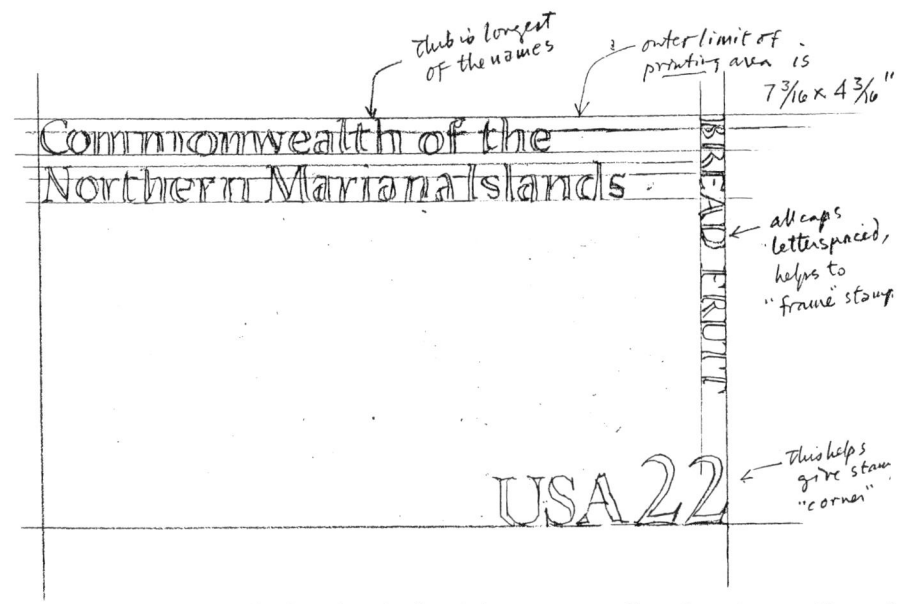

After the concept shifted to four horizontal commemorative-size stamps, Howard Paine sent Herb Kane this type positioning guide. The marginal notes are Paine's.

flag took up so much space, the vignette took up so much space and the lettering fit in the upper quarter. We could have put anything we wanted in those spaces, but it was a system.

"As is turned out, only two stamps were issued, but I still think it worked all right."

As finally printed, the se-tenant pair did incorporate a solid color

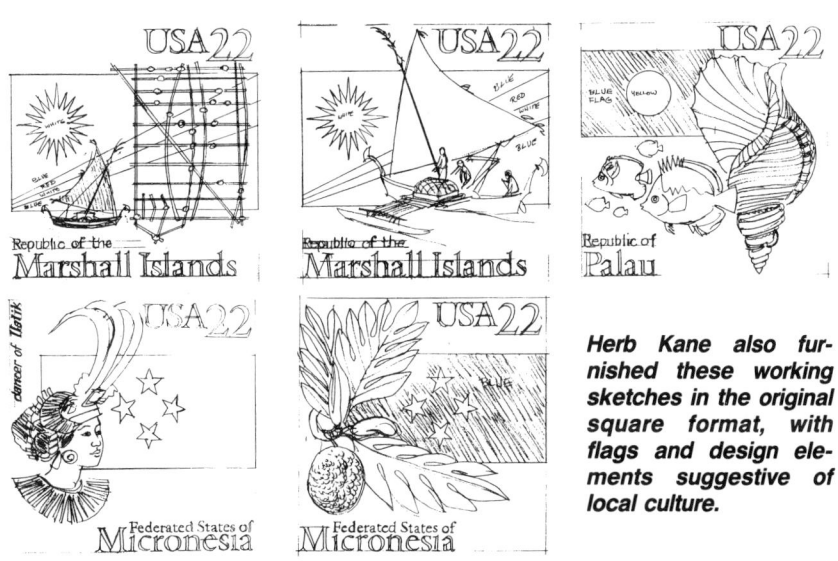

Herb Kane also furnished these working sketches in the original square format, with flags and design elements suggestive of local culture.

107

Herb Kane based his drawing of a stick chart on this chart that was documented in 1901 by an ethnographer named Winkler. The chart was reproduced in Dr. David Lewis' book We the Navigators. *Winkler listed the name of each island as represented by a cowrie shell on the chart.*

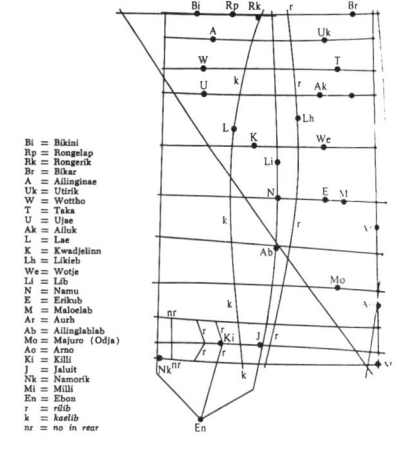

Bi = Bikini
Rp = Rongelap
Rk = Rongerik
Br = Bikar
A = Ailinginae
Uk = Utirik
W = Wottho
T = Taka
U = Ujae
Ak = Ailuk
L = Lae
K = Kwadjelinn
Lh = Likieb
We = Wotje
Li = Lib
N = Namu
E = Erikub
M = Maloelab
Ar = Aurh
Ab = Ailinglablab
Mo = Majuro (Odja)
Ao = Arno
Ki = Killi
J = Jaluit
Nk = Namorik
Mi = Milli
En = Ebon
r = rilib
k = kaelib
nr = no in rear

background, in blue, but with typography in intaglio black rather than dropout white.

The finished design for the Marshall Islands stamp utilized the wa lap canoe — its fanlike ornaments on the prows identifying it as the vessel of a chief — and the stick chart. Stick charts are devices used to teach young men to navigate by reading wave patterns. Using reeds and shells, the charts mark the location of atolls and islands, and show the movement of waves as they are bent or altered by bodies of land. Understanding stick charts was a guarded secret for many years, known only to master navigators and initiates.

As for the FSM stamp, its final design showed the popo canoe, which is still used in the central Caroline Islands and has changed little since 1579, when Sir Francis Drake's crew observed the boats as "cut with great arte, and cunning." Kane had strongly urged that the breadfruit design be used, but it was vetoed by postal representatives of the Federated States of Micronesia, for reasons that are still unclear to USPS officials.

"Breadfruit is grown throughout Polynesia, Micronesia and Melanesia, but it is most favored as a staple in Micronesia," the artist had written to Jack Williams, the USPS project manager for the stamps. "Its identity with Micronesia is much the same as the potato's identity with Ireland, or the taro with Polynesia, or pasta with Italy.

This design for the U.S. Marshall Islands stamp differed from the final version only in that the words "Stick Chart" on the left side were replaced by "Free Association."

Another Herb Kane sketch in which breadfruit was used as a subject representing the Federated States of Micronesia.

"The breadfruit may seem humble today to some Micronesians, perhaps politicians seeking Western status, but it was a fruit revered by their ancestors in myth and legend. Survival at times depended on the breadfruit, which grows on magnificent trees on some atolls where other staples will not grow.

"Canoes are carved from breadfruit logs, so in the old days even successful fishing and voyaging depended on the breadfruit tree. The coconut is used, but no more than it is used in other parts of the Pacific. Only in Micronesia, however, is breadfruit the dominant food . . . It is the symbol of human survival on tiny coral islands and as such deserves to be featured on a Micronesia stamp."

To questions from CSAC members about the authenticity of his stick chart, Kane provided this assurance:

"Many stick charts are made for sale to tourists which are not authentic. This made me cautious in choosing a design for the stamp. I searched the literature on these charts for one that is proved to be authentic, and followed that."

The stamps were printed in five offset colors, magenta, yellow, cyan, blue and black, and one intaglio color, black. The only portion of the design printed in intaglio was the lettering.

Varieties

Two vertical strips of five of the Micronesia stamps were found completely missing the black intaglio portions of the design. These areas comprised the denomination and "USA" (from the lower-right corner) and "Federated States of Micronesia" (from the upper-left corner). The remaining black areas in the design, the rigging on the ship and the words "Free Association," being offset-printed, were present.

The 10 error stamps were found by a non-collector in a vending machine pack that was sold through a southern California post office. The finder split the discovery with a co-worker and sold her share to Tom Hontos of A-1 Stamps in Fountain Valley, California, according to *Linn's Stamp News*.

First-Day Facts

The six joint-issue stamps were released simultaneously in a ceremony at the Dean Acheson Auditorium in the Department of State in Washington September 28, and also in the two Pacific nations — at Palikir, Pohnpei, FSM, and Majuro in the Marshall Islands.

Officials from all three countries had prominent roles in the ceremony. The U.S. stamps were dedicated by Thomas E. Leavey, assistant postmaster general. Doing the honors for the Marshall Islands stamp was Henchi Balos, the republic's minister of finance. Andon L. Amaraich, personal representative of the president of the FSM, dedicated his country's triptych.

Bethwell Henry, postmaster general of the FSM, delivered the invocation. Honored guests included Jesse B. Marehalau, ambassador to the United States from the FSM; Wilfred Kendall, ambassador of the Republic of the Marshall Islands, and other officials from the two Pacific countries.

This vertical strip of five is one of two such strips of the U.S. Micronesia stamp found completely missing the black intaglio portions of the design. These areas comprised the denominations and "USA" (from the lower-right corner) and "Federated States of Micronesia" (from the upper-left corner).

These are the first-day cancellations used for the joint issue by the United States, the Republic of the Marshall Islands and the Federated States of Micronesia.

First-day covers distributed at the Washington ceremony bore the U.S. pair of stamps, the Marshall Islands single and one of the three Micronesia stamps, each canceled with the first-day-of-issue postmark of the government that issued it.

The original USPS announcement of the issue, on September 6, 1990, gave instructions for ordering first-day covers of the U.S. stamps, but made no mention of combination covers. Dealers' advertisements offering such covers quickly appeared, however.

Some time later, USPS issued an unusual news release headed: "Combination Cover Policy Clarified . . ." It announced that collectors would have until May 1, 1991 — more than seven months after the stamps were issued — to obtain a U.S. first-day postmark on combination covers bearing stamps of the United States and the Marshall Islands and/or the FSM.

"Although the Postal Service's initial press release did not preclude a U.S. first-day postmark on combination covers, some confusion had arisen due to the complex nature of a joint stamp issuance with two countries and the different policy which governed the joint stamp issue with the Soviet Union for the recent Creatures of the Sea stamps," the release said.

"Customers submitting combination covers . . . must affix the stamps on their envelopes so that each U.S. first day of issue postmark applied will cancel *at least* one United States stamp. The covers will only be postmarked with the U.S. first day cancellation ('September 28, 1990, Washington, DC 20066')."

Collectors were instructed to send their covers, with stamps affixed, to the Philatelic Sales Division in Kansas City, Missouri. They were required to obtain the FSM and Marshall Islands stamps from the two countries' respective philatelic agents; USPS didn't offer their stamps for sale.

25¢ CREATURES OF THE SEA (BLOCK OF FOUR) (JOINT ISSUE)

Date of Issue: October 3, 1990

Catalog Numbers: Scott 2508-11 (stamps); Scott 2511a (block of four)

Colors: magenta, yellow, cyan, black (offset); black (intaglio)

First-Day Cancel: Moscow, U.S.S.R., and Baltimore, Maryland (National Aquarium)

FDCs Canceled: 706,047

Format: Panes of 40, horizontal, 5 across, 8 down. Offset printing plates of 160 subjects (10 across, 16 around); intaglio printing sleeve of 320 subjects (10 across, 32 around)

Perf: 10.9 by 11.2 (Eureka off-line perforator)

Selvage Markings: ©United States Postal Service 1990, Use Correct ZIP Code®; Joint issue by the United States and Union of Soviet Socialist Republics. Sea Lion and Sea Otter stamp designs prepared by a Soviet Union designer. Killer Whale and Dolphin designs prepared by a United States designer.

Designers: Peter Cocci (BEP) and Vladimir Beilin of the Soviet Union

Modeler: Peter Cocci (BEP)

Engraver: Michael J. Ryan, lettering (BEP)

Art Director: Leonard Buckley (BEP)

Project Manager: Jack Williams (USPS)

Typographer: Bradbury Thompson (CSAC)

Printing: BEP's 6-color offset, 3-color intaglio D press (902)

Quantity Ordered: 287,000,000
Quantity Distributed: 277,904,000

Plate/Sleeve Number Detail: One group of four offset plate numbers and a single-digit intaglio sleeve number on adjacent stamp.

Tagging: overall

The Stamps

The year's most highly publicized stamp issue was a se-tenant block of four stamps depicting marine mammals. USPS referred to the set as "Creatures of the Sea." The block was part of a joint issue with the Soviet Union, which simultaneously released a block of its own bearing the same designs as those on the U.S. stamps. The U.S. stamps were of the 25¢ denomination, covering the first-class rate. The Soviet stamps were valued at 25 kopecks (42¢), the rate for a registered international airmail packet in the Soviet Union.

First-day ceremonies for both sets of stamps were held October 3 at the National Aquarium in Baltimore, Maryland, and in the Moscow Circus in Moscow.

The event in Baltimore launched USPS' 10th annual National Stamp Collecting Month promotion, which borrowed its theme ("Splash into an Ocean of Fun — Collect Stamps!") from the subject matter of the four stamp designs. The Soviet Union also designated October as a month to promote the hobby vigorously.

The joint issue was only the second of its kind between the two superpowers and former Cold War rivals. In the first, in 1975, each country produced a se-tenant pair of stamps to mark the Apollo Soyuz space test project, which linked in orbit manned spacecraft of the two nations. At World Stamp Expo 89 in Washington in 1989, both countries issued imperforate souvenir sheets in similar formats on space-related themes, but these were independent projects.

The 1990 stamps, like the Apollo Soyuz pair, were jointly designed by artists from the United States and the Soviet Union. Peter Cocci of the U.S. Bureau of Engraving and Printing was credited with the stamps depicting killer whales and a common dolphin. The stamps showing northern sea lions and a sea otter were the work of Vladimir Beilin of the U.S.S.R. Ministry of Communications.

On June 1, 1989, when USPS first announced that its 1990 stamp program would include "a salute to marine mammals," no mention was made of a joint issue. However, at that stage, USPS and Soviet officials were already well along in negotiations to go partners on the Creatures of the Sea stamps.

USPS, which had originated the idea of such a block of four, intended to issue its stamps whether or not the negotiations bore fruit. But details were worked out, and an agreement setting forth the terms of the joint issue was signed the following November, when Soviet postal representatives were in Washington to attend the Universal Postal Union Congress and World Stamp Expo.

To arrive at this point had required an evolutionary process at USPS that spanned several years. That process began in 1979 when the Citizens' Stamp Advisory Committee, aware of the concern of environmentalists over the danger to whales posed by unrestrained international hunting, asked three artists, including Peter Cocci of BEP, to work up a design for a single stamp depicting a blue whale or a right whale. But the committee turned out to be ambivalent, with some members reluctant to inject the Postal Service into an international controversy, so nothing came immediately of the whale project. A few years later, however, in exploring themes for future topical issues, CSAC expressed an interest in a se-tenant

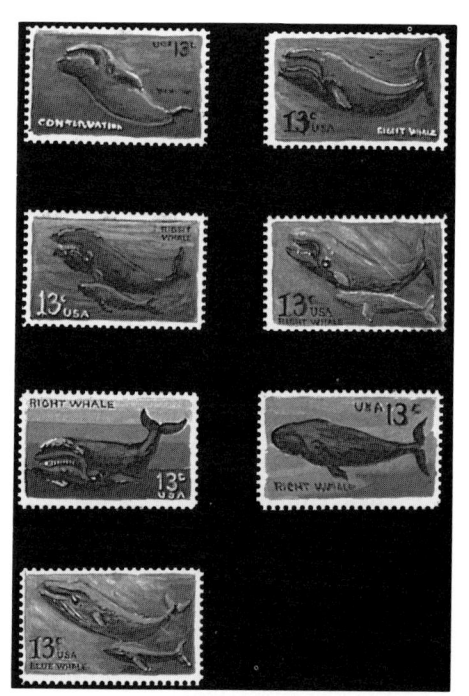

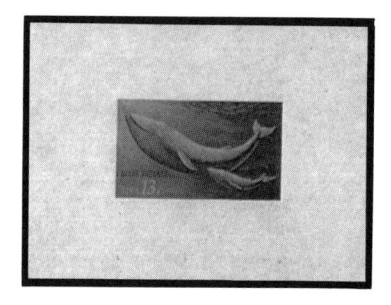

The Creatures of the Sea idea originated in the late 1970s as a single commemorative stamp calling attention to the endangered status of certain whale species. These concept sketches by Peter Cocci depicted right whales and blue whales.

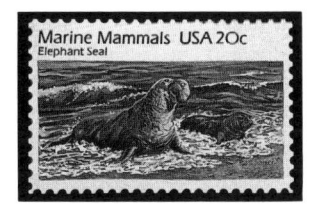

When the Citizens' Stamp Advisory Committee was first considering a block of four stamps showing marine mammals, Peter Cocci offered them concept sketches of these six species for consideration: elephant seal, manatee, sea otter, Dall porpoise, common dolphin and humpback whale.

block that would depict four different species of sea mammal. Cocci did some research and produced paintings of six species for its consideration: elephant seal, manatee, sea otter, Dall porpoise, common dolphin and humpback whale.

"I tried to get a selection of species that surrounded the United States, with examples from the Atlantic Ocean, Pacific Ocean and Gulf of Mexico," the artist explained.

Then the committee decided to consider the sea mammal stamps as candidates for a booklet instead of a block. To show how a booklet pane might look, Cocci did a number of miniature paintings, which he called "thumbnail sketches," using different sizes, configurations, layouts and combinations of the six mammals he had painted earlier.

Eventually, CSAC returned to its original idea of a block, and narrowed the field of species to five: the common dolphin, sea otter and manatee from Cocci's original list, plus a killer whale and a walrus. Finally the manatee was dropped, and the remaining mammals were listed by USPS in its June 1, 1989, announcement of the planned block of four.

In the meantime, however, Soviet postal officials had come up with a proposal for a joint issue. Recalled Don McDowell, head of the USPS Office of Stamp and Philatelic Marketing:

"The Soviets told us they would like to pursue the idea of the United States and the Soviet Union issuing something that would be topically popular with collectors in both countries, as opposed to having another joint issue where one country or the other celebrates its birthday — which is the typical worldwide joint-issue sort of thing. So they started looking at what was in their thinking for the future, and we started looking at ours, and at one point I mentioned that we had in advanced development a Sea Creatures block. They responded by saying that Russian collectors love that kind of stamp issue. And it went from there."

On March 1, 1990, USPS and the U.S.S.R. Ministry of Posts announced plans for the joint issue, featuring animals "common to American and Soviet territorial waters." Collectors learned that the northern sea lion had replaced the walrus, which had been included in the earlier list of four species that USPS had made public.

The public got its first glimpse of the designs in July when post offices began displaying posters featuring enlarged color pictures of the stamps. The official design unveiling took place August 8 at the Baltimore's National Aquarium, with Assistant Postmaster General Thomas E. Leavey doing the honors.

In a departure from usual practice for the United States, both nations followed the Soviet custom of placing the year of issue, 1990, on the stamps. This policy, originally proposed by European catalog publishers, was recommended by the Universal Postal Union, but had not been followed by USPS over the years on the advice of the Citizens' Stamp Advisory Committee.

USPS explained its practice in a February 3, 1989, letter to A.C. Roozen of Atlanta, Georgia, who had suggested that such dates be included. The USPS letter was quoted by *Linn's Stamp News* columnist John Hotchner:

"As you know, the USPS copyright symbol and year are printed in the selvage of stamp panes. The basis for establishing the copyright year is the first public showing of the design, and quite often this differs from the year of issue when stamp designs are 'unveiled' before they are issued. Thus unnecessary confusion might result when the two dates are different. Most European countries using year dates do not print copyright notices and accordingly do not face the confusion problem.

"A more compelling reason for not including the date is the situation the Postal Service faces in years where postage rates change and many new issues are required within a short period of time. Rates are established by the independent Postal Rate Commission, and it is difficult to determine the precise implementation date in advance. There are long lead times for the preparation of printing cylinders, and in a rate-change year, the cylinders are brought to near-completion well in advance so that the presses can begin rolling immediately when denominations are known. Adding both a year date and a denomination (particularly with engraved cylinders) would create additional production workload at a time when speed of production is essential to getting stamps of the right denomination in the hands of customers as rapidly as possible.

"European countries at rate-change time do not have this problem because their output is typically much smaller than ours and the rate-setting process is less complicated.

"In addition to the above reasons, the Advisory Committee over the years has voted to remove as many typographic elements as possible from stamp designs in order to provide a more prominent space for the design itself and the message that it conveys."

Ironically, in 1990 USPS began returning some of those information-providing "typographic elements" to its stamp designs on orders from Postmaster General Anthony M. Frank (see chapter on the 5¢ Luis Munoz Marin stamp).

Two of the many paintings Peter Cocci made while the Creatures of the Sea issue was in preparation. These show blue whales and walruses.

The Soviet stamps were available to U.S. collectors at a number of post office philatelic centers and by mail order from the Philatelic Sales Division. The cost was 42¢ each, $1.68 for a block of four.

A 12-page souvenir folder containing blocks of four of the U.S. and Soviet stamps, and their corresponding first-day cancellations, was offered for sale for $7.95.

COMMON DOLPHIN. This is one of the best-known of the more than 30 species of true dolphin, a highly intelligent mammal that shouldn't be confused with the fish of the same name. Dolphins and whales both belong to the order of marine mammals known as *Cetacea.* The common dolphin is found, often in large numbers, in all the warm and temperate seas of the world. It grows to a length of about eight feet, and its sides are streaked with brown, yellow and white. A dark mark running around the eye and tapering to a point at the beak gives it a pleasant look.

This is the dolphin often seen convoying ships, jumping completely out of the sea and moving almost erect on its tail flippers while searching the horizon. Finding a ship, dolphins encircle it, some leading at the bow, some on the sides, all leaping alternately in arching flights of several yards before plunging back into the water.

KILLER WHALE. The killer whale, also known as the grampus or orc, can grow to 30 feet in length. A fierce predator, it devours a wide range of prey, including squid, fish, sea birds, seals and even whales far larger than itself; sometimes it rockets upward through pack ice, tipping basking seals into the water where they can be converted into dinner. Strangely, it has never been known to attack humans. Killer whales live and hunt in packs ranging from three to 50 and are most common in Arctic and Antarctic waters. Distinguishing features are the tall dorsal fin, with a faint gray patch behind it; the white underbelly, and the white patch behind the eye.

NORTHERN SEA LION. Also known as Steller's sea lion, this mammal belongs to the family *Otariidae,* or eared seals, which consists of 12 species of fur seal and sea lion. Sea lions are so named because of the thick lion-like mane of the male. On breeding beaches each spring they gather by the tens of thousands. The northern variety is the largest sea lion, much larger than the California sea lion, which was depicted on one of the 50 stamps of the 1987 North American wildlife pane (Scott 2329). It breeds on islands in the North Pacific from California as far as Japan.

SEA OTTER. This fascinating creature was nearly wiped out by fur-seekers in the 19th century, but under careful protection its numbers have begun to increase. The sea otter lives on the coasts of the North Pacific from the Kuriles south to lower California. Weighing no more than 100 pounds, it is the smallest of all the marine mammals, and is unique among them in several ways.

It has no thick layer of fat insulating it from the cold water, but relies instead on two layers of fur, particularly a dense, soft lower layer, which traps air and gives the animal buoyancy. If the air layer is lost — as happened to the thousands of sea otters that were trapped in the Exxon Valdez oil spill in Alaska — the animal soon dies. Its hind legs have been transformed into webbed flippers. The fifth toe is the longest, a feature it shares with no other mammal, and this makes the flippers more efficient when the creature is swimming on its back.

The sea otter is also among the very few animals that utilize tools. When feeding, it uses a large rock, held in its rounded forefeet, to detach shellfish from the seabed, and as an anvil against which to smash the hard shells.

The Designs

Two of the four designs Peter Cocci had prepared for the U.S. block had to be dropped to make room for two designs by Vladimir Beilin. These were Cocci's sea otter and walrus, which were replaced by a Beilin-painted sea otter and the northern sea lion.

Both men were experienced at their profession. Cocci had been a banknote designer for several years before joining the BEP staff in 1973, and thereafter designed numerous U.S. stamps, including the 1988 Flag With Clouds and Flag Over Yosemite definitives. He was also credited with designing the Bicentennial $2 bill issued in 1976. Beilin, an artist with the U.S.S.R. Ministry of Communications, was described as a veteran designer of Soviet postal issues.

The U.S. stamps were printed by a combination of four-color offset and intaglio on BEP's D press. The only intaglio elements

These two illustrations show the Creatures of the Sea block nearing finished form, when it was conceived as a U.S. issue only. At this point, the only decision remaining to be made was whether the fourth stamp should depict a manatee or a walrus. In the end, CSAC opted for the walrus, and that species was included in the first public announcement of the block on June 1, 1989. Then came the joint-issue decision, and changes were made. Peter Cocci's sea otter and walrus designs were dropped, to be replaced by Vladimir Beilin's sea otter and northern sea lion. And Cocci's killer whale picture was "flopped," or reversed, to make the appearance of the block of four more symmetrical.

were the lettering and numerals, in black. The Soviet stamps were printed entirely by four-color process offset lithography at the U.S.S.R. State Security Printing House in Moscow. At the Soviets' request, and in the interest of obtaining uniform color in both sets of stamps, BEP prepared the color separations for both countries.

The stamps were the same "semi-jumbo" size as the 1989 Prehistoric Animals stamps and were printed 40 to a pane in both countries. However, the U.S. panes were five stamps across and eight down, and the Soviet panes were four across and 10 down, which meant each Soviet pane contained 10 complete blocks of four while each U.S. pane contained only eight.

Cocci painted his pictures in water-based designer colors, with an acrylic wash, on illustration board. For source material he used photographs supplied by the National Geographic Society plus others he located himself.

To make certain the artwork was accurate — both Cocci's and Beilin's, which the Soviets had forwarded to the Bureau — the project's art director, Leonard Buckley of BEP, hand-carried it to the Smithsonian Institution's Museum of Natural History for review by Dr. James Mead, the museum's curator of mammals. Cocci made several modifications based on Dr. Mead's comments.

To do so he used, not a paintbrush, but the computer at BEP's Design Center, after first scanning the artwork into the system's memory. Through electronic design manipulation he made the dorsal fin on his common dolphin higher and gave the beak more of a point; with his killer whales he also raised the dorsal fins and made the flippers longer and broader. He even altered one of Vladimir Beilin's paintings, the northern sea lion, to adjust the position of one flipper. Finally, he used the computer to "flop" his killer whales design, reversing the entire image so that the whale in the foreground was diving into the lower right corner of the stamp instead of the lower left. This was done to give an overall symmetry to the full block of four.

Although USPS yielded to the Soviets in placing the year of issue in the design, it held firm on its policy of not crediting the artist in either the design or the selvage. The Soviet stamp pane selvage contained the following credit lines (in Russian): " 'Northern Sea Lion' and 'Sea Otter'. Author — Soviet Artist Vladimir Beilin" and " 'Killer Whale' and 'Common Dolphin'. Author — American Artist Peter Cocci." The U.S. selvage, however, contained only these messages: "Sea Otter and Sea Lion stamp designs prepared by a Soviet Union designer," and "Killer Whale and Dolphin designs prepared by a United States designer." A third informational marking in the U.S. selvage read: "Joint stamp issue by the United States and the Union of Soviet Socialist Republics."

Varieties

Stamp Collector reported that Ken Smith of Long Beach, Washington, had discovered a pane of the U.S. stamps with the intaglio typography missing in the first six rows and only partly present in the bottom two rows.

First-Day Facts

The Baltimore first-day ceremony was held at the National Aquarium's new marine mammal pavilion. Limited public seating was available on a first-come, first-served basis.

Postmaster General Anthony M. Frank dedicated the U.S. stamps, and Major General Viktor V. Gorbatko dedicated the Soviet block. General Gorbatko's list of titles was impressive: "Pilot-cosmonaut of the U.S.S.R.; delegate to the Supreme Soviet of the U.S.S.R.; head of the department, Zhukovsky Air Force Academy; chairman of the All Union Federation of Philatelists of the U.S.S.R."

Two of the principal speakers were unable to attend. One was Alexander A. Bessmertnykh, Soviet ambassador to the United States, whose remarks were delivered by Robert N. Ruzanov, trade representative and commercial minister of the U.S.S.R. The other was John H. Sununu, White House chief of staff and an enthusiastic stamp collector, who was attending federal budget "summit" negotiations. The other speaker, Dr. Robert V. Miller of Seattle, Washington, deputy director of the National Marine Mammal Laboratory, National Marine Fisheries, went on as scheduled.

Maryland Governor William D. Schaefer gave the welcome. Captain Nicholas Brown, executive director of Baltimore's National Aquarium, introduced the distinguished guests, who included Vladimir A. Denisenko, deputy director, Institute of Earth Magnetism, U.S.S.R. Academy of Science; Levon K. Manukian, director of the Stamp Issuing and Marketing Bureau (MARKA), U.S.S.R. Ministry of Communications, and Igor D. Panfilov, director of Sovinfilatelia, the Soviet International Philatelic Service.

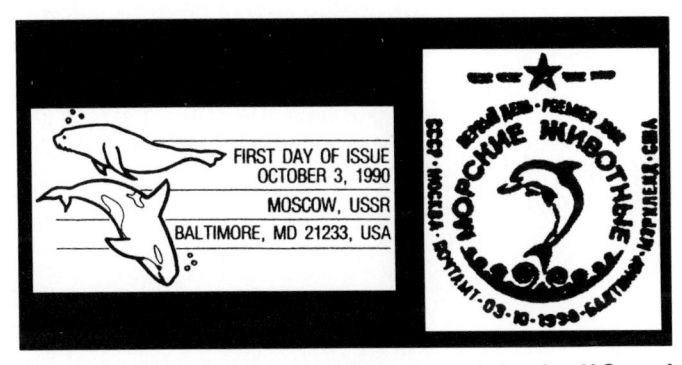

These are the first-day cancellations used for the U.S. and Soviet Creatures of the Sea stamps.

USPS authorized both a pictorial cancellation showing a magnifying glass and stamp, and a special machine cancellation with a Creatures of the Sea theme, to publicize National Stamp Collecting Month.

Meanwhile, in Moscow, a scheduled circus performance at the newly renovated "old" Moscow Circus on Tsvetnoi Boulevard was delayed for the stamp dedication. The circus director, noted clown Yuri Nikulin, presided and introduced the guests, who included Edward Horgan, associate U.S. postmaster general; Vladimir Glinka, vice minister of posts and telecommunications of the U.S.S.R., and Karen Joice, representing the U.S. Embassy in Moscow. Also present were Peter Cocci and his wife as guests of MARKA. The Coccis' 10-day visit to the Soviet Union included dinner at the home of Vladimir Beilin, his collaborator in the design project.

The U.S. first-day cancellation featured simple line drawings of the sea lion and killer whale taken from the stamp designs. The Soviet first-day cancellation showed a leaping dolphin. Both postmarks carried the names of both Baltimore and Moscow.

First-day cover collectors were offered the opportunity to obtain covers with the U.S. stamps and cancellation alone, the Soviet stamps and cancellation alone or a combination on one envelope, by submitting their self-addressed envelopes to the postmaster in Baltimore. Collectors affixing their own stamps to combination covers were cautioned to leave enough space on the envelope for both cancellations to be applied so that neither cancellation touched the stamps of the other country. For covers bearing Soviet stamps, customers were required to include a self-addressed, stamped envelope in which USPS could return the covers after processing them.

USPS also authorized a special machine cancellation with a marine mammals theme to be used nationally to promote National Stamp Collecting Month. The cancellation die, in use from September 1 through October 31 at 146 participating postal facilities, showed a leaping dolphin and bore the slogan: "Splash into an Ocean of Fun! Collect Stamps!"

25¢ GRAND CANYON
AMERICAS SERIES

Date of Issue: October 12, 1990

Catalog Number: Scott 2512

Colors: magenta, yellow, cyan and black

First-Day Cancel: Grand Canyon, Arizona (El Tovar Hotel)

FDCs Canceled: 164,190

Format: Panes of 50, horizontal, 5 across, 10 down. Gravure printing cylinders of 200 subjects (10 across, 20 around) manufactured by Armotek Industries Inc., Palmyra, New Jersey.

Perf: 10.9 (L perforator)

Selvage Markings: PUAS logo, Postal Union of the Americas and Spain, natural surroundings seen by explorers; Grand Canyon, American Southwest, ©United States Postal Service 1990, Use Correct ZIP Code®

Designer: Mark Hess, Katonah, New York

Art Director and Typographer: Richard Sheaff (CSAC)

Project Manager: Joe Brockert (USPS)

Modeler: Richard C. Sennett (Sennett Enterprises) for American Bank Note Company

Printing: Stamps printed and sheeted out by American Bank Note Company on a leased Champlain gravure press (J.W. Fergusson and Sons, Richmond, Virginia) under the supervision of Sennett Enterprises (Fairfax, Virginia). Perforated, processed and shipped by ABNC (Chicago, Illinois).

Quantity Ordered: 143,995,000
Quantity Distributed: 143,995,000

Cylinder Number Detail: One group of four cylinder numbers preceded by the letter "A" over/under corner stamps.

Tagging: overall

The Stamp

In 1990 the 24 member nations of the Postal Union of the Americas and Spain (PUAS), including the United States, issued their second round of postage stamps in the America series. Under the agreement that created the series, each country would issue a set of stamps with a common theme each year leading up to the 500th anniversary in 1992 of Christopher Columbus' arrival in America.

The series began in 1989 with the theme of pre-Columbian peoples and their customs, images and traditions. That year USPS issued a 25¢ commemorative stamp depicting a ceremonial wooden statuette from the Mimbres culture of the American Southwest, and a 45¢ airmail stamp showing the Key Marco cat, a wooden figure made by the Calusa Indian tribe of southern Florida.

The theme for 1990 was natural wonders that the early European explorers of the Americas might have seen. As it had done in 1989, USPS produced two stamps with different designs, a 25¢ value for the first-class rate that featured a Southwestern subject, and a 45¢ airmail stamp whose design subject was Southeastern.

The 1990 stamps, like the 1989 pair, were printed by the American Bank Note Company, using the gravure process. A form of "quadrant printing" was used, by which three of the four 50-stamp positions on each printed sheet of 200 stamps bore the 25¢ stamp, and the fourth position (the top left position only) carried the 45¢ value. Thus the four cylinder numbers for the 45¢ stamp appeared in the same position on every pane.

This was the first time a private printer producing stamps for USPS had printed panes of different stamps from the same printing cylinder. The Bureau of Engraving and Printing, however, had "ganged" the gravure-printed 20¢ Federal Deposit Insurance Corporation, Soil and Water Conservation, Credit Union Act and National Archives commemorative panes in 1984, and the 33¢ Verville and 39¢ Sperry airmail panes of 1985.

Since its creation in 1931, PUAS member-nations have worked together to improve the exchange of mail and promote common interests. Originally founded in 1911 as the South American Postal Union, with 10 South American member states, it today comprises 24 nations stretching geographically from Canada to Spain to Argentina. The United States joined in 1922.

With Spanish as the predominant language in the postal union, its official name is "Union Postale de las Americas y Espana," and the posthorn logo designed for use on the America stamps bears the initials "UPAE." Before the first sets were issued in 1989, USPS received a special dispensation from the members to change these initials to PUAS on its stamps to correspond to the English language version of the organization's title. This change meant little, however, to users of the 1989 stamps, who had no idea from looking at them what PUAS was or what the purpose of the issue might be. The 1990 stamps themselves presented the same problem, only more so. Whereas the wooden artifacts on the 1989 designs were labeled, albeit in extremely small type, the two scenic views on the 1990 stamps bore no identifying wording.

However, USPS did take a modest step toward enlightening buyers of the 1990 stamps by printing brief messages in the sheet selvage. The margins of the 25¢ stamp panes showed the PUAS logo and the name of the organization, Postal Union of the Americas and Spain, plus the notation: "Natural surroundings seen by explorers: Grand Canyon, American Southwest."

The Grand Canyon, the most spectacular canyon in the world, is a 217-mile gorge cut by the Colorado River through the high plateau of northern Arizona. It was first seen by Europeans when a scouting party of the great expedition of Francisco Vasquez de Coronado came upon it in 1540. A reservation of 1,008 square miles along the rim was set aside by the federal government in 1919 as a national park, and in 1932 an additional 306 square miles on the downstream side of the park was made a national monument.

The canyon had been featured on two previous U.S. stamps. A view from the park lodge was shown on the 2¢ value of the 1934 National Parks series (Scott 741). Some collectors declared that if this stamp was looked at endwise, the rock formations at the right resolved themselves into the strong-chinned profile of President Franklin D. Roosevelt, the stamp collector then in residence in the White House, but this requires a somewhat whimsical imagination to see. The other stamp, a 6¢ commemorative of 1969 (Scott 1374), marked the 100th anniversary of the trip of John Wesley Powell, who led the first party to go through the gorge end to end.

The Design

"For 1990, as opposed to cultural artifacts, it was on to land forms — distinctive terrain — in each of the countries," said Richard Sheaff, art director for the stamps.

"It was my thought that it would make sense to show the Caribbean, for one thing. I kept thinking of how interesting it must have been for northern Europeans to have found the paradise of the

A view of Grand Canyon from the lodge was shown on this 2¢ stamp of the 1934 National Parks series (Scott 741). Some observers professed to see an upward-looking profile of President Franklin D. Roosevelt in the rock formations at the right.

Art director Richard Sheaff made this concept sketch using a color photograph of the Rainbow Bridge in Utah.

tropical islands. That certainly was one of the kinds of terrain that they encountered. And then it was only logical that we have something else from the interior of the country somewhere. And we all had the thought quickly that things in the West also would have looked rather unusual to the early explorers, and different from what they were accustomed to."

For discussion purposes Sheaff prepared some concept sketches using color photographs. One was of the Rainbow Bridge in Utah; another was of a tropical island beach, to show the committee how a sand-and-surf, sky-and-palm tree design might look.

"I took my concepts, photo and verbal, in and talked to the committee about it," Sheaff said, "and once they had decided they wanted to go to artwork rather than photography, then I got Mark Hess involved."

Hess, the Katonah, New York, artist who had designed the Classic Mail Transportation block of four the previous year, wasn't known as a landscape painter, but Sheaff liked his style and wanted to work with him again. Hess prepared a vertical concept sketch for each of the two regions, Western and Caribbean, with each being generic rather than of a specific scene. The first of these showed a stylized Western landscape, with buttes and rock pinnacles.

Mark Hess painted this vertically arranged concept sketch of a Southwestern landscape of buttes and rock pinnacles.

126

"The committee liked it fine," Sheaff said, "but in their discussion the members decided they wanted it to be something that specifically had been seen by one of the early explorers, rather than generic. There were a number of possibilities, but we ended up picking the Grand Canyon, which was seen, not by Coronado himself, apparently, but by one of his scouting parties."

Hess then painted a panoramic view of the canyon as viewed from the south rim; a single bird hovers over one of the rock pinnacles. His first piece of finished art seemed to Sheaff to be somewhat flat and monochromatic. On the same day Sheaff received it in the mail, he also received a catalog of art books that contained a reproduction of a similar Grand Canyon painting done by Thomas Moran, a 19th-century landscape painter.

"The Moran painting had a lot more contrast of lights and darks and zip to it, and so I sent it along to Mark," Sheaff said. "It turns out that Thomas Moran was one of his heroes, and he had been sort of fumbling a little bit about how to make this thing better, and so he went back and redrew it before I showed it to the committee.

"What it shows is still a hole in the ground — it's not America's most exciting stamp — but it has a lot more contrast and life than it did the first time. Mark was sort of inspired by the work of Moran."

Looking back, Sheaff admitted to mild regret at the choice of subject matter. "Frankly, I think the generic Western scene was much stronger looking than what they ended up with," he said.

First-Day Facts

Like the previous year's America stamps, the 1990 pair was issued on October 12, Columbus Day. The first-day ceremony was held at the El Tovar Hotel, located on the south rim of the canyon in Grand Canyon National Park, Arizona.

William T. Johnstone, assistant postmaster general, dedicated the stamps. The principal speaker was David C. Bakke, general manager/postmaster at Phoenix, Arizona. Bill Mason, postmaster at Grand Canyon, presided, and John Reed, assistant superintendent of Grand Canyon National Park, gave the welcome.

25¢ DWIGHT D. EISENHOWER BIRTH CENTENNIAL

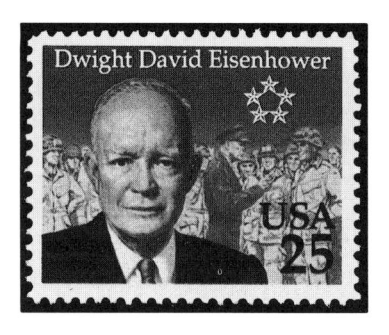

Date of Issue: October 13, 1990

Catalog Number: Scott 2513

Colors: dark brown, yellow, red, blue and black

First-Day Cancel: Abilene, Kansas

FDCs Canceled: 487,988

Format: Panes of 40, horizontal, 5 across, 8 down. Gravure printing cylinders of 160 subjects (10 across, 16 down) manufactured by Armotek Industries Inc., Palmyra, New Jersey.

Perf: 10.9 (L perforator)

Selvage Markings: ©United States Postal Service 1990, Use Correct ZIP Code®. This stamp honors the centennial year of the birth of Dwight David Eisenhower, the World War II supreme Allied commander who in 1953 became 34th President of the United States. Between WWII and 1953, he was commander of U.S. occupation forces in Europe, the U.S. Army Chief of Staff, President of Columbia University and the 1950 commander of newly-formed NATO forces. From the horse-and-buggy days of his youth to the late-1950s dawning of the U.S. space age, President Eisenhower's life spanned times of historic change in the United States and the world.

Designer: Ken Hodges of Los Alamitos, California

Art Director and Typographer: Richard Sheaff (CSAC)

Project Manager: Jack Williams (USPS)

Modeler: Richard C. Sennett (Sennett Enterprises) for American Bank Note Company

Printing: Stamps printed and sheeted out by American Bank Note Company on a leased Champlain gravure press (J.W. Fergusson and Sons, Richmond, Virginia) under the supervision of Sennett Enterprises (Fairfax, Virginia). Perforated, processed and shipped by ABNC (Chicago, Illinois).

Quantity Ordered: 142,692,000
Quantity Distributed: 142,692,000

Cylinder Number Detail: One group of five cylinder numbers preceded by the letter "A" along side corner stamps.

Tagging: overall

The Stamp

Early in 1988 the Citizens' Stamp Advisory Committee received two formal requests for a commemorative stamp in 1990 to mark the 100th anniversary of the birth of Dwight David Eisenhower, 34th president of the United States and supreme commander of the Allied Expeditionary Forces in Europe during World War II.

One, on March 11, came from Calvin A. Strowig, president of the Eisenhower Foundation of Abilene, Kansas, the town where Ike grew up. The other, on April 6, was written by the former president's granddaughter, Susan Eisenhower, who was president of the Eisenhower World Affairs Institute in Washington, D.C. When Congress established the Dwight D. Eisenhower Commission to organize centennial observances, it designated those two organizations — the Foundation and the Institute — to cooperate in the planning.

CSAC approved the request. USPS announced the stamp June 1, 1989, as part of its 1990 program, and issued it in Abilene on Saturday, October 13, 1990, one day before the 100th birthday anniversary. USPS spokesman Frank Thomas told *The Washington Post* that the stamp was released a day early so it could be used on the actual birth date in other cities with ties to Ike, such as Denison, Texas, where he was born, and Gettysburg, Pennsylvania, where he and his wife Mamie lived in retirement.

Dwight Eisenhower hadn't lacked for postal recognition; the centennial stamp was the sixth face-different stamp to depict him. The first, a 6¢ memorial issue in jumbo size (Scott 1383), was issued on October 14, 1969, some 7½ months after his death on March 28 of that year. Like the 1990 stamp, it had its first-day sale in Abilene. In 1970 and 1971, three similar-appearing stamps in the Prominent Americans series were issued in various sheet, booklet and coil formats: a 6¢ blue (Scott 1393), an 8¢ bicolor (Scott 1394) and an 8¢ claret (Scott 1395). Eisenhower was also featured on one of the 36 stamps contained in the four Presidents miniature sheets (Scott 2219g) issued to mark the Ameripex 86 stamp show.

The designs of previous U.S. stamps depicting Eisenhower.

Several other presidents had previously been honored with commemorative stamps issued on major anniversaries of their birth. They were: Abraham Lincoln, in 1909 (100th) and 1959 (150th); George Washington, in 1932 (200th, with a 12-stamp set) and 1982 (250th); James Monroe, in 1958 (200th), and Franklin D. Roosevelt, in 1982 (100th). Three definitives had doubled as commemoratives, in effect: the 10¢ Andrew Jackson stamp of the Prominent Americans series, issued in 1967 on Jackson's 200th birthday; the 13¢ John F. Kennedy stamp of the same series, issued on JFK's 50th birthday, also in 1967; and the 20¢ Harry Truman stamp of the Great Americans series, which had first-day sale on Truman's 100th birthday in 1984. A request for a 200th birthday stamp for Martin Van Buren in 1982 was turned down, but USPS recognized the anniversary by unveiling a Van Buren stamp design as the prototype for the 36 presidential stamps that would be issued four years later in the Ameripex 86 miniature sheets.

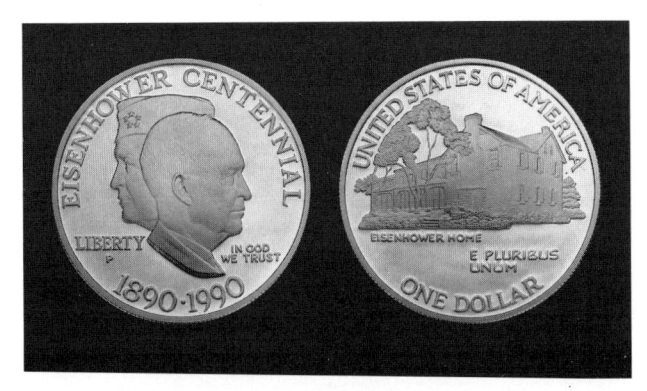

The U.S. Mint issued this commemorative silver dollar in 1990 to mark Eisenhower's birth centennial. The obverse, designed by John Mercanti, shows Eisenhower as five-star general and as postwar president in counterfacing profiles — the first dual portrait of one person ever used on a U.S. coin. The reverse, by Marcel Jovine, depicts the Gettysburg National Historic Site, home of Ike and Mamie.

Eisenhower's 100th anniversary in 1990 was also marked by a commemorative silver dollar produced by the U.S. Mint under authority of a federal law enacted October 3, 1988. The obverse, designed by John Mercanti, featured Ike as a five-star general and as a postwar president in counterfacing profiles — the first dual portrait of one person ever shown on a U.S. coin. The Republic of the Marshall Islands also issued a commemorative silver coin, in the $5 denomination, for the occasion.

The information on Eisenhower that was printed in the margin of each pane of 40 stamps constituted a virtual mini-biography. It was contained in the vertical selvage attached to three adjacent stamps:

"This stamp honors the/centennial year of the birth/of Dwight David Eisenhower,/the World War II supreme/Allied commander who in/1953 became the 34th President/of the United States.

"Between WWII and 1953, he/was commander of U.S. occu-/pation forces in Europe, the/U.S. Army Chief of Staff, Pres-/ident of Columbia University/and the 1950 commander of/newly-formed NATO forces." (Note the unusual hyphenation of "President.")

In response to the request of the Eisenhower Institute, CSAC asked artist Ken Hodges to prepare a concept sketch showing a horse and buggy and a space-shuttle launch to indicate the sweep of technological progress in Eisenhower's lifetime. The ornamentation and lettering at the left side of the design simulated 19th-century engraving style. On the right-hand side, the lettering was in a modern sans-serif face. The committee was dissatisfied with the result.

"From the horse-and-buggy/days of his youth to the late-/1950s dawning of the U.S./space age, President Eisen-/hower's life spanned times/of historic change in the/United States and the world."

The wording of the last of these paragraphs was a concession of sorts to the Eisenhower Institute. The Institute had originally suggested that the design of the stamp convey the sense of Eisenhower's long life span, from horse-and-buggy times to the space era. That idea, as we shall see, was tried and turned down by CSAC.

In the original set of marginal inscriptions, as composed by Jack Williams, USPS project manager for the stamp, the second paragraph began: "Between WWII and the presidency . . ." When the paragraphs were set in type, however, the second paragraph was slightly longer than the others, with a "widow," or short extra line.

So it was revised to read: "Between WWII and 1953 . . ." This was the only change made in the wording.

Dwight Eisenhower was born in Denison, Texas, but his family moved to Abilene while he was an infant. In grade school he was nicknamed "Little Ike" and his older brother Edgar was "Big Ike."

After high school, he applied to both the U.S. Naval and Military Academies, and won appointment to the latter. He graduated from West Point in 1915 and returned to Texas as an officer with the 19th Infantry at Fort Sam Houston. Here he met Mamie Geneva Doud, whom he married in 1916.

During World War I, Ike trained tank battalions. He served in various stateside and foreign posts between the wars, rising steadily in rank and attracting favorable attention from two Army chiefs of staff, General Douglas MacArthur, whom he served as aide, and General George C. Marshall. Five days after Pearl Harbor, Marshall named Eisenhower chief of the War Department's War Plans Division. In 1942, as head of the Operations Division of the War Department, he drew up plans to unify all American forces in Europe under one commander. Three days after submitting his plans, he was named commanding general of American forces in the European Theater of Operations, vaulting over 366 senior officers eligible for the job.

Ike planned and commanded the Allied invasions of North Africa in 1942 and Sicily and Italy in 1943. By now a full general, he was selected by President Franklin D. Roosevelt to command Operation Overlord, the Allied invasion of Nazi Germany-held Western Europe. Ike gambled that a break in stormy weather on June 6, 1944, would hold long enough for him to send his 175,000-man invasion force across the English Channel and onto the Normandy beaches. The gamble paid off, the troops landed and held on, and after 11 months of bloody fighting, Germany surrendered on May 7, 1945.

In November 1945, Eisenhower was made chief of staff, presiding over postwar demobilization. Three years later he retired from active duty to become president of Columbia University, but he returned to uniform in 1950 when the brand-new North Atlantic Treaty Organization made him supreme commander in Europe. Once again he joined many armies into one force, but this time his purpose was to preserve peace, not to wage war.

For several years Ike turned down pleas from both political parties to run for president on their tickets. In 1952 he yielded and came home to campaign for the Republican nomination. The 1952 GOP National Convention chose him on the first ballot. He won easily that fall over Democrat Adlai Stevenson, and fulfilled a campaign promise to go to Korea to observe the U.N. police action in which U.S. troops had fought North Korean and Chinese invaders to a stalemate. A few months later a truce was signed.

J. Anthony Wills' official portrait of President Eisenhower, which hangs in the entrance hall of the White House.

Among the memorable events of Eisenhower's two-term presidency were the first summit conference with leaders of the Soviet Union; the sending of Army troops to Little Rock, Arkansas, to back up the U.S. Supreme Court order that schools be desegregated; the commencement of major public works projects such as the St. Lawrence Seaway and the Interstate Highway System, and the dawning of the space age with the launching of Soviet Sputniks and the start of America's own satellite program. In January 1961 he left the White House and retired with Mamie to Gettysburg. His health gradually declined, and on March 28, 1969, he died of heart failure in Walter Reed General Hospital in Washington, D.C.

The Design

The Eisenhower Institute had asked that the Ike portrait be based on the official White House painting, and had provided a color transparency of it. However, CSAC was dubious about the Institute's proposal for a design stressing the fact that Eisenhower had lived from the horse-and-buggy age to the space age. As members pointed out, this was hardly unique to Eisenhower; every one of his contemporaries could make the same claim.

Nevertheless, art director Richard Sheaff asked the artist assigned to the project, Ken Hodges of Los Alamitos, California, to work up

This is the U.S. Army photograph on which the background sketch on the Eisenhower stamp was based. Ike is talking with battle-ready members of the 101st Airborne Division on the eve of D-Day, shortly before they would take off to be parachuted into Nazi-occupied France.

a concept sketch with a horse and buggy on one side of the Ike portrait and a space-shuttle launching on the other. "It really didn't work," Sheaff said. "It was awkward. It didn't make a lot of sense."

The committee then asked Sheaff for a design that contained a reference to Eisenhower's military career. The other major phase of his life, his presidency, was already covered by the decision to use the White House portrait. To do justice to this design approach and to obtain the aspect ratio Sheaff wanted, USPS agreed to issue the stamp in the semi-jumbo size that comes 40 to a printed pane.

Sheaff forwarded to Hodges some wartime photographs of Ike. One of these, perhaps the best known, was a U.S. Army photo taken on the eve of D-Day. It showed the general talking with battle-ready members of the 101st Airborne Division at Newbury, England, shortly before they took off in C-47s to jump behind enemy lines in Normandy. That one would probably best suit the layout, Sheaff

This is an early version of Ken Hodges' stamp design. In it, the soldiers in the background sketch are very similar to the ones in the photograph; the GI to whom Ike is talking even wears the same number, 23, on his jacket. The figures were later altered to eliminate the problem of showing living people on a stamp. Ike's five stars are arranged here in a straight line, rather than in the cluster in which they were finally placed, and the portrait is slightly larger than on the stamp as issued.

suggested. The center of action would fit on the right side of the portrait, but there would also be figures to fill the space on the left. Hodges agreed, and proceeded on that basis.

Hodges' first version of what would be the ultimate stamp design was faithful to the photograph. Because many of these soldiers were identifiable (D-Day historian Cornelius Ryan had been able to identify at least 11 of them with the help of the 101st Airborne Association) and some were no doubt still living, Sheaff directed the artist to alter their appearance. "To avoid the whole question of showing living people on stamps, we changed them all around," Sheaff said. "We gave some of them helmets and changed their body postures. Some of them, particularly the man Ike is talking to, are in relatively the same position, but even that soldier underwent some changes. No one is literally the same as he is in the photo."

The background picture was printed in a sepia tone reminiscent of old rotogravure-section illustrations. The Eisenhower head-and-shoulders portrait in the foreground, by contrast, was in full color. The portrait on which it was based was painted in 1967, when Eisenhower was 76, by J. Anthony Wills, who had done several previous portraits of the same subject. Ike sat for this one in Palm Springs, California. At the time the stamp was issued, the painting hung in the entrance hall of the White House.

To round out the composition, Hodges included the five stars of Eisenhower's top Army rank, general of the Army. In his concept sketch he placed the stars in a horizontal row, but project manager Jack Williams — a former Army lieutenant colonel — checked with Pentagon sources and returned with the official word that the insignia as worn by holders of the rank has its stars arranged in a cluster, with a configuration that creates a pentagon shape on the inside. Hodges made the change on the finished artwork.

The Eisenhower stamp was Hodges' second design assignment for USPS. He had previously designed the se-tenant block of four Future Mail Transport commemoratives issued in 1989.

Varieties

A single imperforate pane of 40 Eisenhower stamps was found by a collector in California. The lower-left position pane bore the gravure number combination A11111. The pane was sold privately through the Jacques Schiff firm of Ridgefield Park, New Jersey.

First-Day Facts

Senior Assistant Postmaster General Richard J. Strasser Jr. dedicated the stamp at a public ceremony on the grounds of the Eisenhower Center in Abilene. The Center is the popular name given the five-building complex, which includes the Eisenhower presidential

An imperforate pane of the 25¢ Dwight D. Eisenhower stamp was discovered in California. Shown here is a plate block from the full pane.

library, museum, family home and the final resting place of President and Mrs. Eisenhower.

Principal speakers were the late president's son, John S.D. Eisenhower, and U.S. Representative Pat Roberts, Republican of Kansas. Richard Norton Smith, acting director of the Dwight D. Eisenhower Library, gave the welcome.

SPECIAL STAMPS

Special stamps differ from commemorative stamps in that they are issued for use on specific occasions and not to honor persons, places or events. They differ from definitive stamps in that they usually don't remain on sale for many years at a time or until they are rendered obsolete by a postal rate change.

Six special stamps were issued in 1990. For the first time, each of the three continuing categories of special stamp — traditional Christmas, or Christmas Madonna; contemporary Christmas, or Christmas Greetings, and Love — was issued in two forms, sheet and booklet. The Love stamp had never before been produced in booklet form. To print the Love sheet version, USPS gave the United States Banknote Company its first U.S. stamp contract.

25¢ LOVE (SHEET STAMP)

Date of Issue: January 18, 1990

Catalog Number: Scott 2440

Colors: magenta, yellow, cyan and black

First-Day Cancel: Romance, Arkansas (Romance Church of Christ)

FDCs Canceled: 257,788 (sheet and booklet)

Format: Panes of 50, horizontal, 5 across, 10 down. Gravure printing cylinders of 300 subjects (15 across, 30 around) manufactured by Harrison and Sons.

Perf: 12.5 by 13 comb perforated

Selvage Markings: USE CORRECT ZIP CODE®, ©USPS 1988

Designer: Jane Hertko of New York, New York

Art Director and Typographer: Bradbury Thompson (CSAC)

Project Manager: Jack Williams (USPS)

Printing: Gravure printed using 4 of the 5 gravure units of the webfed gravure/intaglio Giori press of the U.S. Bank Note Company.

Quantity Ordered: 928,000,000
Quantity Distributed: 928,000,000

Cylinder Number Detail: One group of four cylinder numbers preceded by the letter "U" over/under corner stamps.

Tagging: overall

The Stamp

The 1990 stamp with the longest elapsed time between unveiling and issuance was the Love stamp.

It was originally scheduled to be released in 1989, and its design was first shown to the public in downtown Washington, D.C., as the final seconds of 1988 ticked away on New Year's Eve. In keeping with a tradition begun in 1983, a large reproduction of the stamp was lowered from the clock tower of the Old Post Office Pavilion on Pennsylvania Avenue to help welcome in the New Year.

However, in June 1989 USPS announced that the stamp's issuance would be postponed until 1990. Accordingly, on the next New Year's Eve, instead of using the same design in the ceremony, USPS lowered from the tower a reproduction of the Love envelope that it had issued the previous September 22 as a late addition to its 1989 stamp and stationery program.

The stamp was finally issued January 18, 1990, in the tiny town of Romance, Arkansas. Thus it was available for 1990 Valentine's Day mailings. USPS gave no reason for the delay in its issuance, but subsequent disclosures suggested one: The printing job had been given to a new contractor, who encountered difficulties in getting the bugs out of newly acquired equipment and launching production.

The 1990 Love stamp was the ninth face-different variety in the series that began in 1973, but it represented several firsts.

• It was the first of the Love group to be printed in the new special size — between a commemorative and a definitive — that was initiated with the 1988 Christmas stamps.

• It was the first Love stamp issued in booklets as well as sheets.

• The sheet stamps were the first stamps to be printed under a contract awarded in 1989 to the United States Bank Note Company (USBNC) of Philadelphia, a successor firm to the Hamilton Banknote Company. The booklets were made by the Bureau of Engraving and Printing, and are described in the next chapter.

• Finally, the sheet stamp introduced some perforation innovations. It was the first U.S. stamp to be perforated 12½ (horizontal) by 13; the first true comb-perforated U.S. stamp, and the first U.S. stamp to be perforated in multiple sheets.

The stamps were printed at the plant of the Jeffries Banknote Company of Los Angeles, which USBNC had acquired as a wholly owned subsidiary in 1989. In 1990 USBNC added another wholly owned subsidiary, the American Bank Note Company, a long-time supplier of U.S. stamps.

For collectors, there were a number of subtle indications that the Love stamps had come from a new supplier. One was the prefix letter "U" before the printing cylinder numbers in the selvage. Another was a different typeface on the marginal inscriptions, and a narrower-than-usual selvage where these markings were printed.

Charles Yeager, Washington correspondent for *Linn's Stamp News,* wrote this account of an interview with Thomas C. Harris, USBNC vice president for government sales:

"To get the 1990 Love sheet stamp out on schedule, USBNC

worked closely with a number of suppliers, including two foreign security printing houses, Harrison and Sons Limited in England and the British American Bank Note Company of Canada.

"(In the spring of 1989) USBNC began setting up a used webfed gravure/intaglio press in its Los Angeles Jeffries Banknote plant. The press, acquired from a foreign firm, is one of five such presses manufactured by Giori during the early 1970s. The press is like the BEP's A press, having five gravure printing stations and one three-color intaglio printing unit. For the Love stamp, only four of the five gravure units on the USBNC press were used. And, as with most complex modern printing equipment, getting the press to work as it should required time, effort and endless tests.

"USBNC used a coated, pre-gummed, phosphored paper, supplied by Fitchburg Coated Products (an American company) . . .

"Harrison and Sons supplied USBNC with photomechanically etched 300-subject printing cylinders. These cylinders were laid out in the new special stamp size used for the Christmas stamps the last two years: 15 subjects across the cylinder by 20 subjects around. This works out to six printed panes of 50 stamps each per revolution of the printing cylinder. Under normal conditions, only one or two sets of printing cylinders are required by the BEP and the ABNC to produce a stamp by the gravure method. Because of startup snags and wrinkles, however, USBNC needed more than three complete sets of Love printing cylinders . . .

"For the 1990 Love stamp, USBNC did not have an on-line press perforating chassis capable of producing a perforation pattern compatible with the U.S. special stamp size. Rather than use L perforators, which produce overlapping corner perf holes, USBNC opted to use sheetfed stroke comb-perforators that produce perfect corner perforations. Harrison and Sons had comb perforators in mothballs. USBNC borrowed two Grover stroke double-comb perforators from Harrison, and a third Grover machine (another stroke double-comb perforator) was obtained from the Canadian security printer, British American Bank Note Company. All three of these machines were capable of perforating multiple sheets at a time.

"The perforator obtained from Canada (USBNC Number 7614)

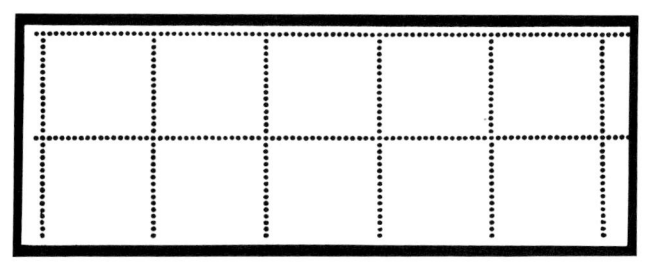

A double-comb perforator, as was used on the 1990 Love sheet stamp, perforates two rows at a time.

perforated six sheets at a time. One of the Grover machines borrowed from Harrison perforated seven sheets at a time (USBNC Number 7612). The other Harrison machine (USBN Number 7611) was never able to handle more than six sheets at a time.

"Collectors of European and other foreign stamps are familiar with comb-perforated stamps. Collectors of U.S. stamps, however, may need help in understanding how comb perforators work.

"Starting with a stroke single-comb perforation, the word 'comb' is used because the effect of one stroke of a single-comb perforator produces what resembles a comb with teeth. The long row of holes is sometimes called 'the line,' with the short rows of holes at right angles to the long row called 'the legs.'

"On a stroke single-comb perforator, the first stroke perforates three sides of one row of stamps. The paper is then moved forward and the next stroke completes the perforation of the first row and adds the legs or sides of the next row of stamps. This action continues until the sheet of stamps is completely perforated.

"On a stroke double-comb perforator, one stroke of the pins perforates one row of stamps, plus the legs of the next row.

"Illustrated is a partial pane of Love sheet stamps, shown from the back, with blank spots between perforations. This defect, caused by a broken or missing perf pin, repeats every other row, due to the nature of a double-comb perforator.

"The perforators used by USBNC require prepunched holes in the outer sheet margins to accommodate the pin alignment registration system of the Grover machines. The holes are punched into the outer margins of the printed paper web on the printing press before sheeting-out occurs.

"After perforating, the 300-subject sheets are trimmed and cut into post office panes of 50 stamps. One of the reasons for the unusually narrow selvage on the Love panes (where marginal markings are printed) is because a larger amount of selvage than on regularly printed BEP and ABNC stamp issues must be trimmed away to eliminate the prepunched pin registration holes."

Distinguishing among the six different panes on the printing sheet was easy, because the location of the cylinder numbers was different

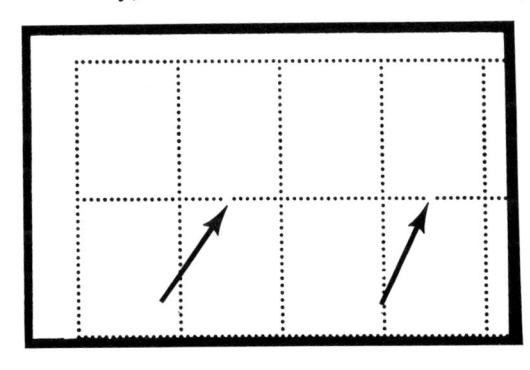

A perforation defect, such as a missing perf pin, repeats in every other row of stamps that are processed by double-comb perforators.

on each one: the upper left corner reading down in the vertical margin, upper left reading across in the horizontal margin, upper right reading down in the vertical margin, lower left reading down in the vertical margin, lower left reading across in the horizontal margin and lower right reading down in the vertical margin.

The day after the stamps went on sale, USPS began selling at post offices and philatelic centers a "1990 Love Folder" that included a block of four of the Love stamps, a sentimental message and a 1989 Love envelope — total face value, $1.25 — for $3.50.

The folder represented "a unique Valentine's Day gift and an expression of affection that is appropriate year 'round," USPS said. This was its message: "Lovebirds sing/Of hearts entwined,/Giving wing/To affection sublime." Whatever the strengths of the Postal Service might be, creating poetry obviously wasn't one of them.

The Design

The design — two blue lovebirds suspended face to face above a pink heart and stylized green garland, all on a white background — was prepared by Jayne Hertko when she was a graduate student in Yale University's Department of Graphic Design.

One of Hertko's instructors was Bradbury Thompson, the typographer and veteran stamp designer who served as a design coordinator for the Citizens' Stamp Advisory Committee. Thompson had suggested to the committee members a few years earlier that they let some of his students take part in a stamp design project involving Love and Christmas stamps. The students would submit their sketches in enlarged form, mounted on cardboard, accompanied by stamp-size reductions, as any other stamp designer would do. The committee agreed, and in November 1986 Hertko's class produced a quantity of Love stamp designs for the committee's consideration. She herself prepared "seven or eight," she told her hometown newspaper, *The Regional News* of Palos Heights, Illinois.

"We got a lot of interesting ideas out of those bright minds," said Jack Williams of USPS, project manager for the 1990 Love stamp. "Brad brought them in and laid them out on the table, and the committee spent some time going through them." CSAC chose two or three as promising, Williams said, including Hertko's lovebirds

Two of the Love stamp design ideas presented by Bradbury Thompson's graphic design students at Yale.

design, which turned out to be the first of the group to actually emerge as a stamp. By the time it was issued Hertko was 27, out of school and working in graphic arts in New York City.

Hertko made her design of cut paper after reviewing illustrations of folk-art matchboxes and other ornamental household storage containers. "Her work is representative of a lovebird motif common in early 20th-century New England and Pennsylvania folk art," the USPS announcement said. The artist's original design was for a commemorative-size stamp, and the dimensions had to be altered to those of the new 300-subject Christmas/Love stamp format. The principal visible effect of the change on the stamp's appearance was a reduction in the amount of greenery at the bottom.

The design, like previous simple, posterlike artwork used in the Love stamp series, wasn't universally popular. One *Linn's Stamp News* reader noted wryly that the news story about the stamp credited a designer-typographer, art director, design coordinator, project manager and modeler. The design had "a very substantial provenance," he wrote, "and was created by a multitude, evidently in great pain . . . At the risk of being irreverent, and considering that Michelangelo painted the Sistine Chapel — alone — I am tempted to paraphrase Churchill's famous statement: 'Never have so many claimed so much for so little.' "

Varieties

An imperforate pane of Love stamps was purchased — not without difficulty — from a Modesto, California, post office.

According to Fred W. Baumann, writing in *Linn's,* the pane was among several bought by an engaged couple for mailing their wedding invitations. The fiancee, who had once worked in a stamp store, recognized the potential value of the find, but she also needed stamps to replace the imperforate pane. When she returned to the post office window to buy more stamps, she made the mistake of mentioning her discovery. As the story was told to Baumann, the clerk then snatched the imperforate pane from the woman's hand, declaring that it was illegal for her to possess it. (The clerk seems to have been the spiritual descendant of the postal inspectors who, back in 1918, tried unsuccessfully to retrieve the sheet of 100 inverted Jenny airmail stamps from its purchaser, William Robey.)

Unable to persuade local postal officials to return the pane,

Jane Hertko's original design was in commemorative size and contained more greenery than appeared on the finished stamp.

A top margin block of 10 of the imperforate Love stamp photographically cropped from the original discovery pane of 50.

Baumann wrote, the couple telephoned the postmaster general's office in Washington the next day. Shortly after that, the stamps were given back to the couple. Local stamp dealer Henry Leer referred the owners to San Francisco auctioneer Aubrey Bartlett, who sold the pane at his firm's auction at the Westpex 90 stamp show April 27-29. It fetched $12,650, including the buyer's 10-percent surcharge. The pane was from the top middle position in the original six-pane production sheet of 300 stamps.

Another production error created a pane with 10 blank stamps across the bottom two rows. Two rows of stamps were trimmed off the pane at the top, with partial stamps appearing in the narrow top selvage. The remaining 40 stamps were normal, with normal center-

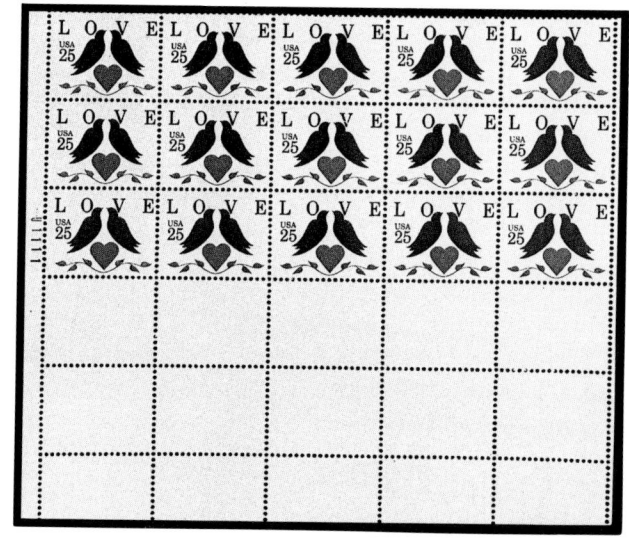

A full pane, half of which is shown here, was discovered with two horizontal rows of blank stamps. The cause was a shift during processing of the printed stamps. Two full rows of good stamps were trimmed from the top.

ing. The pane was from the lower left position of the printing sheet. Since the top two rows were missing, only the cylinder numbers remained as marginal markings, along with an "S" from "USPS" and a trim mark. The pane was bought in a Richmond, Virginia, post office by a non-collector, who paid $12.50 for what was only $10 worth of stamps. The buyer immediately realized the value of the purchase, according to Mike Davis of Virginia Stamp Auctions, Chester, Virginia, which was asked to handle the sale of the pane.

George Brett, writing in *The United States Specialist,* described the error and explained how it had occurred:

"One of the consequences of using an A-type press, if it has off-the-shelf printing cylinders, is that the results do not divide into aliquot (exact-number, with no remainder) sheets in the U.S. for issuance. There is a three-stamp row overrun beyond even sheet and pane divisions which can result in a repeating unprinted span with each printing cylinder rotation . . .

"This unprinted span has shown up on Love sheets, ostensibly from miscutting . . . The strange thing about (the Richmond pane) is the rather well applied perforations, because the perforation control holes would seemingly have been out of synchronization. But that provides the answer as to when this happened in production. In other words, it was after perforating. It resulted from one of the large 300-subject sheets, as perforated, being turned around in a stack during the final processing — inspection, counting, cutting into panes. Additionally, the top and bottom cutting is off a bit as the perforated fractions should be of approximately equal width rather than narrow at the top and wide at the bottom."

Five other miscut panes would have had to be produced along with this one, but as of this writing none had been reported found.

First-Day Facts

Maintaining his record as the postmaster general most likely to be found at a first-day ceremony, Anthony M. Frank turned up in Romance, Arkansas (population 75) January 18 to speak at the Love stamp dedication at the Church of Christ, across the highway from the post office. Also participating was U.S. Senator David H. Pryor of Arkansas and Deborah K. Bowker, assistant postmaster general.

After the dedication of the stamp, a Little Rock couple, Deanna Cole and James Cantrell, were married at the church. They had won a Valentine's honeymoon contest sponsored by a local radio station.

According to *The Arkansas Gazette,* the Romance post office is a popular mailing point for senders of valentines around the country, and also gets many requests to postmark wedding invitations every May and June.

$5 LOVE BOOKLET

Date of Issue: January 18, 1990

Catalog Number: Scott 2441

Colors: green, magenta, cyan and black

First-Day Cancel: Romance, Arkansas (Romance Church of Christ)

FDCs Canceled: 257,788 (sheet and booklet)

Format: Two panes of 10 stamps each arranged horizontally 5 by 2. Gravure printing cylinders of 300 subjects (15 across, 20 around)

Perf: 11.2 (Eureka off-line perforator)

Selvage Markings: 4 cylinder numbers on binding stub of each pane. Registration mark remnants on 17% of all pane binding stubs.

Cover Markings: ©United States Postal Service 1990 on inside of front cover. Universal Product Code (UPC) printed on outside of back cover.

Designer: Jane Hertko of New York, New York

Art Designer and Typographer: Bradbury Thompson (CSAC)

Project Manager: Jack Williams (USPS)

Printing: Stamps printed on BEP's 7-color Andreotti gravure press (601). Booklet covers printed on a 6-color Goebel Optiforma offset press in yellow, magenta, cyan and black. Booklets formed on standard book binding equipment.

Quantity Ordered: 30,000,000 booklets
Quantity Distributed: 49,758,900 booklets

Cylinder Number Detail: One group of four cylinder numbers on each pane binding stub.

Tagging: overall

The Stamp

The Love booklets were produced on the McCain off-line book-binding equipment, as modified by the Bureau of Engraving and Printing, which had been used earlier for the booklet versions of the two 1989 Christmas stamps.

The stamps were printed on BEP's 20-year-old Andreotti gravure press. Colors weren't process colors but red, blue, green and black self-colors. Differing marginal markings gave booklet collectors six varieties of panes to collect, and the two-pane booklets came in 18 different combinations of marginal markings.

The perforations on the booklet stamps measured the standard 11.2, unlike the sheet stamps, which at 12½ by 13 had the smallest perforation gauge of any U.S. stamps in the 20th century.

Besides the size of the perforations and the fact that each booklet stamp had at least one straight edge while the sheet stamps were completely perforated, there were other, subtle differences in appearance between the two versions. The colors on BEP's booklet stamps were darker, especially the blue and green. The black "USA" was heavier. The printed design on the booklet stamps was slightly larger in both dimensions, and the booklet gum was smoother and shinier.

Stamp printing expert George Brett, writing in *The United States Specialist,* noted that, although the United States Bank Note Company used water-based inks on the sheet stamps, the gravure printing cylinders supplied by Harrison and Sons of England "produced the old-time jagged edges to the printed segments, lettering, etc.," while BEP's edges were smooth.

Brett also observed that the paper used by USBNC for the sheet stamps readily fluoresced under both long- and short-wave ultraviolet light, while the BEP paper fluoresced only under short-wave.

Varieties

Six booklets with the red heart completely omitted on the first pane were found by Jeri Fortier in the Kent, Ohio, post office.

Fortier told *Linn's Stamp News* that she purchased three error booklets May 24, 1990. She said that after she saw a line at the post office counter she decided to use a post office vending machine to buy her stamps instead. After receiving one booklet and opening it, Fortier noticed the missing color. She double-checked it with an illustration in a copy of the USPS *Philatelic Catalog* on the counter. Fortier then showed the booklet to the post office clerk, asking whether it was supposed to be the way it was.

The clerk told Fortier the stamps were errors and asked to see them. She then took the booklet to the back of the post office so it could be examined. Meantime, Fortier purchased two more error booklets from the machine. Shortly thereafter, the machine was opened by postal employees, who looked through the remaining booklets and found three more with the error. These booklets were reportedly purchased by the employees.

Fortier said she planned to keep one of the booklets but would probably sell the other two. One of the color-omitted Love booklets was privately sold through dealer Jacques Schiff.

First-Day Facts

For covers fully serviced by USPS, only full panes were affixed, at a cost of $2.50 per cover. Collectors wanting a combination of sheet and booklet stamps on covers had to prepare their own envelopes and send them to the Romance, Arkansas, postmaster.

25¢ CHRISTMAS MADONNA AND CHILD (SHEET STAMP)

Date of Issue: October 18, 1990

Catalog Number: Scott 2514

Colors: red, yellow, pink and blue (offset); red and brown (intaglio)

First-Day Cancel: Washington, D.C. (National Gallery of Art)

FDCs Canceled: 378,383 (sheet and booklet)

Format: Panes of 50, vertical, 10 across, 5 down. Offset printing plates of 300 subjects (15 across, 20 around) and intaglio printing sleeve of 600 subjects (15 across, 40 around).

Perf: 11.2 (Eureka off-line perforator)

Selvage Markings: USE CORRECT ZIP CODE®, ©UNITED STATES POSTAL SERVICE 1990

Designer: Bradbury Thompson (CSAC)

Project Manager: Jack Williams (USPS)

Engravers: Thomas Hipschen, vignette (BEP); Michael J. Ryan, lettering and numerals (BEP)

Modeler: Ronald C. Sharpe (BEP)

Printing: BEP 6-color offset, 3-color intaglio D press (902)

Quantity Ordered: 600,000,000
Quantity Distributed: 600,000,000

Plate/Sleeve Number Detail: One group of four offset plate numbers on large margin, with single-digit intaglio sleeve number on selvage of adjacent stamp.

Tagging: block

The Stamp

As it had done in 1989, USPS issued each of its two Christmas stamps — which it calls "traditional" and "contemporary" — in both sheet and booklet forms. All four varieties had their first-day sale October 18.

The first U.S. Christmas stamps were sold in 1962 and at least one new face-different specimen has been issued in each holiday season since then. From 1970 on, mailers have had a choice of a traditional, or religious-oriented, design and a contemporary, or secular, design. The traditional designs have usually featured a madonna and child as their subject.

Both the 1990 types were of the "in-between" size, larger than a definitive but smaller than a standard commemorative, that was introduced in 1988. The change came in response to the complaints of customers who thought the definitive-size Christmas stamps that had been issued in the two prior years were too small to do justice to their designs. Even so, the new dimensions required less paper and ink to produce than the commemorative size that had been used frequently on earlier Christmas stamps, and this was good news to USPS accountants.

Like the 1988 and 1989 Christmas stamps, the 1990 stamps that were issued in sheet form were printed in sheets of 300, divided into six panes of 50 (10 across by five deep). Following another precedent that was set in 1988, the 1990 traditional versions were produced by a combination of offset and intaglio on BEP's D press, rather than by the gravure method that was used to print all Christmas stamps from 1970 through 1987 (and which continued to be used for the contemporary versions).

"The committee decided that you really need intaglio to bring out the detail in the Old Masters' paintings," said Jack Williams of USPS, who has been the project manager for recent Christmas stamps.

In the case of the previous year's traditional Christmas stamp, both the sheet and booklet versions were perforated 11½ by 11, and single copies of each were identical except that those from booklets had one or two straight edges. For that reason, the 1989 booklet pane was given only a minor listing under the sheet variety in the 1991 *Scott Specialized Catalogue of United States Stamps*.

But with the 1990 traditional Christmas stamp, although the sheet and booklet versions also had the same design and perforation gauge, they differed in an important respect. The sheet stamps were block tagged on regular stamp paper; the booklet stamps were block tagged on prephosphored paper. (See next chapter.)

Some experts also reported that they could see a difference between the engraved portions of the sheet and booklet stamps. One was Richard L. Sine, editorial director of the Scott Publishing Company, whose column in the *Scott Stamp Monthly* for January 1991 carried an enlarged picture of each version.

"Note in the booklet version," Sine wrote, "that the area by the frame line to the right and bottom is far less defined against the vignette than it is on the sheet version . . . where there is a sharp distinction between the edge of the painting and the beginning of the frame." The difference, Sine added, had proved to be constant in several examples of the booklet stamp purchased in various parts of the United States, making it unlikely that variations in amount of ink was the cause.

Bureau of Engraving and Printing technicians told *Linn's Stamp News* that they had been unaware of the reported difference and couldn't account for it. The same transfer roll was used to rock in the subjects on the printing sleeves for both the sheet and booklet stamps, BEP said. As of this writing, no satisfactory explanation had been found.

The Design

The design followed a formula that was devised by CSAC's Brad-

The Madonna and Child *of Antonello da Messina, which hangs in the West Building of the National Gallery of Art.*

bury Thompson and used since 1986 for the traditional Christmas stamps. In this formula a Renaissance painting of a madonna and child from the National Gallery of Art collection, which Thompson crops so as to focus on those two figures, fills a rectangular frame that also contains the denomination and "USA." The word "CHRISTMAS" in red capitals on white reaches across the top, and the artist's last name and "National Gallery" appears in uppercase and lowercase letters across the bottom.

The 1990 design was based on a portion of Antonello da Messina's *Madonna and Child* (circa 1475), done in tempera and oil on wood, which is part of the National Gallery's Andrew W. Mellon Collection and was acquired in 1937. The painting hangs in the West building of the National Gallery.

Antonello (circa 1430-1479), wrote art historian Frederick Hartt, was "one of the greatest portraitists in history . . . one of those extraordinary geniuses who turn up every now and then as if to refute theorists who like to relate history in terms of necessary developments from stage to stage." The son of a stonecutter, he was born in the Sicilian city of Messina, where there had been no artistic tradition for some three centuries. In some manner — scholars aren't sure how — he acquired a mastery of the Flemish technique of oil painting. In 1475 he arrived in Venice and changed the course of Venetian painting by teaching the local artists the subtle effects that could be achieved with oils.

Antonello, wrote Hartt, "was able to blend a Netherlandish passion for the infinitesimal details of visual reality and for the saturation of vision in light and shadow with a quintessentially Mediterranean purity and clarity of form." Among his other works is *Virgin Annunciate,* whose Mary, her hair and shoulders covered by a blue veil, bears the same contemplative expression that is seen on her face in the painting reproduced on the Christmas stamp.

Although the past five madonna paintings on which traditional Christmas stamp designs have been based were from the National Gallery, there is no policy saying this must be the case, and in fact the subject of the 1991 traditional stamp will be from another museum, USPS sources said. CSAC selects subjects for the traditional Christmas stamp several years in advance. In 1989 the members reviewed transparencies of madonna paintings from a number of art galleries, including the National Gallery, and made a series of selections for the future. The assignment of a painting to a specific year of issue is completely arbitrary.

First-Day Facts

The first-day ceremony for the traditional sheet and booklet stamps was held in the auditorium of the East building of the National Gallery of Art, which is the newer of the institution's structures. For the occasion, the Antonello painting was brought to the ceremony from its customary location in the West building.

Senior Assistant Postmaster General Richard J. Strasser Jr. dedicated the stamps. The principal speakers were Frances Feldman, a lecturer at the National Gallery, and Joseph Harris, postmaster of Washington, D.C. Esther J. Richards, general manager/postmaster for the Southern Maryland Division of USPS, introduced the distinguished guests, who included Dr. C. Douglas Lewis, the National Gallery's curator of sculpture and decorative arts and a member of the Citizens' Stamp Advisory Committee.

USPS made provision for first-day cover collectors who wanted to combine booklet and sheet stamps and/or traditional and contemporary Christmas stamps on one cover. Customers planning to prepare their own combination envelopes in advance were told to send the envelopes, with any combination of stamps affixed, to the postmaster in Evergreen, Colorado, (the first-day city for the contemporary sheet and booklet stamps) and specify whether the Evergreen or the Washington, D.C., first-day cancellation was desired.

Collectors who wished to have USPS affix the stamps were given eight options. They could obtain either of the two sheet stamps on a separate cover with the appropriate first-day postmark, either of the two booklet stamps as a full pane on a separate cover with the appropriate first-day postmark, single copies of both sheet stamps on one cover with either the Evergreen or Washington postmark, and full panes of both booklet stamps on one cover with either the Evergreen or Washington postmark.

$5 CHRISTMAS MADONNA AND CHILD BOOKLET

Date of Issue: October 18, 1990

Catalog Number: unassigned by Scott

Colors: red, yellow, pink and blue (offset); red and brown (intaglio)

First-Day Cancel: Washington, D.C. (National Gallery of Art)

FDCs Canceled: 378,383 (sheet and booklet)

Format: Two panes of 10 stamps each arranged vertically 2 by 5. Offset printing plates of 300 subjects (15 across, 20 around) and intaglio printing sleeve of 600 subjects (15 across, 40 around).

Perf: 11.2 by 11.2 (Eureka off-line perforator)

Selvage Markings: Sleeve number on binding stub of each pane. Registration mark remnants on 17% of all binding stubs.

Cover Markings: ©United States Postal Service 1990 on inside of front cover. Universal Product Code (UPC) printed on outside of back cover.

Designer, Art Director and Typographer: Bradbury Thompson (CSAC)

Project Manager: Jack Williams (USPS)

Engravers: Thomas Hipschen, vignette (BEP)
Michael J. Ryan, lettering and numerals (BEP)

Modeler: Ronald C. Sharpe (BEP)

Printing: BEP 6-color offset, 3-color intaglio D press (902). Booklet covers printed on a 6-color Goebel Optiforma offset press (043) in magenta, yellow, cyan and black. Booklets formed on standard bookbinding equipment.

Quantity Ordered: 12,000,000 booklets
Quantity Distributed: 12,000,000 booklets

Plate/Sleeve Number Detail: One sleeve number on each pane binding stub.

Tagging: block tagged on prephosphored paper

The Stamp

The booklet version of the traditional Christmas stamp had a unique double tagging. It was printed on prephosphored paper, and in addition was block tagged. *Linn's Stamp News* writer Wayne Youngblood was the first to report this discovery, which was later confirmed by Bureau of Engraving and Printing officials. Viewed under shortwave ultraviolet light, the booklet stamp has the appearance of all-over tagging with block tagging printed on top of it, which produces a very strong and clear phosphor signal.

BEP used paper type LP703, which was a prephosphored paper rather than phosphor-coated, to print all the traditional Christmas booklet stamps. LP689, a standard paper, was used to print the sheet version of the stamp.

During the make-ready process, BEP printers had determined that the phosphor signal emitted by the prephosphored paper was insufficient. The density of the design impaired the signal. Rather than change the paper type at press time (which wasn't as simple as

The two types of tagging on the Christmas Madonna booklet stamp are shown here by the use of graphic film.

taking a different roll of paper from the pallet), BEP decided to use the prephosphored paper as planned, but to add the block tagging to ensure a good signal. The entire press run of traditional Christmas stamp booklets was produced in this manner.

No change was needed for the sheet version, which had been scheduled from the beginning to be printed on ordinary, non-prephosphored paper and to receive block tagging.

If a single sheet stamp and single booklet stamp are compared side by side, the booklet stamp has a noticeably brighter appearance, quite aside from their differences under ultraviolet light.

The Design

Like the cover of the 1989 traditional Christmas stamp booklet, the 1990 cover bore an enlarged reproduction of the design used on the stamps inside, printed by offset in full color. And, as was the case in 1989, the image was somewhat misleading because it was shown with perforations on all four sides. All the stamps inside the booklet, of course, had at least one straight edge.

The printed material on the back and inside the booklet cover included a plug and coupon for USPS' "Best of the Decade" mint set, and a paragraph urging mailers to "help speed mail delivery" by using all capital letters with no punctuation in addresses.

First-Day Facts

Information on the first-day ceremony for the sheet and booklet versions of the traditional Christmas stamp can be found in the preceding chapter.

The first-day ceremony programs for both the traditional and contemporary Christmas stamps that were distributed on subscription, both to collectors and dealers, contained a major mistake. Each was supposed to bear a single of the sheet stamp and a pair of the booklet stamp. The programs handed out at the ceremonies themselves were correctly assembled. But the pairs that were affixed in the subscription programs were of sheet stamps, not booklet stamps.

Official USPS ceremony programs bear stamps affixed by Minnesota Diversified Industries, which employs disabled persons, although the programs are canceled by the Postal Service's Philatelic Sales Division. "Somehow a missed communication didn't make it clear that the two separate stamps were supposed to come from the booklet," Frank Thomas of USPS told *Stamp Collector* columnist Lloyd A. De Vries. "We don't have enough programs left over from the ceremony to meet the subscription needs."

To remedy the mistake, USPS reprinted the programs and sent a reprint, with a pair of booklet stamps in the appropriate place, at no additional cost to each subscriber who was on record as being active at the time the error version was sent. Approximately 2,000 programs had to be replaced.

25¢ CHRISTMAS GREETINGS (SHEET STAMP)

Date of Issue: October 18, 1990

Catalog Number: Scott 2515

Colors: red, purple, yellow and green

First-Day Cancel: Evergreen, Colorado

FDCs Canceled: 230,586 (sheet and booklet)

Format: Panes of 50, vertical, 5 across, 10 down. Gravure printing cylinders of 200 subjects (10 across, 20 around) manufactured by Armotek Industries Inc., Palmyra, New Jersey.

Perf: 10.9 (L perforator)

Selvage Markings: ©United States Postal Service 1990, ®Use Correct ZIP Code

Designer: Libby Thiel of Bryan's Road, Maryland

Art Director and Typographer: Derry Noyes (CSAC)

Project Manager: Jack Williams (USPS)

Printing: Stamps printed and sheeted out by American Bank Note Company on a leased Champlain gravure press (J.W. Fergusson and Sons, Richmond, Virginia) under the supervision of Sennett Enterprises (Fairfax, Virginia). Perforated, processed and shipped by ABNC (Chicago, Illinois).

Quantity Ordered: 600,000,000
Quantity Distributed: 600,000,000

Cylinder Number Detail: One group of four cylinder numbers preceded by the letter "A."

Tagging: overall

The Stamp
In 1990, as in 1989, the sheet and booklet versions of the contemporary Christmas stamp were made by the gravure process by different printers. The American Bank Note Company again contracted to produce the sheet stamps, and the Bureau of Engraving and Printing manufactured the booklets.

The Design
Only a limited number of design subjects exist that can be effectively used for a Christmas stamp, and after 29 years — the last 21 of which have seen separate "traditional" and "contemporary" categories — repetition is unavoidable. The 1990 contemporary stamp depicted a family Christmas tree, a subject that had been previously used in 1973 and 1982.

The 1973 design had shown a tree done in needlepoint; the 1990 design was also unconventional. It featured a brightly decorated hand-cut paper tree in dropout white against a red background, surrounded by stylized snowflakes that were also dropped out of the red. As has been the practice since 1986, the stamp carried the single word "Greetings."

The artist was Libby Thiel of Bryan's Road, Maryland, whose previous stamp design credit was the block of four Lacemaking stamps of 1987. Her art director for that assignment, Derry Noyes, later asked her to submit a Love stamp design, and Thiel produced three samples, including one based on cut paper.

None of the three was chosen by the Citizens' Stamp Advisory Committee for final art. However, Thiel said, Noyes "wanted to try to pursue the same sort of hand-cut playfulness that my Love stamp

This photocopy of Thiel's original hand-cut Christmas tree shows how the green strips were twisted and creased to form the garlands.

had," and she asked the artist to design a Christmas stamp, using the same technique. (Coincidentally, a Love stamp design was then in the works that was also based on cut paper; the creation of Jayne Hertko, it too would end up being issued in 1990.)

Thiel tried to approach the Christmas stamp project as a child would, with a child's creative delight. "It was easily done," she said. "When you have a 7-year-old son around, as I did, singing Christmas carols, it kind of gets you in the spirit.

"I basically tried to stay with bright colors, very Christmasy colors. I thought of the old-fashioned colored light bulbs that my parents had on their Christmas trees, with the yellows and greens and reds and blues."

To make her design, Thiel simply cut a tree from paper, beginning at the bottom. When she got to the star, she said, she just "started in one direction and kept cutting points." The ornaments were scraps of colored paper, snipped with scissors or made with a hand-held hole punch; the snowflakes were white scraps; the garlands were strips of green paper cut irregularly and then twisted and creased to give the effect of winding around the tree.

After she got the artistic feeling she wanted from her cut-and-paste image, Thiel re-created it as a silk-screen print, laying down the colors through the screen one at a time. She then sent the print to USPS. Silk-screen is a technique Thiel uses extensively in her work because she likes the "rich, vibrant, flat colors" it produces.

When the stamp was printed, both BEP and ABNC used a purple self-color for some of the ornaments instead of the "periwinkle blue" Thiel had given USPS. "That didn't bother me, though," she said. "The color was well within the range."

The Christmas stamp design was based on this silk-screen print, which Libby Thiel based on her hand-cut Christmas tree image.

When the two varieties were laid side by side, one could easily see differences in the printed images. On ABNC's sheet stamp, the red was brighter, the purple lighter, the green deeper — actually more of a blue-green — and the lettering on the word "Greetings" was thinner. The sheet stamp also faithfully reproduced a piece of green garland that, on Thiel's original silk-screen print, was separated from the main strip. This "orphan" piece did not appear on BEP's booklet version of the stamp.

There were also differences in perforation and paper. The sheet stamp was perf 11 and printed on soft paper that left visible fibers when the stamps were separated. The booklet version was perf 11½ and printed on harder, more brittle paper that separated cleanly. And, of course, all the booklet stamps had at least one straight edge.

First-Day Facts

In recent years the Postal Service has chosen post offices with appropriate names as first-day sites for contemporary Christmas stamps. Thus, dedication ceremonies have been held in such places as Berlin, New Hampshire (for the "White Christmas" stamp of 1988); Holiday, California; Snow Hill, Maryland; Nazareth, Holly and Christmas, Michigan; Santa Claus, Indiana; Snow, Oklahoma, and North Pole, Alaska. The sheet and booklet versions of the 1990 contemporary Christmas stamp were dedicated October 18 at Evergreen, Colorado, a small town just west of Denver, by Kenneth J. Hunter, associate postmaster general.

The ceremony had a strong local presence to it. Speakers were Sylvia Booth Brockner of the Evergreen Naturalists Audubon Society and the Evergreen Garden Club, and David C. Snyder Sr., coordinator, Ben Franklin Stamp Club. Karol Lyon, president of the Evergreen Area Chamber of Commerce, gave the welcome, and Evergreen Postmaster Ray Teetsel presided. Evergreen High School performers provided the music. The honored guests included Nancy Clough, president, Jefferson County Historical Society; Sandy Crain, director, Hiwan Homestead Museum; Jack Rosenthal, chairman of the Citizens' Stamp Advisory Committee, and designer Libby Thiel.

$5 CHRISTMAS GREETINGS BOOKLET

Date of Issue: October 18, 1990

Catalog Number: Scott 2516

Colors: red, purple, yellow and green

First-Day Cancel: Evergreen, Colorado

FDCs Canceled: 230,586 (sheet and booklet)

Format: Two panes of 10 stamps each arranged vertically 2 by 5. Gravure printing cylinders of 300 subjects (15 across, 20 around).

Perf: 11.2 by 11.2 (Eureka off-line perforator)

Selvage Markings: 4 cylinder numbers on binding stub of each pane. Registration mark remnants on 17% of all pane binding stubs.

Cover Markings: ©United States Postal Service 1990 on inside of front cover. Universal Product Code (UPC) printed on outside of back cover.

Designer: Libby Thiel of Bryan's Road, Maryland

Art Designer and Typographer: Derry Noyes (CSAC)

Project Manager: Jack Williams (USPS)

Printing: Stamps printed on BEP's 7-color Andreotti gravure press (601). Booklet covers printed on a 6-color Goebel Optiforma offset press in red, purple, yellow and green. Booklets formed on standard bookbinding equipment.

Quantity Ordered: 15,500,000 booklets
Quantity Distributed: 15,500,000 booklets

Cylinder Number Detail: One group of four cylinder numbers on each pane binding stub.

Tagging: overall

The Stamp

The contemporary Christmas stamp booklet was printed by the Bureau of Engraving and Printing, unlike the sheet version, which was produced by the American Bank Note Company.

As with the traditional Christmas stamp booklet, the size of the pane was longer and slightly wider than most panes, reflecting the slightly larger size of the individual stamps.

The Design

The differences between the BEP and ABNC versions of the contemporary Christmas stamp were discussed in the preceding chapter.

With both the traditional and contemporary Christmas stamp booklets, BEP reproduced the stamp that was inside in enlarged form on the booklet cover. This was done to forestall the kind of criticism some buyers had directed at previous booklet covers that bore pictures differing from those on the stamps inside. In both Christmas booklets, however, the image on the cover wasn't exactly accurate; the stamp was shown with perforations all around, whereas each of the stamps inside had at least one straight edge.

In 1989, the contemporary Christmas stamp booklet cover had carried the word "Christmas," which supplemented the word "Greetings" on the stamp reproduction beside it. In 1990, however, the cover message was "Season's Greetings," which merely repeated the word "Greetings" on the stamp.

First-Day Facts

Information on the dedication ceremony for both versions of the contemporary Christmas stamp can be found in the preceding chapter.

By mistake, the first-day ceremony programs that were distributed to subscription customers contained a pair of sheet stamps instead of booklet stamps. Details on this error can be found in the chapter on the Christmas Madonna booklet stamp.

DEFINITIVES

The seven definitive stamps of 1990 included two prototypes for future series.

One, a $2 Bobcat stamp, was the first of a new set of dollar-value stamps in commemorative size depicting wildlife. The other was a 15¢ postcard-rate booklet stamp that showed a beach umbrella, the forerunner of what USPS calls "mini-scape" stamps that will show colorful little vignettes from everyday American life.

The Postal Service's two long-running definitive series, Transportation coils and Great Americans sheet stamps, had two additions each, bringing the total number of design-different varieties in the two sets to 47 and 48, respectively.

The seventh definitive of the year, the plastic U.S. Flag self-adhesive, didn't really fit the definition of a definitive, since it wasn't meant to be reprinted periodically as needed. On the other hand, it was neither a commemorative nor a special stamp. It was experimental, much like 1989's pressure-sensitive Eagle and Shield stamp. In time, if USPS continues to test the market for radically new products in this way, a separate category of experimental stamps may well be required.

$3 BEACH UMBRELLA BOOKLET

Date of Issue: February 3, 1990

Catalog Numbers: Scott 2443 (stamp); Scott 2443a (booklet pane)

Colors: light yellow, cyan, yellow, magenta, green and blue

First-Day Cancel: Sarasota, Florida (Sarasota Exhibition Hall)

FDCs Canceled: 72,286

Format: Two panes of 10 stamps each arranged vertically 2 by 5. Gravure printing cylinders of 800 subjects (10 across, 80 around).

166

Perf: 11.2 (Eureka off-line perforator)

Selvage Markings: Six cylinder numbers on binding stub of each pane. Cyan electric-eye mark remnants (diagonal-end or rectangle-end) on 10% of all pane binding stubs

Cover Markings: ©United States Postal Service 1990 inside front cover. Universal Product Code (UPC) on outside of back cover.

Designer: Pierre Mion of Lovettsville, Virginia (stamps). Bradbury Thompson (CSAC) (cover)

Art Director and Typographer: Howard Paine (CSAC)

Project Manager: Jack Williams (USPS)

Modeler: Clarence Holbert (BEP)

Printing: Stamps printed on BEP's 7-color Andreotti gravure press (601). Booklet covers printed on 6-color Goebel Optiforma offset press (043) in magenta, yellow, cyan and black. Booklets formed on standard bookbinding equipment.

Quantity Ordered: 30,000,000 booklets
Quantity Distributed: 15,763,800 booklets

Cylinder Number Detail: One group of six gravure cylinder numbers on each pane binding stub

Tagging: phosphor taggant added to light yellow and cyan inks

The Stamp

The Postal Service's first postcard-rate stamp to be issued solely in booklet form, for use by tourists and vacationers, made its appearance February 3 in Sarasota, Florida, as part of the Sarasota Philatelic Club's Sarapex 90 show. The design of the 15¢ stamp featured a seashore scene with a large red and yellow beach umbrella as its most prominent feature.

The stamp was issued in booklets of 20 that sold for $3. It was created in response to requests for more color and variety in regular-issue stamps, USPS said in its January 10 news release.

The Beach Umbrella was the first of a series of small, colorful definitives called "mini-scapes," which USPS planned to issue as the need and opportunity arose. The series had its origin in the summer of 1988 when the Citizens' Stamp Advisory Committee decided to look for a way to give the stamp users an alternative to what one member termed "bewhiskered unknowns" and Flag-over-Capitol type scenes on their postage. Even substituting landmarks like Yosemite National Park for buildings on the Flag stamps wasn't a wholly satisfactory answer; some at USPS felt these designs didn't reduce well to definitive-stamp size.

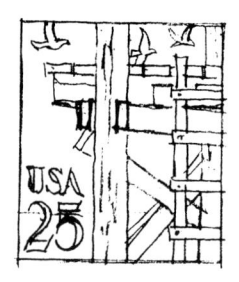

Two Mion concept sketches for "mini-scape" stamps showed a boy on a carousel horse and a pier.

Accordingly, Howard Paine, a CSAC design coordinator, commissioned three artists to prepare concept sketches of stamps that would be bright, cheerful and colorful. These were to show "generic landscapes" common to many sections of the country, or "tight little vignettes" of familiar objects and scenes, he told them. To one artist, Pierre Mion of Lovettsville, Virginia, Paine's list of suggestions included a hot-air balloon in flight, a child with an umbrella in the rain, and a piggy bank.

Mion submitted colored-pencil sketches in double stamp size of these subjects, and also threw in some drawings based on ideas of his own: a beach umbrella; the prow of a small boat of the kind used on the East Coast for oystering and crabbing; the end of a pier; a boy on a carousel. At Paine's request, Mion made finished paintings on the first three, at the customary five times stamp size. When the need arose for a postcard-rate stamp for use in booklets, Mion's beach umbrella artwork was selected as the design.

Mary Ann Owens, a member of the CSAC and a topical collector whose specialties include umbrellas on stamps, disclaimed any credit for choosing the beach umbrella as a subject but said she was happy to see such a stamp issued.

She pointed out that umbrellas had appeared several times previously on U.S. stamps. The most obvious examples are the umbrella-carrying mailman on the 5¢ City Mail Delivery commemorative of 1963 (Scott 1238) and the umbrella-protected pushcart on the 12.5¢ Transportation series coil of 1985 (Scott 2133). Less readily apparent are the open umbrellas that can be seen by closely examining the 3¢ Transcontinental Railroad stamp of 1944 (Scott 922) and the 4¢ Lincoln-Douglas Debate stamp of 1958 (Scott 1115), and the furled parasol in the hand of one of the women on the 5¢ General Federation of Women's Clubs stamp of 1966 (Scott 1316). And only the most diligent umbrella-searcher would find the tiny reproduction of Scott 1238 on the child's album page that is shown on the second stamp in the 1986 Stamp Collecting booklet (Scott 2199).

Owens further noted that a beach umbrella can also be seen on the photograph of Miami Beach that appears on the address side of the Travel Service postal cards of 1966-1971 (Scott UXC5, 8, 11).

The Beach Umbrella stamp was printed on BEP's Andreotti gravure press in six colors: light yellow (sand), cyan, yellow, magenta, green and blue. The phosphorescent tagging compound was mixed with two of the colors, light yellow and cyan, rather than being applied as a coating on the finished stamp. On two previous occasions BEP had employed phosphorescent material mixed with a single color. These were the 6¢ Leif Ericsson stamp of 1968 (Scott 1359) and the 36¢ Igor Sikorsky airmail of 1988 (Scott C119). The Beach Umbrella was the first stamp issued by USPS in which the taggant was mixed with two different colors of ink.

The resulting effect on the Beach Umbrella stamps, as shown in the accompanying shortwave ultraviolet photograph, was two distinct areas and intensities of tagging, although both glowed green under the UV light. The tagging in the sky was less intense than in the sand, probably due to the darker pigment present in the cyan ink. The yellow ink in the umbrella reacted strongly to longwave UV light; this wasn't tagging, but it created an attractive appearance.

Use of phosphorescent printing ink saves the additional production step of applying taggant to the printed stamps. Because the entire surface area of stamps tagged in this manner isn't coated with the phosphorescent solution, the stamps theoretically should accept cancellation ink better, thus making it more difficult for "stamp washers" to remove the cancel and re-use the stamp.

The first of the six gravure cylinder digits printed on the Beach Umbrella pane binding tab was the light yellow (sand) color. This digit was very hard to see with the naked eye. Because the ink was luminescent, however, the first digit was much easier to make out when it was illuminated with shortwave UV light.

The 400-stamp printing cylinders were laid out 10 booklet panes wide by four panes deep, with alternating rows of panes inverted, similar to the layout of the Jack London 10-stamp booklet pane intaglio sleeves of 1988. Down the center of the sheet was a gutter containing two electric-eye marks in cyan — one a rectangle, the other a parallelogram on the diagonal. When the sheets were cut into panes, these two marks were bisected, and four of the 40 panes on each sheet contain the tips of these markings at their left or right selvage edges. For booklet pane specialists, these EE-marked panes constitute collectible varieties.

After printing, the Beach Umbrella stamps were processed on the Eureka perforator and bound into booklets by modified bookbind-

The tagging on the Umbrella stamps is contained in the pigmented inks used to print the sky and the sand. This stamp was photographed under ultraviolet light.

ing equipment. After printed and perforated sheets of stamps were matched with booklet cover stock, they were glued in by the bookbinding equipment. The glued booklets then were sliced, making the cover and pane edges match perfectly. BEP first used this process to produce the 1987 Flag With Fireworks booklet in order to help make up for a 40 million booklet per year shortfall.

Panes of Beach Umbrella stamps were also produced unbound and unfolded, with binding stub intact, for sale to collectors.

The Design

Pierre Mion's seashore scene, painted in gouache, featured a wide, sandy beach in the foreground, with tufts of sea grass on drifting dunes. A laughing gull, identifiable as such by the black head and black wingtips, hovers over the beach, and the ocean with a line of white surf is visible in the distance under a cloudless sky. Propped against the heat of the sun is a large beach umbrella with red and yellow alternating panels. Presumably, one or more beachgoers lounge on the other side of the umbrella, but the only sign that humans are present are a few puckers in the sand, which, Mion confirmed, are footprints.

The beach was generic, of course, but Mion acknowledged that as he painted it he might have had in mind his own favorite beaches, the isolated stretches of North Carolina's Outer Banks. Asked if he had imagined who was seated on the other side of the umbrella, he laughed and replied: "Definitely. My girlfriend and I!"

Mion was generally satisfied with the finished stamp, but had one complaint. The sea grass as he had painted it was more delicate in

Pierre Mion made these preliminary pencil sketches before deciding on the final arrangement of design elements (last picture) for the Beach Umbrella stamp.

appearance than it was on the stamp. BEP "fattened up" the grass, in Mion's phrase, on its electronic scanner, presumably to make sure it would print satisfactorily.

Bradbury Thompson, another CSAC design coordinator, designed the booklet cover, which was inscribed: "For Post Cards" and reproduced a picture of the Beach Umbrella stamp in four-color offset.

First-Day Facts

Gordon C. Morison, assistant postmaster general, dedicated the stamp at the Sarasota Exhibition Hall. The principal speaker was Marc Bostrom, president of the Sarasota Philatelic Club. Peter Fernandez, postmaster at Sarasota, presided, and Mayor Lou Ann R. Palmer welcomed the guests.

For first-day covers that were completely serviced by USPS, only full panes of 10 stamps were affixed and collectors were charged $1.50. Collectors affixing their own stamps had to make sure they provide enough postage to cover the 25¢ first-class rate.

5¢ LUIS MUNOZ MARIN
GREAT AMERICANS SERIES

Date of Issue: February 18, 1990

Catalog Number: Scott 2173

Color: red

First-Day Cancel: San Juan, Puerto Rico

FDCs Canceled: 269,618

Format: Panes of 100, vertical, 10 across, 10 down. Printing sleeve of 800 subjects (20 across, 40 around).

Perf: 11.2 (Eureka off-line perforator)

Selvage Markings: Luis Munoz Marin (1898-1980). First elected Governor of Puerto Rico, 1948. Founder of Puerto Rico Commonwealth. ©United States Postal Service 1990, Use Correct ZIP Code®

Designer: Juan Maldonado of New York, New York

Engravers: Gary Chaconas, vignette (BEP)
Gary Slaght, lettering (BEP)

Art Director: Derry Noyes (CSAC)

Project Manager: Jack Williams (USPS)

Modeler: Ronald C. Sharpe (BEP)

Typographer: Bradbury Thompson (CSAC)

Printing: 3-color intaglio unit of the BEP's 8-color gravure/intaglio A press (702).

Quantity Ordered: 155,000,000
Quantity Distributed: 155,780,000

Sleeve Number Detail: Single-digit intaglio sleeve number

Tagging: overall

The Stamp

On February 18, 1990, with the issuance of a 5¢ stamp in the Great Americans series honoring Luis Munoz Marin, the U.S. Postal Service made two significant changes in design policy. For the first time, USPS printed identifying information about the subject of a Great Americans stamp in the design. It provided additional information in the selvage, another first. And, with the inscription "05," it introduced a new way of expressing the denomination of stamps with a value below 10¢.

These two developments came in response to two different concerns at USPS and just happened to coincide in one stamp. The first one was no great surprise. Whether, and how, to better identify the "Great Americans" had been a recurring topic of discussion, inside and outside the Postal Service, for several years. But the denomination change was something else; collectors had been unaware that any such thing was under consideration.

The identification problem had been neatly illustrated in 1983 by this letter from a reader to syndicated columnist Abigail Van Buren:

"Dear Abby: The U.S. post office has issued a 17¢ postage stamp with a picture of a woman on it. Her name is Carson. Who is she? Someone said she's Johnny Carson's mother. Is that true?"

"False!" Abby replied. "The stamp was issued to honor Rachel Louise Carson, an American biologist and science writer."

The exchange underlined the paradox of the Great Americans series, which had been obvious from its beginning in 1980. The purpose of the series was to honor people, including women and members of minority groups, whose names weren't household words but who had made significant contributions to various aspects of American life. The effort was to a large extent neutralized, however, by the fact that the stamps contained no information as to who the person was, or what he or she had done to merit the honor.

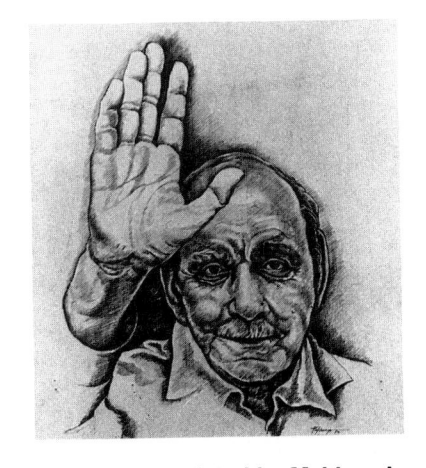

These are two of several Munoz portraits previously painted by Maldonado.

That was the case because of another objective of the Citizens' Stamp Advisory Committee. A majority of CSAC in the 1980s felt it was important to create a clean, uncluttered look in stamp design and, specifically, in the Great Americans series. For more than nine years, this aim took priority. To fulfill it, stamp designers included only four things in a Great Americans stamp's small design area: the head or head and shoulders of the subject, his or her name, "USA" and the denomination.

Rachel Carson, as it turned out, was a well-known personality indeed compared to some of the people who followed her onto Great Americans stamps. Some, like Chester Carlson and Belva Ann Lockwood, couldn't even be found in most standard encyclopedias. Others — Abraham Baldwin, Sylvanus Thayer, Alden Partridge, Grenville Clark, Harvey Cushing, Bernard Revel — were almost as obscure to the general public.

A few CSAC members, such as C. Douglas Lewis, curator of sculpture at the National Gallery of Art, believed strongly that postal customers should somehow be given appropriate information about the Great Americans. But the committee majority subscribed to a minimalist view of stamp design — that the less typography there was, the better. They liked the "series look" of the Great Americans stamps and didn't want to make "any abrupt clanging change in the middle of it," as Don McDowell, then-manager of the Stamps Division, told *Linn's Stamp News* several years ago.

The identification problem wasn't limited to Great Americans stamps. Some commemoratives also failed to indicate what their subjects had done to merit attention: these included the Black Heritage stamps for Whitney Young, Mary McLeod Bethune and Carter G. Woodson, the Literary Arts stamps for T.S. Eliot and William Faulkner, and individual stamps honoring Joseph Priestley and Abigail Adams.

One frequently suggested alternative to adding more words to the design was to print thumbnail biographies in the selvage. That would help the buyer who obtained stamps with the selvage at-

The 5¢ Buck, 5¢ Black and 5¢ Munoz U.S. stamps issued in 1983, 1986 and 1990 illustrate the three ways the 5¢ denomination has been depicted in the Great Americans series.

tached, and it would also help stamp clerks give an answer when customers asked: "Who is this person?"

But McDowell and other USPS staffers were reluctant for a long time to create new marginal inscriptions. They remembered the many complaints they had heard from plate block collectors in the 1970s, a decade in which multiple plate numbers stretched along the sheet margins of multicolor stamps. They were afraid that the addition of new printing in the selvage would revive the old accusations that USPS was "ripping off" collectors by forcing them to buy extra-large blocks in order to get the marginal imprints they needed. At one point, McDowell wrote a column, published in *Linn's,* inviting collectors to comment on whether subject information should be printed in the selvage. The response, he said later, was inconclusive.

Then, in 1989, everything changed. The vehicle for change was a new Great Americans definitive then in the works that would depict Luis Munoz Marin, the first popularly elected governor of the Commonwealth of Puerto Rico.

CSAC had approved Munoz for stamp honors years earlier at the behest of one of its members, Raul Gandara, a prominent Puerto Rican stamp collector. In 1984, Gandara's final year on the committee, USPS announced that the Munoz stamp would be issued in 1990, the first year the subject would be eligible under USPS' rule that no person other than a president could be postally honored within 10 years following his death. The design that was worked up by the Stamps Division carried no information about Munoz other than his name, as per custom.

But in the meantime USPS acquired a postmaster general, Anthony M. Frank, who, more than any of his recent predecessors, took a strong interest in the stamps produced by his agency. When Frank is presented with the design of a stamp for his approval, Don McDowell said, he "will go unerringly to the reaction of the person who buys it — and he has a real aversion to a postage stamp that's going to leave an unanswered question in the mind of the customer."

The postmaster general "started looking at the Great Americans series," McDowell continued, "and he said, if a stamp doesn't explain itself, if it leaves the customer saying 'Why is this person on this stamp I'm buying?' then the stamp design has failed. And even if we made it possible for a window clerk to answer that question, Mr. Frank said, it wouldn't help a person who received a letter with that stamp on it. He's not going to drive all the way down to his post office to ask a window clerk, and he's not going to the library and look it up. Mr. Frank said to us: You've got to fix it."

In other words, there should be no more of what USPS staffers came to refer to as "huh?" stamps. With the Munoz stamp, USPS began inserting identifying words into the Great Americans designs.

And, though Anthony Frank didn't order it, the Postal Service also began providing additional information in the selvage.

In the case of Munoz, the already-completed design was revised by elevating the portrait slightly and placing the words "Governor, Puerto Rico" across the bottom of the stamp. Adding a selvage inscription was an easier task. The Bureau of Engraving and Printing merely placed words in margins that would otherwise have been blank. These inscriptions, appearing opposite three stamps in sequence, were: "Luis Munoz Marin/(1898-1980); First elected Governor/of Puerto Rico, 1948; Founder of Puerto/Rico Commonwealth."

The postmaster general's directive to give the postal customer more information was followed with commemoratives as well. (See chapters on the Supreme Court and Marianne Moore stamps.) In time, McDowell suggested, it would also affect the wording on Transportation series coils and other categories.

CSAC member C. Douglas Lewis welcomed the postmaster general's order. But, he said, the order did no more than speed up a development that was already in the works.

Over an extended period, Lewis said, the committee had been studying Great Americans stamp designs and how their various elements could and should be arranged. One of its conclusions was that the designers should make greater use of shading behind the subject's head, to better define heads that were white-haired or bald (such as the head of Igor Stravinsky, which could have used a dark background back in 1982 but didn't get one). In the process of the study, Lewis said, committee members also decided that the designs could accommodate what he called "an educational rubric" about the subjects without doing any aesthetic harm.

Out of that same impulse to improve the Great Americans series' designs grew the other policy change that was implemented with the Munoz stamp: the use of a zero and numeral to express the denomination of stamps with a value less than a dime.

For many years, the words "cent," "cents," "dollar" and "dollars" were spelled out on U.S. stamps. In the early 1930s, the "¢" sign began appearing as an alternative to "cents." From the late 1950s on, a new alternative — the letter "c" — turned up from time to time, and beginning around 1970 "c" came into almost exclusive use.

In the meantime, there had also been a small number of designs (such as Scott 1415-1418, Scott 1425) that bore no denomination symbol at all, only a number. Late in 1984, in the course of its quest for clean, simple design statements, CSAC adopted this method for all its stamped paper. All methods of designating cents were eliminated, and only the appropriate number or numbers were used to indicate the denomination for those definitives and commemoratives costing less than $1.

The first item issued in accordance with this practice was the 13¢ Rancho San Pedro postal card in the Historic Preservation series, issued September 16, 1984. The committee's aim, said Don McDowell, was to create from the initials USA and the numbers-only denomination "a national identifier that as far as possible was a logo — the U.S. equivalent of the queen's head on the stamps of Great Britain — that would give U.S. stamps a distinctive look."

The Postal Service assumed, McDowell said, that postal customers would understand that a solitary figure 1 on a stamp meant 1¢, not $1. But, to the surprise of postal officials, people began trying to pass off the cheaper stamps as more expensive ones, sometimes on the advice of unscrupulous "consultants" who advertised and sold "tips" such as that one for saving money on postage. Eventually, concerned officials decided that another change was needed, one that would make it clear that a low-value stamp represented the prepayment of pennies, not dollars.

The obvious move would be to go back to "cents," "¢" or "c." But with the Great Americans and Transportation series, there was a special factor to consider. Typically, subjects for these definitive stamps are approved long before the stamps are issued, or even before a need for a particular denomination is established by a rate change or some other factor. Often, the stamps are designed ahead of time; on a few occasions, they are engraved with everything except the denomination and then put on the shelf to await the addition of that final element. A designer working within the tight confines of a Great Americans stamp — confines that would henceforth be even tighter because of the need to add information on the subject to the design — needed to know precisely how much space should be left blank for the value designation.

If the "¢" or "c" was restored, CSAC members reasoned, there would be a problem. The designer might reserve space for two characters, which would be fine if the stamp ended up being between 1¢ and 9¢ in value, but any denomination between 10¢ and 99¢ would require three characters, not two.

"For consistency, we couldn't put the 'c' back just with single-digit numbers," said Joe Brockert, a program manager for philatelic design. "We'd have to restore it to the entire program, and the bulk of our program is two-digit numbers. With all of our commemora-

Maldonado's original design for the Luis Munoz Marin stamp didn't include the biographical information that was later added, or the dark background. Note also that the tilde over the "n" in "Munoz" is missing.

Both the sleeve number and ZIP code slogan appear on the same piece of selvage on all lower-position panes of the Munoz stamp, because of a siderographer's error.

tives we'd have to go back to the 'c.' And we could never position the denomination ahead of the 'USA' because it would then read, for example, '25 CUSA.'

"All that was hashed out by the committee, too. Everything had an advantage, and everything had a problem."

The course CSAC finally chose was recommended by Bradbury Thompson, its expert on typography, and endorsed by Belmont Faries, its long-time chairman. This was to standardize the space for the denomination on Great Americans stamps to accommodate two characters, no more, no less. Denominations of 1¢ through 9¢ would be indicated by 01 through 09. Higher values — 10¢, 25¢, 99¢ — would be designated in the normal way: 10, 25, 99. Dollar-value stamps — $1, $2, $5 — would use the dollar sign and the single digit. For consistency, the same system was adopted for Transportation series coils, as well. But because many of the Transportation stamps are for use by holders of precancel permits, the artists who prepared advance designs would be instructed, in some cases, to leave enough space to accommodate a three-digit fractional denomination and a service inscription.

The new system came under some criticism. Fred Baumann, writing in *Linn's Stamp News,* pointed out that the Munoz stamp was the third in the Great Americans series to cover the lightly used 5¢ rate, following the 5¢ Hugo Black of 1986 and the 5¢ Pearl Buck of 1983. To Baumann, the real purpose of the change to "05" was to justify issuance of yet another 5¢ stamp.

"The bent logic that imagined the need for this contrivance has, no doubt, already commissioned other unneeded stamps that will be similarly denominated, to replace still more perfectly good 1¢ to 9¢ definitives that are now in service," Baumann predicted.

The writer also suggested that the aim of putting subject information in the stamp selvage was "to sell collectors (plate strips of) 20 stamps instead of four." Thus, the apprehension that Don

McDowell had expressed several years earlier — that additional selvage markings would be criticized — was quickly borne out.

Several *Linn's* readers agreed with Baumann, but others defended USPS. "There are many outstanding United States citizens worthy of recognition on a postage stamp," one wrote. "Frequent change in definitives is one way to give some of them that recognition . . . I am glad to now have Gov. Munoz Marin brought to my attention with a new 5¢ stamp. I am tired of the 5¢ Hugo Black stamp — for which I have also had use."

In fact, the supply of 5¢ Hugo Blacks was abruptly and unexpectedly exhausted. The March-April issue of the USPS *Philatelic Catalog* carried the words "SOLD OUT" printed over the listing for the stamp. Ordinarily, the *Philatelic Catalog* gives collectors two months' notice when a stamp or other sale item is to be discontinued.

The Munoz stamp had a third unique feature — but this one was unintentional, the result of a siderographer's mistake. That mistake created the first combination ZIP/plate number blocks in the history of U.S. stamp production. On all lower-left and lower-right panes, the corner selvage contained both a sleeve number and the "Use Correct ZIP Code" inscription. Plate blocks from upper-position panes appeared normal, with just the sleeve number.

According to official sources, a layout of the upper-pane positioning was shown to USPS and was approved for use. A BEP currency siderographer, who wasn't familiar with stamp production, apparently knew that sleeve numbers were supposed to appear in the four corners of a printing sheet. He didn't know, however, to move the positioning of the marginal markings, and he entered them on the printing sleeves in the same positions on all panes. This resulted, on all lower panes, in a blank upper corner and the double-inscription lower corner. To prevent similar mistakes in the future, USPS began asking for entire-sheet layouts from BEP before production.

The Munoz stamp had its first-day sale in San Juan, capital of Puerto Rico. Its sale date — February 18, Munoz's birthday — fell more than two months short of the 10th anniversary of his death, which occurred April 30, 1980. But USPS has made it clear in the past that the 10-year minimum period it requires for stamp eligibility applies only to the year of issue, not to the precise date.

This stamp (Scott 983) was issued in 1949 to commemorate the first gubernatorial election in Puerto Rico, held November 2, 1948, and the inauguration of Governor Luis Munoz Marin January 2, 1949.

CSAC also considered these two sketches by another artist.

Luis Munoz Marin, an advocate for Puerto Rico's landless jibaros (peasants), has been called the most popular politician in the island's history. He began as an ardent advocate of Puerto Rican independence and a socialist, but he later became a firm believer in gradually increasing autonomy and combining public and private enterprise. *Time* described him as a man who thought in both English and Spanish and could explain his ideas "in either language with literary dignity or colloquial directness . . . that can go straight to the heart and mind of the humblest and least educated hearer."

He was the son of Luis Munoz Rivera, himself a popular political leader who had won from Spain the island's first measure of autonomy. After the United States acquired Puerto Rico in 1898, the same year young Luis Munoz Marin was born in San Juan, the father became resident commissioner in Washington. In time the son studied at Georgetown University and later worked as a writer and translator in New York City.

In 1926 he returned to San Juan to edit the newspaper *La Democracia.* He was elected to the Puerto Rican Senate in 1932, and through his connections in Washington and talks with President Franklin D. Roosevelt, he worked successfully to get New Deal money for the Depression-hit island. In 1938 he organized the Popular Democratic Party and campaigned throughout the Puerto Rican back country for land reform, the minimum wage, industrial development and regulation of the sugar industry.

Munoz's party swept to a landslide victory in the legislature in 1944. In 1948 he won the first popular election for governor and was re-elected three times, serving from 1949 to 1965. Munoz is considered the chief architect of the unique commonwealth status achieved by Puerto Rico in 1952.

That first gubernatorial election and inauguration were marked by a 3¢ U.S. stamp in 1949 (Scott 983). Munoz himself was responsible for the stamp's design. Julius A. Krug, who was U.S. secretary of the Interior at the time the stamp was issued, has written:

"It was his (Munoz's) idea that the stamp depict a 'jibaro' symbolizing the Puerto Rican agricultural background, a ballot box symbolizing the value and power of the vote, and something to symbolize Puerto Rico's industrialization program. He had several people in his office work on the idea and shortly afterward several sketches were prepared and submitted to this department (Interior).

"Governor Munoz indicated that one of the sketches, that of the 'jibaro' holding a ballot box in one hand and a cogwheel as a symbol of industry in the other, was his preference." At the first-day ceremony for the 1949 stamp in San Juan, officials gave Munoz a souvenir album signed by Postmaster General Jesse M. Donaldson.

The Design

CSAC considered concept sketches by two artists, but in the end picked the man recommended by Raul Gandara, the committee member who had originally advocated the stamp. This was Juan Maldonado, a Puerto Rican artist with a studio in Brooklyn, New York. Maldonado had previously painted several portraits of Munoz, and this fact, plus the appropriateness of his island origin, influenced the committee's decision.

The portrait on the stamp was a composite of two photographs taken when Munoz was a relatively young man. Maldonado's artwork showed the head of the subject against a white background, but when the die for the stamp was engraved at BEP, a dark background was provided for better contrast.

First-Day Facts

The first-day ceremony in San Juan was a particularly satisfying event for stamp collectors in the Commonwealth because disaster had wiped out the last such ceremony scheduled for the Puerto Rican capital. On October 12, 1989, the 25¢ and 45¢ America series commemoratives were to be dedicated in San Juan, but the event

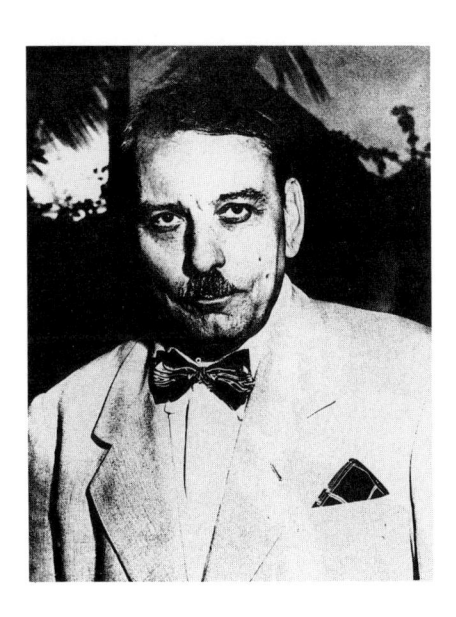

This portrait of Munoz Marin was used by Maldonado as the principal source of his stamp portrait.

181

had to be canceled because of the damage done by Hurricane Hugo a few weeks before.

Sadly, the man who had persuaded CSAC to approve a stamp for Luis Munoz Marin wasn't present for the stamp's dedication. Raul Gandara had died December 22, 1989, at the age of 79.

Frank Thomas of the Stamp Market Development Branch delivered the dedication address in place of Postmaster General Frank, who had been the scheduled speaker. Rafael Hernandez Colon, governor of Puerto Rico, and Teodoro Moscoso, former director of the Alliance for Progress, also spoke. Juan Diaz, executive director of the National Parks Trust, gave the welcome. Among the guests were Munoz Marin's widow, Ines Mendoza de Munoz, and a daughter, Victoria Munoz Mendoza, who was a senator in the Commonwealth. Six months later, on August 13, 1990, Ines Mendoza de Munoz died of a heart attack at the age of 82. Mrs. Munoz had been an active advisor to her husband and was Puerto Rico's first lady for the 16 years he was governor.

The brief description of Munoz Marin's career on the first-day programs was printed in both English and Spanish. For first-day covers on which USPS affixed stamps, one 5¢ Munoz Marin stamp and one 20¢ Cable Car stamp of 1988 were combined to make the 25¢ first-class rate.

$1 SEAPLANE (COIL)
TRANSPORTATION SERIES

Date of Issue: April 20, 1990

Catalog Number: Scott 2468

Colors: red, blue

First-Day Cancel: Phoenix, Arizona

FDCs Canceled: 244,775

Format: Coils of 500, printing sleeve of 936 subjects (18 across, 52 around).

Perf: 9.8 (Huck rotary perforator)

Designer: Chuck Hodgson of Newhall, California

Engravers: Gary Chaconas, vignette (BEP)
John Masure, lettering (BEP)

Art Director and Project Manager: Jack Williams (USPS)

Modeler: Frank J. Waslick (BEP)

Typographer: Bradbury Thompson (CSAC)

Printing: BEP'S three-color intaglio B press (701)

Quantity Ordered: 48,000 coils of 500
Quantity Distributed: 47,800 coils of 500

Sleeve Number Detail: Single-digit intaglio sleeve number on every 52nd stamp.

Tagging: overall

183

The Stamp

On April 20 USPS issued its first new face-different stamp in the Transportation coil series in almost 18 months. The stamp was unusual in several ways.

• It pictured a 1914 seaplane. None of the previous 45 different Transportation coil designs had featured an aircraft.

• It showed the pilot and a passenger, unlike previous Transportation coil stamps, which had shown the vehicles only, with no human figures.

• Its $1 face value was four times higher than that of any previous stamp in the series.

• With "$1 USA" printed in red and the rest of the design in blue, it was the first Transportation stamp to have its basic design in two colors. (A second color had been used on some of the earlier stamps for service inscriptions, or "precancels," as USPS calls them.)

The stamp was first placed on sale in Phoenix, Arizona, at Aripex 90, the annual show of the Arizona Federation of Stamp Clubs. Originally USPS had planned to dedicate another stamp in the Transportation series, the 5¢ Circus Wagon, at the show. Later it decided to substitute the Seaplane because of a need for a $1 coil.

Coil stamps of this denomination are used in USPS vending machines at post offices with facilities for mailing parcels or first-class flats at hours when the office is closed. The new stamp replaced the first-ever $1 coil stamp, the Eugene O'Neill (Scott 1305C), issued in 1973 as part of the Prominent Americans series and printed on BEP's old Cottrell press. The O'Neill coil had been the oldest item still listed in the USPS *Philatelic Catalog*.

The Seaplane became the highest face-value stamp by far to be printed with sleeve numbers appearing on individual stamps at regular intervals in the coil roll. Because of this, USPS ruled that collectors need buy only a minimum of five stamps to receive a number, instead of the 25, 49, 53 or 60-stamp purchase requirements that applied to the various lower-denomination stamps. (The same five-stamp purchase requirement had been established for the old O'Neill coil to obtain a line pair.)

The Bureau of Engraving and Printing applied a new kind of tagging to the stamp. It was an overall tagging applied on the B press by a roller that left an untagged vertical stripe about 2 or 3 millimeters wide across every 26th stamp in a coil roll. In the past, tagging done on the B, C and D presses had been block tagging, smaller than the shape of the stamp, so that perforating pins wouldn't have to penetrate the abrasive tagging material.

The specific plane shown on the stamp was a Benoist Type XIV Airboat, a biplane with a boat's hull, powered by two pusher-type propellers. The plane was first proposed as a Transportation series subject by W. Donald Thomas, museum director of the Florida Aviation Historical Society, in a letter to USPS April 9, 1987. It was this type of craft that on January 1, 1914, began regular flights with passengers and freight across Tampa Bay between Tampa and St. Petersburg, Florida, inaugurating what is generally accepted to be the world's first scheduled air passenger service.

According to historian Roger Bilstein, the organizer of the Florida venture was P.E. Fansler, a speedboat enthusiast who had seen press notices of exhibition flights of a Benoist flying boat piloted by Tony Jannus. Fansler got in touch with Tom Benoist of St. Louis, the plane's builder, and the two men agreed to team up in an effort to test the possibilities of commercial aviation.

For a site Fansler chose St. Petersburg, a busy vacation city of 30,000 population that was located on the requisite body of water. The promoter found some local backers, none of whom had ever seen a flying boat. They promised the support of the board of trade, gave a $1,200 guarantee and agreed to subsidize the line at $50 a day for the first month and $25 per day thereafter for each day of four regularly scheduled flights. The only stipulation was that there be no flights on Sundays.

This advertising flyer was distributed January 2, 1914.

The plan was to appeal to vacationers whose only access to St. Petersburg from the railroad station at Tampa was by boat, which took three hours, or by road, a 49-mile trip around the bay. By airplane, they could make the 19-mile direct flight in 30 minutes. The airline's "fleet," as it turned out, would consist of one plane, which had seen extensive service the previous summer giving passenger-exhibition flights on lakes and rivers in the Middle West. Advertisements said the plane would make two round trips daily, carrying two passengers each way. A round trip would cost $10, and passengers were allowed a gross weight of 200 pounds, including personal baggage. Excess was charged at $5 per 100 pounds, with a minimum charge of 25¢. Special flights could be arranged for $15, with trips available, the ads said, "from the waters' surface to several thousand feet high AT PASSENGERS' REQUEST."

Although some believed at first that the promotion was a hoax, the St. Petersburg-Tampa Airboat Line began operations on schedule and flew during the three months of the tourist season, carrying some 1,200 intrepid passengers. It never had a fatality, although there were one or two forced landings. There was also a brisk freight business; a Tampa florist frequently sent up to $50 worth of flowers to St. Petersburg, where there was no first-class florist, and Swift & Company of Tampa airlifted hams and bacon across the bay to the Hefner Grocery Company, which advertised the products under the headline: "It comes high but we must have it." *The St. Petersburg Times* boasted that by sending 25 papers each day to Tampa newsstands it was "the first newspaper in the world to use flying machines for delivery purposes."

The passenger service helped draw tourists. In due time the rival resort of Miami signed up an itinerant pilot and his plane, and a Miami paper headed the story with the announcement: "Miami Has an Airplane Too." *The St. Petersburg Independent* reprinted the item with its own heading: "Ours Flies: Does Yours?"

"Things worked out so well," wrote Roger Bilstein, "that operations were planned to extend throughout the year and two more planes were readied for service. Nevertheless, Fansler's efforts were not enough to maintain a sizable air transport company, and with the coming of World War I, the venture dissolved."

The Design

For the stamp design, Chuck Hodgson of Newhall, California, made a drawing of a Benoist Airboat, as seen from below, climbing toward the upper left. Hodgson's drawing was based on a reversal of a photograph of the aircraft that appeared in an advertising flyer distributed by the St. Petersburg-Tampa Airboat Line January 2, 1914. The picture was furnished to USPS by W. Donald Thomas of the Florida Aviation Historical Society in his 1987 letter that pro-

In this early model of the Seaplane stamp, the typography was placed above the aircraft.

posed the airboat as a stamp subject.

The old USPS practice of omitting humans from the designs of the Transportation stamps had worked well with static subjects, but produced amusing results on a 1988 stamp (Scott 2263), which showed a San Francisco cable car coming over the crest of a hill without an operator. In planning a stamp that would show a seaplane in flight, the Citizens' Stamp Advisory Committee wisely decided to have the artist put people in the cockpit.

Chuck Hodgson had previously designed the 44¢ Trans-Pacific airmail stamp (Scott C115), the 33¢ China Clipper postal card (Scott UXC22) and the 36¢ DC-3 postal card (Scott UXC24).

First-Day Facts

Gordon C. Morison, assistant postmaster general, dedicated the stamp as part of the opening ceremony for Aripex 90 at the Civic Plaza in Phoenix.

25¢ FLAG (ATM-VENDED SHEETLET) STAMP

Date of Issue: May 18, 1990

Catalog Number: Scott 2475

Colors: red, blue

First-Day Cancel: Seattle, Washington

FDCs Canceled: 97,567

Format: Made of polyester film, self-adhesive. Unfolded pane of 12, horizontal, 4 across, 3 down. Gravure printing cylinders of 180 units, 12 across, 15 down. All selvage removed before distribution.

Perf: die cut, no perforations

Markings: DO NOT WET, DO NOT WET, EXTRAordinary Stamp for ATM, Self-adhesive Do not moisten, Patent Pending ©USPS 1989 printed on reverse liner.

Designer: Harry Zelenko of New York, New York

Art Director: Joe Brockert (USPS)

Project Manager: Joseph Peng (USPS)

Typographer and Modeler: John Boyd of Anagraphics Inc., New York, New York

Printing: Photogravure by Avery International, Pasadena, California, on USPS-owned Chesnut press.

Quantity Ordered: 3,014,000 sheetlets
Quantity Distributed: 3,014,000 sheetlets

Tagging: overall

The Stamp

On May 18, 1990, USPS and the Seattle First National Bank (Seafirst) began a six-month marketing test of stamps sold through bank automated teller machines (ATMs). The primary goals of the

Almost a year and a half prior to the release of the 25¢ Flag ATM stamp, Equibank ABMs in Pittsburgh began dispensing U.S. coil stamps at face value to customers using money access cards. The stamps were lightly affixed, in groups of nine, to carrier paper, which was cut in the size and shape of a dollar bill.

test, USPS said, were to find out how customers liked the option of buying stamps while making an ATM transaction, and to learn whether the banking industry was interested in a widespread application of the idea.

Although the Seattle test was a first for USPS, stamps had been privately vended through ATMs before. Almost a year and a half earlier, on December 14, 1988, Equibank ABMs in Pittsburgh, Pennsylvania, began dispensing regular U.S. coil stamps at face value to customers using money access cards. The stamps were lightly affixed, in groups of nine, to carrier paper, which was cut in the size and shape of a dollar bill. The system bore the trademarked name "The Stamp Stop."

For the purpose of the Seattle test, USPS developed a postage stamp that was radically different from any it had issued over the preceding 143 years. The stamp was a die-cut imperforate self-adhesive on a backing sheet, like the experimental Eagle and Shield stamp of 1989. But it was sold in panes of 12 that had the shape and thickness of the paper currency normally dispensed by ATMs.

What was truly unique was the material of which it was made. It was plastic — specifically, a specially formulated polyester film. Never before had the United States produced a stamp made of anything other than paper (although a forerunner of sorts was the Space Station stamped envelope of the preceding year, a key component of which was a piece of foil bearing a holographic image).

The ATM stamp was of the 25¢ denomination. Its base color was white and its gravure-printed image depicted a portion of a stylized American flag in red and blue. It was printed for USPS by the Avery International Corporation of Pasadena, California, a leading manufacturer of pressure-sensitive labels, on laminated material made at Avery's Fasson Division plant in Painesville, Ohio.

Fasson had worked with USPS on its two previous self-adhesive stamp projects. For the experimental Christmas "precancel" of 1974 the firm took gravure paper supplied by the Bureau of Engraving and Printing and applied the pressure-sensitive adhesive and lacquered paper backing. In 1989, Fasson furnished the printing stock for the Eagle and Shield stamp, which was printed by the American Bank Note Company.

USPS designated the ATM Flag stamp pane as part of its so-called EXTRAordinary line of stamps and postal stationery, which at that time also comprised the Eagle and Shield stamp, the Space Station envelope and three picture postal cards. Unlike those other items, however, the ATM stamp wasn't sold at a premium price; buyers were charged face value of $3 for a pane of 12.

"This stamp will provide Seafirst and postal customers with the convenience of round-the-clock access to stamps," Postmaster General Anthony M. Frank said in announcing of the experiment. "For years, customers have enjoyed the convenience of 'banking by mail.' Now, they will have the convenience of 'mailing by bank.'"

Under the plan, a Seafirst customer, or any ACCEL-member cardholder, could use his cash machine bank card to select stamps from a menu of banking options and have the cost of the stamps deducted automatically from his account. The stamp panes were dispensed from the ATMs just like cash.

With each stamp transaction, the customer received a Seafirst bank receipt, showing the date and location of the machine and the transaction amount. Some collectors considered these receipts an interesting addition to an album page containing ATM stamps.

In addition to 24-hour accessibility, USPS said, ATM stamps offered the conveniences of peel-and-stick application, ease of repositioning (although some users found repositioning difficult), no

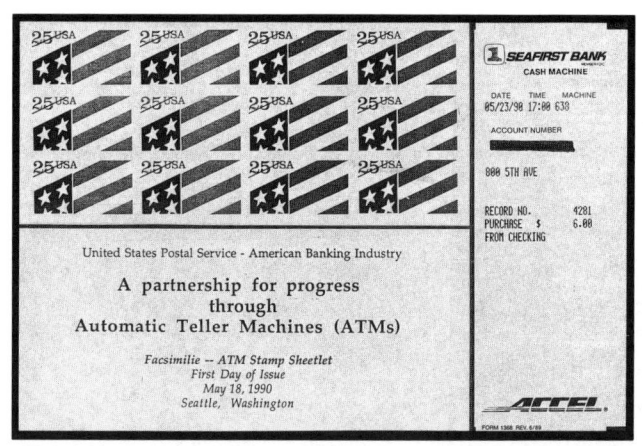

The front and back of a cardboard facsimile pane of ATM stamps (left). These facsimile panes were distributed in May and June by some California philatelic windows and at the National Postal Forum in Anaheim, California. At right is a bank receipt for an ATM stamp transaction.

licking, no tearing and resistance to humidity. And as a concession to collectors, this pressure-sensitive stamp, like its Eagle and Shield predecessor, had a water-soluble coating between stamp and adhesive that permitted used stamps to be soaked from envelopes.

The stamps were made available on May 18 at five ATMs at Seattle's Columbia Seafirst Center, where the first-day ceremony was held. Beginning the next day, they were sold from 22 ATMs at 10 locations in Seattle. They were also available at philatelic centers and by mail order from the Philatelic Sales Division in Kansas City, Missouri. In all cases, only full panes were sold.

Almost six months earlier, specimens of the stamps had been seen by many visitors to World Stamp Expo at the Washington, D.C., Convention Center. These were overprinted "SPECIMEN/FOR ATM TEST," with two black lines over the denomination. The overprinting, like printing of the basic stamp, was done at Avery.

On November 28, 1989, USPS officials moved an ATM into the Convention Center to demonstrate how the panes would be vended by the machines. In addition, an enlarged design of the new stamp was shown in a video display at the show as part of USPS' continuous presentation of the "Post Office of the Future."

The first-day date and city were announced April 2, 1990. On May 11, *USA Today* carried a story at the top of page one, headlined "ATMs help lick sticky stamp problem," and accompanied by a color picture of the stamp. It reported that plans to test the "no-lick" label would be announced that day in Washington.

For the Seattle test, the stamp panes were designed to meet the specifications of ATMs manufactured for Seafirst by Fujitsu Services of America. If consumer response was positive and the banking industry was interested, the Postal Service said, it would work with ATM manufacturers and banks to develop stamp panes compatible with several types of machines.

The ATM project was made possible by the development of a workable pressure-sensitive stamp, but in the spring of 1986, when USPS began its effort to develop such a stamp, it didn't have ATMs in mind. The ATM project actually got its impetus in November 1987, when the Stamps Division was handed a new responsibility: the USPS vending machine program.

"Suddenly, we were all thinking about something we had never paid much attention to before," said Don McDowell, who was then manager of the Stamps Division and later became director of the USPS Office of Stamp and Philatelic Marketing. "We suddenly found ourselves owning 47,000 stamp machines, and we began paying attention to vending machines and the products you put in them. We couldn't go out to dinner or anywhere else without seeing some kind of automatic vending application. When those of us who had debit cards used an ATM, we didn't see an automatic teller machine; we saw a money vending machine.

"I don't remember who in our organization first asked the question, 'Can you make an ATM vend stamps?' But about two weeks after Mr. Frank came aboard as postmaster general (on March 1, 1988) we were called on to give him and the senior management committee of the Postal Service a detailed briefing on the vending program and its future prospects. At the end of it we said, almost in passing, 'One of these days it might be possible to make stamps that ATMs could dispense like currency.' Now, Mr. Frank had come to us from the banking industry. And he immediately recognized what that could mean both to the Postal Service and to banking. He gave us a rapid 'Go see if you can do it!'

With that mandate, Stamps Division officials joined with the Postal Service's Engineering Development Center to educate themselves on ATMs and how they worked. They discovered that the machines rely on the precise thickness of currency to prevent the "double-vending" of bills that banks would abhor. The Bureau of Engraving and Printing manufactures bills within a certain range of thicknesses, and ATMs were built around that range.

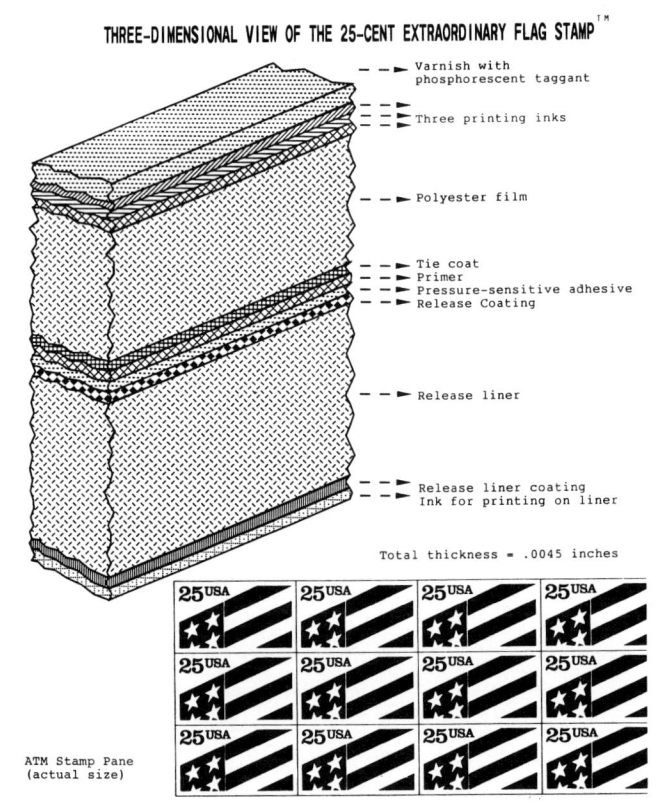

THREE-DIMENSIONAL VIEW OF THE 25-CENT EXTRAORDINARY FLAG STAMP™

Varnish with phosphorescent taggant
Three printing inks
Polyester film
Tie coat
Primer
Pressure-sensitive adhesive
Release Coating
Release liner
Release liner coating
Ink for printing on liner

Total thickness = .0045 inches

ATM Stamp Pane (actual size)

This three-dimensional view of the 25¢ Flag stamp identifies the 10 layers comprising the 12-stamp panes.

"We thought, initially, that we could make a dollar bill-sized little sheetlet of conventional 'lick 'em and stick 'em' stamps for the machines to dispense," McDowell said. "Well, that idea lasted about two days. There's much more thickness control in the manufacture of dollar bills — what engineers call 'caliper control' — than there is in stamps. Currency is printed on a special paper with an internal supporting structure of security threads that makes it act almost like a piece of reinforced concrete. The intaglio impression it receives on both sides requires tremendous pressure, which irons it flat and results in paper with more caliper stability than ordinary paper can ever have. And, unlike stamps, currency doesn't have adhesive laid upon one side in a very imprecise coating operation.

"Then we discovered the existence of plastic pressure-sensitive pharmaceutical labels. Plastic sheets are made by extrusion, and the thickness can be controlled very precisely. If you can control the thickness of the stamp face stock and the liner, and if you then can develop some very careful ways of applying that pressure-sensitive adhesive to it, you've got something you can hold a caliper to."

Working with Avery International Corporation, the USPS Engineering Development Center created a materials "sandwich," 45 ten-thousandths to 48 ten-thousandths (.0045 to .0048) of an inch thick, on which to print the ATM stamps. The "creative genius" behind the product, in McDowell's words, was Joseph Y. Peng, program manager for materials at the Engineering Development Center, who later would become general manager of the USPS Stamp Manufacturing Division.

A pane of stamps as it emerged from an ATM had 10 distinct layers (see illustration). As identified by USPS, they were: (1) varnish containing the phosphorescent taggant; (2) the colored printing inks; (3) the polyester film of which the stamp itself was made; (4) a tie coat to make the film receptive to the adhesive; (5) a water-soluble primer coat; (6) the pressure-sensitive adhesive; (7) a silicone release coating that prevented the adhesive from permanently bonding to the release liner; (8) the release liner; (9) a coating on the release liner, and (10) the ink used to print the message on the back of the release liner.

"In tests, this material proved to be three times as consistent in its thickness as currency," McDowell said.

A bonus was the ability of the plastic to accept a gravure image. Avery was able to use a 350-line screen in the printing operation — the finest screen ever used to print a U.S. stamp.

"Gravure loves a smooth surface, and this surface is incredibly smooth," said McDowell. "The first crack out of the box, we got a better gravure image than we, or I think anybody else, ever put down on a postage stamp. Because of the surface, we did what theoretically couldn't be done: We made the gravure dots touch."

The Seattle bank was chosen as the test site because the postmaster general and Richard P. Cooley, chairman and chief executive officer of Seafirst, were old friends, according to a Seafirst vice president, Inder Singh, quoted in *The Seattle Times*. "The push from the top from both sides really made it happen," Singh said.

The stamps were printed on a six-color webfed gravure press manufactured by Chesnut Engineering Company of Fairfield, New Jersey, purchased by USPS and installed at Avery's plant in Pasadena. "It's the first time we ever owned a stamp press," said Don McDowell. "Part of our deal with Avery is that we can sell the press to them at the end of the project, at the same price we paid for it originally; or they will act as our agent to put it up for sale generally; or they will ship it at their expense to any address in the continental United States that the Postal Service provides.

"In all probability we're going to have it shipped to Williamsburg, Pennsylvania, and use it in some development work at Westvaco on stamped envelopes. There are many things we might do with it there."

The arrangement was part of the USPS' effort to transfer more of the production business to the private sector, McDowell said.

"Government-furnished equipment, or GFE, is a concept that's hardly new," he said. "But it means that 'I don't keep buying that printing press.' There's not a penny in the billing rate that Avery is charging us to pay for a press that they had to buy to do the job. There won't be a penny in the billing rate at Westvaco or wherever else we might send it.

"We have, in effect, bought and paid for every piece of stamp production equipment that the Bureau of Engraving and Printing has, but we don't have title to it. We've bought and paid for everything the GPO has for postal cards, but we don't have title to it. Also, we didn't want to, in effect, pay for label business that Avery would have had to turn down in order to put our job on their press. That would have been factored into the billing rate if we hadn't furnished our own equipment.

"We're being smarter now about our assets. As far as is possible, we're not going to buy things any more and not own them."

Avery used two different cylinders to print the red portion of the stamp. One, made with a 350-line-per-inch screen, was used for the 25USA, to give the best possible resolution along the edges of the type. The other, with a 250-line screen, was used for the stripes. A third cylinder, also 250 lines, printed the blue; a fourth applied the taggant, and a fifth printed the message on the back, which was accomplished by arranging the web so that at one point in its course through the press it turned over and ran in the opposite direction.

The web on which the stamps were printed was 15 inches wide. The cylinders consisted of 180 units (20 nine-stamp sheetlets). The units were arranged sideways on the cylinders, 12 across by 15 deep. There were margins at the sides of the web, which, on a plate proof, appeared at the top and bottom. These margins, with their markings, were trimmed off before the sheets were cut into sheetlets and the individual stamps were die-cut.

The "lost" marginal markings included two sets of three cylinder numbers, one for each of the two red cylinders and one for the blue, printed in mirror image at the top and bottom; color registration circles and crosshairs, and L-shaped markings for registering the die cuts. A number for the message cylinder appeared on the reverse before it was trimmed away. Two combinations of cylinder numbers were used in printing the stamps: PP 08 (reverse), PP 09 (blue), PP 10 (red stripes) and PP 11 (red lettering), and, in the same sequence, PP 15, 16, 17 and 18. "PP" stood for "Postal Production."

Wayne Youngblood of *Linn's Stamp News,* an expert on stamp tagging, reported that the ATM stamp was tagged with the standard zinc-orthosilicate solution that glows yellow-green under shortwave light, but that the glow could only be seen if the stamp was held at an angle and viewed in complete darkness. Postal officials told him that the zinc-orthosilicate compound was ground much finer than usual for application to the plastic stamp. It triggered facer-canceler equipment, but was harder for the eye to see, they said.

The fact that the ATM stamp was of a plastic material disturbed some environmentalists. One of the first critics was Bernard Newman of Newman & Co., a firm that makes paperboard from waste

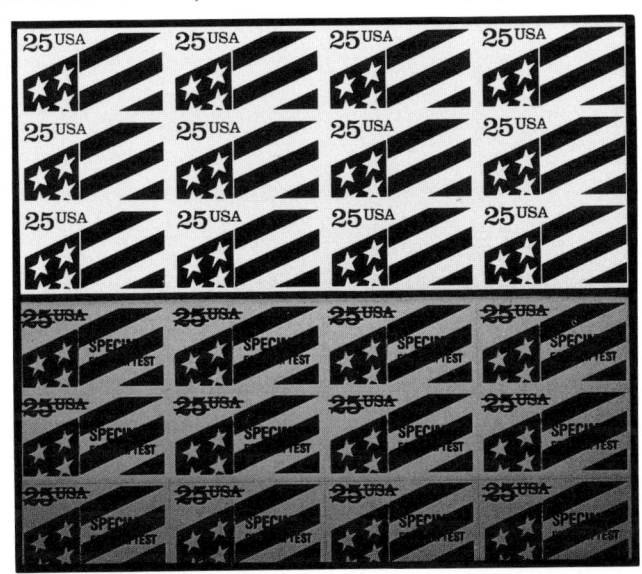

Shown here, under ultraviolet light, are examples of the untagged ATM prototype and the tagged stamp as it was released. The prototype is overprinted SPECIMEN/FOR ATM TEST, and two black lines cover the denomination.

paper. In a letter to *Linn's* in January 1990, he warned: "If plastic stamps are affixed to the millions of envelopes that are currently being consumed by paper mills, there is a very good chance that these envelopes will be rendered useless (for recycling)."

The *Seattle Post-Intelligencer,* in an editorial titled "No! to plastic stamps," declared: "Until the Postal Service develops a biodegradable stamp, the experiment should be dropped. It is particularly repugnant to test-market plastic stamps in the Seattle area, recognized as a national environmental leader in the recycling of solid wastes." And Peter A. Luft, associate director of the Oakland, California, Recycling Association, termed the stamps "an unmitigated disaster environmentally" in a letter to *The New York Times.* Along with other problems, he said, "double the volume of trash is ultimately created because for every sheet of stamps printed there is a sheet of backing material to throw away . . . These days people really should know better."

USPS did its best to deflect the criticism. In its May 14 announcement containing details about the new stamp, the Postal Service noted that the same water-soluble layer that it had provided for the benefit of stamp collectors would, serendipitously, make the envelope the stamp was on recyclable in certain operations. Which ones would depend on the technology used at the recycling facility and the end product produced from the recycled material.

In the same news release, Postmaster General Frank was quoted as saying: "If the ATM test proves successful and there is a demand for the stamp from consumers and the banking industry, the Postal Service will be in a position to create a commercial market — that previously did not exist — for a recyclable pressure-sensitive adhesive.

"We have the opportunity to build an enormous customer base for which the pressure-sensitive adhesive industry can develop an adhesive for use on labels of all kinds and thus make recyclable any piece of paper, including an envelope, to which a label is attached. We are also optimistic that a paper ATM stamp can be developed.

"Across the board with our emerging line of pressure-sensitive stamps, we are committed to environmentally friendly products."

Added Don McDowell: "We never expected that this polyester laminate would be the ultimate material. It gave us the quickest, easiest way to make stamps for tests in a particular kind of ATM machine. Part of the deal with Seafirst was that we would find something their Fujitsu machines could use with no modification."

There were no published reports of post office personnel rejecting the ATM stamps as invalid for postage, as had happened late in 1989 with the Eagle and Shield self-adhesive and the three imperforate souvenir sheets issued at World Stamp Expo. This time, USPS made a special effort on local and regional levels to familiarize its workers with the strange-looking new stamps. Several USPS newsletters and memos to associate-office postmasters included information on the stamps, along with a reminder that they were authentic proof of prepayment of postage.

One sectional center, in Middlesex-Essex, Massachusetts, sent a memo to associate offices with a plastic stamp attached. In a cover letter, Peter C. Milner, director of marketing in that office, wrote:

"A stand-up talk should be in order to inform all employees that it is imperative that none of these stamps be rejected in the mailstream as has been the embarrassing case with other kinds of stamps that have been introduced in recent months."

Despite the upbeat nature of USPS' publicity, postal customers and stamp collectors alike found the ATM stamp wasn't all that easy an item to deal with.

Several persons wrote to *Stamp Collector* complaining that the stamps were difficult to remove from their liner. "Do not ever cut an individual stamp from this sheetlet," one of them warned, "or you may never, in a lifetime, separate it from its backing. Imagine a little old lady trying to remove one of these stamps from the sheetlet, especially if she is in a hurry to mail the letter and has an unsteady hand."

As for collectors, those who soaked used copies from envelopes found that the stamps didn't float free but had to be peeled off, even after a long period in the water, and that sometimes gum residue remained on the back. The reason for the relative difficulty in soaking the stamps was simple, said Joseph Peng. Because water couldn't penetrate the stamp itself to reach the soluble adhesive, it had to get there by the slower process of soaking through the portion of the envelope to which the stamp was attached.

The pressure-sensitive Eagle and Shield stamp of the year before had been issued in the form of a "do-it-yourself" booklet. At that time, USPS had also created a coil version, with a single row of stamps spaced at regular intervals along a strip of backing paper. This was for the benefit of the Philatelic Sales Division, which could use conventional label-affixing equipment to apply the stamps from the coils to first-day covers and other philatelic products.

USPS handled the ATM stamp differently, however. Rather than order a coil version, USPS specified in its contract with Avery International that Avery should affix stamps to the Postal Service's

Harry Zelenko's concept sketch. Only the typography was changed in the final version.

philatelic products. Avery, in turn, contracted with Minnesota Diversified Industries of St. Paul, an employer of the disabled, to peel individual stamps off the backing paper and apply them to first-day programs, souvenir pages and the first-day covers which USPS sets aside for replacing collectors' covers that are damaged in the mails.

For the covers that USPS serviced for collectors in the first instance, however, the stamps were peeled and affixed manually by Philatelic Sales Division personnel in Kansas City, Missouri.

The Design

USPS wanted a design that was "quick and easy and simple for a new printer who had never printed postage stamps before to be able to produce," said Joe Brockert, project manager.

"I had to make sure we got something very uncomplicated," Brockert continued, "because there were going to be more than enough other complications in the whole project — technical problems such as repeat length, die cutting, backing liners and adhesives — and the printers didn't need additional worries about color registration or other questions of aesthetics and cropping and image area. So we kept it simple."

Harry Zelenko of New York City, who had previously designed

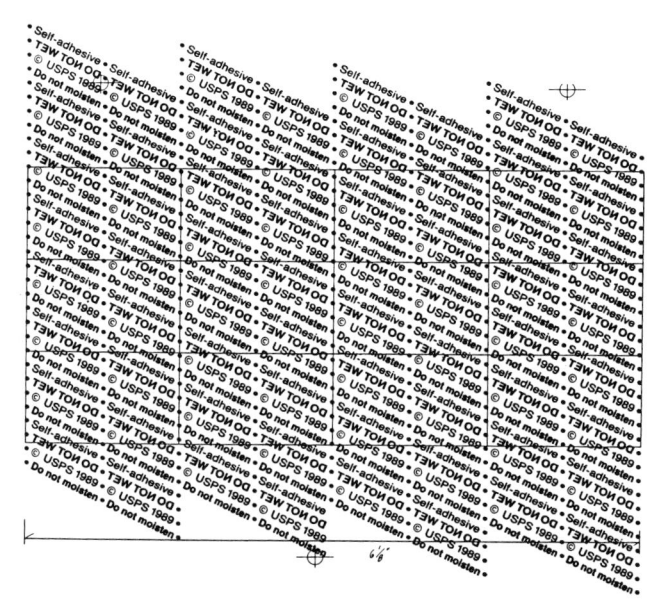

This printing pattern was prepared for the liner, or backing, of the ATM stamps when it was thought that transparent liner material might be used. For that reason the DO NOT WET line was printed in reverse so it could be correctly read from the front after one or more of the stamps had been removed. Because the liner finally selected was opaque, the reversed type wasn't necessary.

the Special Occasions booklet stamps of 1988, submitted a concept sketch that filled the bill. With red stripes and type and a blue field, the design required a relatively basic printing job with a minimum number of self-colors.

For the final art, Brockert sent the concept sketch to John Boyd of Anagraphics Inc., New York, who altered the dimensions slightly to meet size requirements and created the typography, using the same basic type style USPS was using on its current stamped envelopes.

Boyd also helped develop the repeating messages for the backside of the reverse liner, or backing. These consisted of four lines:

"DO NOT WET/EXTRAordinary Stamp (TM) for ATM/Self-adhesive • Do not moisten/©USPS 1989 • Patent Pending."

"In creating those messages, we wanted to make sure that all the information would appear in the space of one stamp on a repeating basis," Brockert said. "That was because we were not sure initially whether the backing would be transparent or not. If the backing had been transparent, we considered doing the messages with the DO NOT WET line printed in reverse.

"That way, most of the information would read properly from the back, but after you took off the stamps the legend DO NOT WET, as a reminder that these are self-adhesive, would read face up. In the end it was decided not to use the transparent material and so we abandoned that idea."

First-Day Facts

A public first-day ceremony was held at the Columbia Seafirst Center in Seattle May 18. Postmaster General Frank dedicated the stamp after remarks by Richard P. Cooley, Seafirst chairman and CEO, and Dr. Alan Gotcher, senior vice president, research, for Avery International Corporation. Gotcher was standing in for Charles D. Miller, Avery's chairman and CEO. The three men then joined in making the first stamp transaction from an ATM.

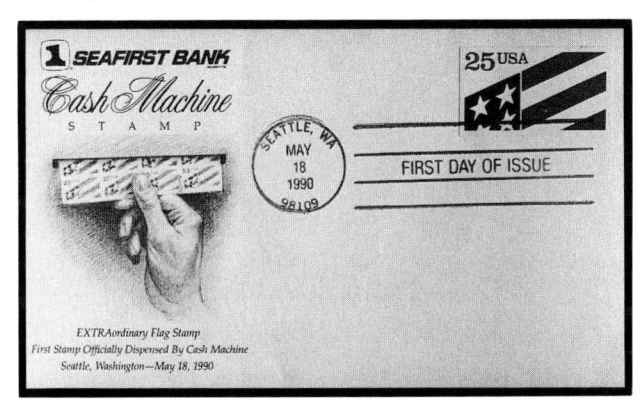

A cacheted first-day cover created by the Seafirst bank, where the ATM stamps were tested.

Honored guests included other officials of Seafirst and of Avery International and its Fasson Division.

Seafirst produced and distributed cacheted envelopes for use on first-day covers. They bore the bank's logo and a picture of a hand receiving a pane of stamps from an ATM.

Details about the stamp, first-day arrangements and the marketing test were contained in a USPS news release dated May 14. However, according to *Linn's Stamp News,* this information didn't reach philatelic publications in time for dissemination before May 18, and as a result many collectors missed the opportunity to attend the first-day ceremony or create special covers on that day.

Because of this late release of first-day information, and the unavailability of the stamps except through philatelic centers, USPS allowed collectors 60 days after the first-day date instead of the normal 30 to submit covers for first-day cancellations.

$2 BOBCAT
WILDLIFE SERIES

Date of Issue: June 1, 1990

Catalog Number: Scott 2476

Colors: magenta, yellow, cyan and black (offset); black (intaglio)

First-Day Cancel: Arlington, Virginia (Napex 90 Stamp Show)

FDCs Canceled: 49,660

Format: Mini-panes of 20, horizontal, 4 across, 5 down. Offset printing plates of 80 subjects, 8 across, 10 down; intaglio printing sleeves of 160 subjects, 8 across, 20 around.

Perf: 11.2 (Eureka off-line perforator)

Selvage Markings: ©USPS 1990; American Wildlife: Bobcat (Lynx rufus)

Designer: Chuck Ripper of Huntington, West Virginia

Engravers: Gary Chaconas, vignette (BEP)
Dennis Brown, lettering (BEP)

Art Director and Project Manager: Jack Williams (USPS)

Modeler: Peter Cocci (BEP)

Typographer: Bradbury Thompson (CSAC)

Printing: BEP's 6-color offset, 3-color intaglio D press (902)

Quantity Ordered: 50,000,000
Quantity Distributed: 26,618,000

Plate/Sleeve Number Detail: One group of four offset plate numbers on the large margin of each pane, a single-digit intaglio sleeve number on the selvage of the adjacent stamp.

Tagging: overall

The Stamp

On June 1, USPS issued a new $2 multicolor stamp depicting a bobcat. The first-day ceremony preceded the opening of Napex 90, the 1990 show of the National Philatelic Exhibitions of Washington, D.C., in the Sheraton National Hotel in Arlington, Virginia.

"This is the first issue planned in the conversion of high-value sheet stamps from the Great Americans series to the colorful, commemorative-size Wildlife series," the Postal Service said. "The $2 Bobcat stamp is a regular issue and will remain in use for a number of years. Eventually, the format of the $1 and $5 regular issues will follow in the tracks of the Bobcat stamp."

USPS officials hoped that the change to the large size, coupled with the use of large, bold denomination symbols, would make it easier for postal workers to distinguish between dollar-value stamps and 1¢, 2¢ and 5¢ stamps. Canada had been making its high-value regular stamps larger than lower-value ones for several years.

The $2 Great Americans stamp that was replaced by the Bobcat stamp depicted William Jennings Bryan (Scott 2195) and was issued in 1986. The stock of Bryan stamps was depleted from the Bureau of Engraving and Printing's inventory about six weeks before the Bobcat stamp was released, and post offices needing $2 stamps during the interim were asked to substitute $1 stamps if necessary.

The idea of high-value stamps picturing wildlife evolved from a project that began in 1987 to design a special stamp for Priority Mail service. Howard Paine, a design coordinator for CSAC, asked three artists who specialized in wildlife each to prepare three sketches showing birds or animals for a Priority Mail stamp that would be printed in intaglio or offset-intaglio combination and show "lots of detail and color." One of the artists, Chuck Ripper of Huntington, West Virginia, was asked to do a pheasant, a bobcat and a jackrabbit. Ripper and the others submitted their sketches in proportions that would fit the extra-large size that USPS had in mind for Priority Mail — the same size used for duck and Express Mail stamps.

"Originally we weren't sure what the image would be on Priority Mail stamps," said Joe Brockert, a USPS program manager for philatelic design. "We thought at one point that Priority Mail might use eagles, like Express Mail . . . The folks who controlled Priority Mail had no preference as to what would be used as an identifier for that particular service. They said there really isn't any intent to establish any other corporate identifier, something other than an eagle, like a fast land animal or something like that, to identify with Priority Mail. So we had kind of an open-ended project there."

The artists' sketches were received and filed away. Then, in 1988, USPS had a need for a booklet stamp to meet the new 25¢ first-class rate. Officials pulled out Ripper's pheasant painting, asked him to revise it so it could be shrunk to definitive size and had it printed by gravure by the American Bank Note Company. Unfortunately, the size was too small to show the details in the pheasant's plumage to good effect, and the problem was compounded by use of gravure and the difficulty encountered by the printers in keeping the colors in register. The result was a disappointing product.

The following year, USPS did issue a Priority Mail stamp, but its theme was space, not wildlife. The occasion was the 20th anniversary of the first manned moon landing, and the Postal Service saw an opportunity to commemorate the event and promote Priority Mail with one stamp. The result was the $2.40 Moon Landing issue (Scott 2419) — and some left-over wildlife designs.

One of those was Ripper's bobcat painting, and it was chosen for the first of the new high-value definitives. "We wanted to take our high-value stamps in a new direction, which was more color and larger size," Joe Brockert said. Officials considered using the special-issue size that had been adopted for Christmas and Love stamps, which was part way between a definitive and commemorative, but decided to go all the way to commemorative size "to give the collector and the user of these stamps more for their money," as Brockert put it.

Following the format introduced with the $5 Bret Harte stamp of 1987, the stamps were issued in mini-sheets of 20. A single-digit intaglio sleeve number appeared in each corner of the pane, making plate blocks more easily accessible for collectors, with less waste for USPS. The selvage also included the words "American Wildlife" and "Bobcat (Lynx rufus)." No wording identifying the animal appeared on the stamp itself.

Bobcats, named for their short, stumpy tails, range from southern Canada to Mexico. Adults vary in size, weighing from 12 to 39 pounds, and prey on small game, including rodents and birds.

The Design

Chuck Ripper's original painting placed the bobcat, stretched out on a log, against a full background of trees and other forest flora. The Citizens' Stamp Advisory Committee reviewed two croppings

Chuck Ripper's original Bobcat stamp painting was done in Priority Mail stamp dimensions and included a full background. BEP changed the dimensions, cropped the image tightly, removed the background and altered some of the details, all on its electronic scanner.

of the design, one for the special-issue (Christmas and Love) size and the other for the commemorative size. It chose the latter. The artwork was turned over to the Bureau of Engraving and Printing, which returned with two alternative models. One was basically Ripper's painting in commemorative dimensions, with "USA $2" at upper right in dropout white against the forest background. The other incorporated extensive changes.

In the second model, the cropping was much tighter, with the bobcat's body filling virtually the entire frame from left to right. A broken branch in Ripper's painting was reduced in size and moved closer to the animal's extended paw. One cluster of rhododendron leaves in the foreground was moved. BEP modeler Peter Cocci made all these alterations electronically, using the Design Center's scanner. CSAC decided that the second model was cleaner, simpler and more effective, and that was the one BEP was instructed to use in producing the stamp.

The stamp was printed on the Bureau's combination offset-intaglio D press. The only part actually printed in intaglio was the $2 USA, in black. To prepare the offset plates, however, BEP's Gary Chaconas first engraved the bobcat image, with multiple individual lines and dots representing the animal's spotted coat, and the plates were made from the engraving rather than from Ripper's original art. This was a procedure the Bureau frequently used to give a sharper definition to offset images.

Ripper hadn't known that BEP was changing his artwork so extensively until he saw the finished stamp, but he wasn't displeased. "All things considered, it doesn't look all that bad," he said. Among the many wildlife stamps he had previously designed for USPS was another bobcat. It appeared on one of the 50 different stamps in the American Wildlife pane of 1987 (Scott 2332), although in a quite different pose from the 1990 version.

"I've got stacks of photographs and drawings of bobcats to work from," Ripper said. "They have a state game farm at French Creek, West Virginia, about an hour and a half, two hours from where we live, where they take orphaned animals that people have taken

This earlier Chuck Ripper-designed Bobcat stamp (Scott 2332) was part of the 50-stamp American Wildlife pane.

home and then found they couldn't really care for them, and they have bobcats there. We stop every time we're driving by and I look and sketch and take pictures."

First-Day Facts

Gordon C. Morison, assistant postmaster general, crossed the Potomac River to Arlington to dedicate the stamp at the Napex 90 stamp show. Milton Mitchell, president of Napex 90, gave the welcome, and Roy Geiger, naturalist for the National Wildlife Federation, delivered the principal address.

Although USPS brought adequate supplies of first-day programs to the ceremony, there were complaints afterward that some persons attending didn't receive copies because of others who took multiple copies for sale to dealers.

5¢ CIRCUS WAGON (COIL)
TRANSPORTATION SERIES

Date of Issue: August 31, 1990

Catalog Number: Scott 2452

Color: red

First-Day Cancel: Syracuse, New York (Empex Stamp Show)

FDCs Canceled: 71,806

Format: Coils of 500 and 3,000. Printing sleeve of 936 subjects (18 across, 52 around).

Perf: 9.8 (Huck rotary perforator)

Designer: Susan Sanford of Washington, D.C.

Engravers: Gary Chaconas, vignette (BEP)
Gary Slaght, lettering (BEP)

Art Director and Project Manager: Joe Brockert (USPS)

Modeler: Frank J. Waslick (BEP)

Typographer: Bradbury Thompson (CSAC)

Printing: BEP's three-color intaglio B press (701)

Quantity Ordered: 48,000 coils of 500; 30,000 coils of 3,000
Quantity Distributed: 46,750 coils of 500; 4,960 coils of 3,000

Sleeve Number Detail: Single-digit intaglio sleeve number on every 52nd stamp.

Tagging: overall

The Stamp

On August 31 USPS issued its second Transportation series coil stamp of 1990, a 5-center depicting a circus wagon of the early 1900s. Its issuance brought to 47 the total of design-different stamps in this series that began in 1981.

It also marked the first time in the series that the same denomination had been covered by three different designs. The first 5¢ Transportation stamp, in 1983, showed a vintage 1913 motorcycle and was printed on BEP's old Cottrell press. After BEP switched production of the series to the B press, a new 5¢ stamp was designed, with a bread wagon as the subject, and was issued in 1987.

The Circus Wagon stamp was also printed on the B press, in rolls of 500 and 3,000. It was the first in the Transportation series to display the new zero-and-a-digit style for denominations less than 10¢, a style that USPS had inaugurated with the 5¢ Luis Munoz Marin sheet stamp earlier in 1990.

The Postal Service had hoped that the stamp would be widely used in 1991, which would have been the case if its request for an increase in the first-class rate from 25¢ to 30¢ had been approved. The 5¢ stamps would then be in great demand to use with leftover 25¢ stamps to cover the new rate. However, the decision of the Postal Rate Commission January 4, 1991, to approve only a 29¢ rate canceled that hope.

As was noted in the chapter on the $1 Seaplane stamp, the Circus Wagon stamp was originally scheduled to be released April 20 during the Aripex stamp show in Phoenix, Arizona, but was replaced by the Seaplane because of USPS' need for a $1 coil.

These picture postcards from the Circus World Museum in Baraboo, Wisconsin, were used by Susan Sanford to design the composite circus wagon on the Transportation coil stamp.

The Circus Wagon stamp had overall tagging. Vertical tagging gaps appeared at 26-stamp intervals on a roll. These gaps, on different rolls, appeared in different locations relative to the numbered stamps, because during production the movement of the tagging cylinders was independent of that of the printing sleeves.

The first circuses in America were opened in permanent locations in Philadelphia and New York City in 1793. Later, traveling circuses were organized, and these brought into being such necessities as the circus wagon and the tent or "big top."

With the development of railroads, large circuses traveled widely. P.T. Barnum's associate, W.C. Coup, introduced a method of loading circus trains from the end in which the gaps between flatcars were bridged, and each wagon in turn was pushed onto the end car and down the length of the train. As circus owners began to advertise the arrival of their shows with street parades, the wagons became more and more ornate, contributing to the spectacle that was designed to lure patrons to the circus grounds.

The Design

"We told the designer specifically to make a generic composite," said Joe Brockert, project manager for the stamp. "Obviously, we didn't want any circus names, we didn't want anything that could be identified with a specific circus or a specific company. So, we said, take the most interesting things from all of the images we've supplied you with and make a composite circus wagon."

The artist, Susan Sanford of Washington, D.C., was given a selection of picture postcards from the Circus World Museum of Baraboo, Wisconsin, with which to work. The wagons shown on the cards were basically from the first decade of the 1900s.

The circus wagon she drew borrowed its side designs and its retractable ladder from a wagon used by the Sparks Circus, its wheels from wagons of the Hagenback-Wallace and Gollmar Brothers Circuses and its windows and some of the decorative work at the top from a Cole Brothers Circus vehicle. It also contained some touches of the artist's own devising.

The Citizens' Stamp Advisory Committee studied the artist's pre-

Susan Sanford submitted this preliminary drawing on which Bradbury Thompson superimposed type, using a 20¢ sample denomination. Sanford later revised the drawing slightly at CSAC's request. BEP made some further changes to simplify the design.

liminary drawing and called for a few changes. Her wagon bore the number "72," and its front wheels were turned to the right. She was asked to remove the number and to straighten out the front axle so that the four wheels were all aimed in the same direction.

In the modeling process, the Bureau of Engraving and Printing removed a few small details that wouldn't have reproduced successfully, such as chains hanging behind the ladder and some knobs and projections where the wagon tongue joined the undercarriage.

The stamp was Sanford's first design for USPS to be executed, but her second stamp to be issued. The 21¢ Chester Carlson stamp in the Great Americans series, issued in 1988, was designed by Sanford after she had completed the Circus Wagon artwork.

First-Day Facts

The first-day ceremony was held in conjunction with the opening of the Empex 90 stamp show and the 35th convention of the American First Day Cover Society (AFDCS) at the Sheraton Inn in Liverpool, New York, a suburb of Syracuse. The first-day postmark read "Syracuse," however. It was pointed out that this was the first first day for that city since the Burgoyne Campaign commemorative of 1927 (Scott 644).

William T. Johnstone, assistant postmaster general, dedicated the stamp, and E. James Strates, president of the James E. Strates Shows and son of its founder, was the principal speaker. The welcome was delivered jointly by the presidents of the two groups most closely involved with Empex, Ronald J. Traino of the Federation of Central New York Philatelic Societies, Inc., the sponsoring organization, and Thomas L. Foust of AFDCS.

A full-sized circus wagon was brought in for the ceremony, and a display of miniature circus wagons lined a hall in the hotel.

Columnist Allison W. Cusick reported in *Linn's Stamp News* that a wide variety of items were "franked" with Circus Wagon stamps and submitted for first-day cancellations at the show, including posters, puzzles, clown masks, brochures and boxes of animal crackers. Five different postmarkers were available. In addition to the standard first-day-of-issue device, there were a small bull's-eye, the AFDCS convention cancel, the Empex show cancel and a pictorial marking from the philatelic center in downtown Syracuse.

For first-day covers on which USPS affixed stamps, a strip of five was used to cover the 25¢ first-class rate.

40¢ CLAIRE LEE CHENNAULT
GREAT AMERICANS SERIES

Date of Issue: September 6, 1990

Catalog Number: Scott 2186

Color: blue

First-Day Cancel: Monroe, Louisiana (Northwest Louisiana University)

FDCs Canceled: 186,761

Format: Panes of 100, vertical, 10 across, 10 down. Printing sleeve of 800 subjects (20 across, 40 around).

Perf: 11.2 (Eureka off-line perforator)

Selvage Markings: Claire Lee Chennault (1890-1958) Lt. Gen.; Led AVG Flying Tigers in China, 1941-43; Headed WWII China Air War, 1943-45; ©United States Postal Service 1990, Use Correct ZIP Code®

Designer: Chris Calle of Stamford, Connecticut

Engravers: Thomas Hipschen, vignette (BEP)
Dennis Brown, lettering (BEP)

Art Director: Derry Noyes (CSAC)

Project Manager: Jack Williams (USPS)

Typographer: Bradbury Thompson (CSAC)

Printing: 3-color intaglio unit of BEP's 8-color gravure/intaglio A press (702)

Quantity Ordered: 80,000,000
Quantity Distributed: 45,300,000

Sleeve Number Detail: Single-digit intaglio sleeve number alongside each corner stamp.

Tagging: overall

The Stamp

On September 6, USPS issued a 40¢ stamp in the Great Americans series depicting Lieutenant General Claire Lee Chennault, the U.S. Air Force officer who led the Flying Tigers in China against the Japanese during World War II.

USPS chose the date because it was the 100th anniversary of Chennault's birth in Commerce, Texas, according to the birth date given in Pentagon records and Chennault's own autobiography, *Way of a Fighter*. In the biographical information printed in the selvage of the stamp panes, USPS listed Chennault's birth year as 1890. However, researchers have concluded that he was actually born three years later than that, on September 6, 1893 — which was the year that his widow, Anna, directed be put on his tombstone.

The three-year difference between Chennault's "official" birth year and the actual one was pointed out to USPS by William M. Smith Jr., a Ph.D. candidate at the University of Arkansas. In their replies to his letters, postal officials acknowledged the discrepancy.

This is the photo, made probably in late 1943, on which the stamp portrait (and, presumably, the Time *cover) was based. Chennault wears the two stars of a major general.*

Although no birth certificate exists for the flyer, Smith wrote, two documents support the case that he was born in 1893, not 1890. One is the wedding license of Chennault's parents, John and Jessie, which was issued in Tensas Parish, Louisiana, December 6, 1892; this was a short time before the newlyweds moved to Texas. The other was the 1900 federal census for Louisiana, whose listing for the John S. Chennault family (which by now had moved back to Tensas Parish) listed a 6-year-old C.L. Chennault, born in Texas in September 1893.

Biographer Martha Byrd, in her 1987 book *Chennault: Giving Wings to the Tiger,* provided this additional information:

"For reasons of his own, Chennault used different birthdates at different times. When he went to Louisiana State University in 1909, he gave his birthdate as 2 June 1893; at the normal school he gave it as 1892. When he first joined the Army he used the date 6 September 1890, and that date remained on his official record, much to his father's chagrin, for at the time the elder Chennault had still been married to his first wife, and Claire's mother had been a mere 14 years old. Chennault's U.S. passport bears the date 6 September 1893, the date recorded in the family Bible and confirmed by reconstructed events.

"Why the inconsistencies? Chennault was sensitive at having married and fathered so many children while still so young, and it embarrassed him that Nell" — his own first wife — "was slightly older than he. Still, the incorrect dates had begun to appear before he married . . . A member of the family who was close to him felt that he 'simply forgot,' gave whatever date popped into his head, and allowed the incorrect dates to stay on the records because he never considered them worth correcting."

When William Smith informed USPS officials they had chosen the wrong year as the Chennault centennial, Mike Smith, marketing director for the Postal Service's Shreveport, Louisiana, MSC, replied: "You were indeed correct in pointing out the discrepancy we had previously discovered in talking with family members in preparation for the first day ceremony."

And Dickey B. Rustin, manager of the Stamp Product Development Branch, wrote to Smith: "We had been advised by another source that 1893 was the correct year of birth, but we could not verify it for the record. As you may surmise, we receive a lot of public comment about many of the stamps we issue, particularly those where we might be deemed to be in error. Consequently, we elected to proceed with 1890 because that is what appears in all standard reference works, in General Chennault's official military records and . . . in his *Way of a Fighter.*"

The inscriptions in the selvage of the Chennault stamp presented other factual problems as well. Located opposite three stamps on

each pane, the inscriptions read as follows:
"Claire Lee Chennault (1890-1958) Lt. Gen."
"Led AVG Flying Tigers in China, 1941-43"
"Headed WWII China Air War 1943-45."

As William Smith pointed out in a letter to this writer, the AVG (American Volunteer Group), popularly known as the Flying Tigers, was activated on December 1, 1941, by the Nationalist Chinese Government, and dissolved July 4, 1942 — not 1943. It was replaced by the China Air Task Force, a U.S. Army Air Corps unit, which Chennault, who by this time was a brigadier general, was named to head. "Everyone agrees on these dates — except the USPS," Smith said.

As for the third inscription, Smith noted that Chennault had actually "headed the World War II China air war" since 1937,

The portrait of Claire Chennault that appeared on the December 6, 1943 cover of Time *was probably based on the same photograph that Christopher Calle used as his principal reference in drawing the stamp portrait.*

213

when, as a retired Army Air Corps officer, he was hired by Chiang Kai-shek's Kuomintang — the ruling nationalist party — to build and train a Chinese air force to fight the invading Japanese.

In this latter enterprise Chennault had a relatively free hand, but the going was difficult, and planes, ammunition, skilled pilots and other personnel were in desperately short supply. Finally, in 1941, before Pearl Harbor, Chennault and the Chinese government received tacit support from Washington to organize the American Volunteer Group: American pilots to fly American P-40 fighter planes for the Chinese.

The so-called Flying Tigers never had more than 87 pilots. However, in less than seven months of existence they were credited with destroying 284 enemy planes, with 19 casualties in the group. The Tigers created a memorable trademark for themselves when they turned the sharply pointed spinners of their P-40s into the noses of tiger sharks by adding a sinister eye and rows of large white teeth around the open cowling. It was an idea they borrowed from P-40 pilots in the Royal Air Force in Africa, but made their own.

Chennault drilled his men on the P-40's assets. The Japanese Zero had speed and maneuverability, he reminded them, but the P-40 had diving speed and firepower. He convinced them that if they used these strengths, they could get by. Recalled one: "He told us: Never stay in and fight; never try to turn; never try to mix with them . . . Get altitude and dive on them and keep going — hit and run tactics; never lose speed . . . or take for granted that the planes you could see were all there were, because we would always be outnumbered."

These are two "portrait concepts" that Chris Calle made as part of his extensive preliminary work in designing the Chennault stamp.

Chennault resigned as commander of the 14th Air Force in 1945 and retired as a major general. The following year he divorced Nell and married Anna Chen, a Chinese newspaperwoman who had been a nurse for the Flying Tigers. He helped found and chaired the Civil Air Transport, a Chinese civilian airline, and he moved with the CAT to Taiwan after the Communist takeover of mainland China.

In 1957 Chennault developed inoperable lung cancer. He died July 27, 1958, a few days after Congress had approved a bill promoting him to the rank of lieutenant general on the retired list.

Chennault was the third World War II military leader to appear on a Great Americans stamp. Preceding him were Admiral Chester W. Nimitz (1985) and General H.H. "Hap" Arnold (1988).

In honoring Chennault the Postal Service kept a promise made six years earlier by then-Postmaster General William Bolger to Anna Chennault. Anna and the Flying Tigers Association had requested such a stamp, and on July 12, 1984, Bolger wrote this to her:

"It gives me great pleasure to inform you that the U.S. Postal Service plans to issue a regular postage stamp honoring your late husband, General Claire Lee Chennault, on the 100th anniversary of his birth in 1990. Representatives of our Stamps Division will keep you informed of future developments."

The 40¢ stamp met the current one-ounce overseas surface rate. It

Chris Calle made these rough sketches for the Claire Chennault stamp, using different portraits, shading and arrangements of wording.

replaced another stamp of that denomination in the Great Americans series, issued in 1984 and depicting Lillian Gilbreth.

The Design

The portrait used on the stamp was based on a wartime photograph showing Chennault in uniform with the two stars of a major general on his shoulder. The same photo appears to have been the basis for a *Time* magazine cover December 6, 1943, painted by Boris Chaliapin. It was selected by Anna Chennault and obtained from the Smithsonian Institution's Air and Space Museum. The photo showed to good effect the weatherbeaten appearance of the pilot's face, which, friends had said, "looked as if he had been holding it out of the cockpit and into a storm for years."

The artwork was by Christopher Calle of Stamford, Connecticut, who had designed nine previous Great Americans stamps, including those for Nimitz and "Hap" Arnold. Like Calle's previous designs, this one was executed in pencil.

In the final version, Calle added some background shading at the left side. This design touch was one that CSAC had come to prefer on all Great Americans stamps. "It's a good way to 'hold' the face, and bring out the features," Calle said.

Calle had offered CSAC some alternative sketches of Chennault to choose among. He based these on photographs furnished by USPS, plus others he had unearthed in his own research. "I presented about six different designs, different portraits, a variety, which is

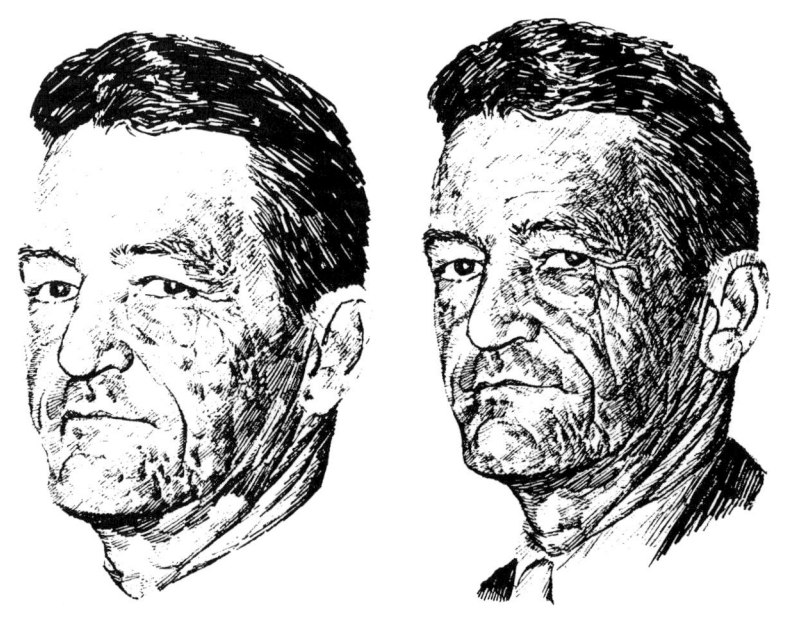

These are what Chris Calle called the "warm-up" sketch for his final drawing of General Claire Chennault, and the final drawing itself.

usually what I like to do," Calle said.

Calle's stamp portraits aren't exactly composites, but he usually refers to several different pictures as he works. "I like to gather as much visual information as I can," Calle said. "Usually the portrait is based primarily on one photograph or one sitting of photographs. But the more information you have, the better portrait you can do of a person, because there might be something very characteristic that's not captured in a single photograph. It's always good to have a variety of angles of the person, in different lighting situations.

"That was especially true with Chennault. He had such a strong, determined face. That's what I tried to bring out, and whether it's based on one photograph or 10 photographs, the end result was an attempt to capture that strength and that determination."

Calle uses an HB or 2-H pencil, neither very soft nor very hard. "For me it's very flexible," he said. "I can get a lot of different stroke variations in the graphite, different textures, using the same strength of lead. I don't really like to switch off, but that's just me; other people like to mix different leads to get different effects."

Calle's pencil drawings, with their many individual strokes, give a lot of guidance to the BEP engravers who must translate them into dies for making the intaglio printing sleeves. "I like to use slick-surface paper so that my strokes can show the engraver the directional flow of the lines of the face that he's going to follow," Calle said. "They see exactly what I'm trying to capture. If you had a very soft half-tone drawing or photograph, then the engraver would have to interpret that into line. This way they have it basically into line

This Postal Service picture, used for placing the typography in the correct position, shows how the descriptive wording on the stamp evolved.

and they can just transfer it down to size."

The Bureau's Thomas Hipschen engraved the portrait and Dennis Brown did the lettering. The stamp was printed in blue on the intaglio portion of BEP's gravure-intaglio A press. Calle had no vote in the color selection, but he termed it "a great choice — that steel blue, strong color was appropriate to Chennault."

As with the Luis Munoz Marin stamp, the Chennault stamp was originally designed without any explanatory wording, then had to be modified after Postmaster General Frank decreed that future Great Americans stamps contain some information about their subjects.

What descriptive wording to use under Chennault's portrait in the design required some discussion among Citizens' Stamp Advisory Committee members and USPS staff. One proposed version was: "AVG 'Flying Tigers' 1941." Another version that was actually set in type read: "Flying Tigers WWII." "The committee pointed out," said project manager Jack Williams, "that World War II didn't start for us until December of 1941, and these guys were flying as volunteers in China prior to that time. So we changed it to '1940s,' which was more descriptive, even though Chennault had been in China since 1937. They really started flying in the 1940s."

First-Day Facts

The first-day ceremony, open to the public, was held at the Anna Gray Noe Alumni Center on the campus of Northeast Louisiana University in Monroe. It was an elaborate affair, featuring music and presentation of the colors by U.S. Air Force units and a military "fly-by" by World War II aircraft of the Confederate Air Force, based in Harlingen, Texas, and planes of the 23rd Tactical Air Wing stationed at England AFB in Alexandria, Louisiana.

Speakers were Anna Chennault, the general's widow; Wayne G. Johnson, past president of the Flying Tigers of the 14th Air Force Association, and John Richard Rossi, president of the Flying Tigers, AVG, Chinese Air Force. The stamp was dedicated by Joseph Y. Peng, general manager of the USPS Stamp Manufacturing Division, whose father had been an officer in the Chinese Air Force and an associate of Chennault. Honored guests included two of Chennault's brothers, Joe Y. Chennault and Nelson Ernest Chennault, and William H. "Trey" LeBlanc, a member of the Postal Rate Commission.

45¢ CARIBBEAN COASTAL SCENE (AIRMAIL)
AMERICAS SERIES

Date of Issue: October 12, 1990

Catalog Number: Scott C127

Colors: magenta, yellow, cyan and black

First-Day Cancel: Grand Canyon, Arizona (El Tovar Hotel)

FDCs Canceled: 137,068

Format: Panes of 50, horizontal, 5 across, 10 down. Gravure printing cylinders of 200 subjects (10 across, 20 around) manufactured by Armotek Industries Inc., Palmyra, New Jersey.

Perf: 10.9 (L perforator)

Selvage Markings: ©United States Postal Service 1990, Use Correct ZIP Code®, PUAS logo, Postal Union of the Americas and Spain, Natural surroundings seen by explorers: Tropical islands, American Caribbean

Designer: Mark Hess of Katonah, New York

Art Director and Typographer: Richard Sheaff (CSAC)

Project Manager: Joe Brockert (USPS)

Modeler: Richard Sennett (Sennett Enterprises) for American Bank Note Company

Printing: Stamps printed and sheeted out by American Bank Note Company on a leased Champlain gravure press (J.W. Fergusson and Sons, Richmond, Virginia) under the supervision of Sennett Enterprises (Fairfax, Virginia). Perforated, processed and shipped by ABNC (Chicago, Illinois).

Quantity Ordered: 48,000,000
Quantity Distributed: 48,000,000

Cylinder Number Detail: One group of four cylinder numbers preceded by the letter "A" over/under corner stamps.

Tagging: overall

A concept sketch made by art director Richard Sheaff, using a color photograph of a Caribbean island beachfront. Sheaff included a similar picture on the pages describing the America series in USPS' 1990 Mint Set book, which he designed.

The Stamp

The second series of America stamps to be issued by USPS as part of the annual omnibus issue sponsored by the Postal Union of the Americas and Spain (PUAS) featured scenery that the early European explorers of the Western Hemisphere might have encountered. Like the first series in 1989, the 1990 series comprised a 25¢ first-class rate stamp and a 45¢ airmail stamp. General information on the two stamps can be found in the chapter on the 25¢ item in the Commemoratives section.

The Design

In the preliminary design stages, art director Richard Sheaff used a color photograph of a Caribbean island, with palm trees, blue ocean and pounding white surf, to show the Citizens' Stamp Advisory Committee how a stamp of that kind might look. (Sheaff later used a similar picture to illustrate the pages on the America stamps in the Philatelic Sales Division's 1990 Commemorative Mint Set book, which he designed.)

The committee decided to use paintings rather than color photographs in the finished designs, and Mark Hess of Katonah, New York, was commissioned for the project. His first concept sketch for the stamp that would become the 45¢ airmail was vertically ar-

A Mark Hess concept sketch, arranged vertically, showing lush vegetation crowding a sandy beach on a Caribbean island.

ranged and depicted a generic tropical island beach, dominated by lush green foliage just behind the narrow strip of sand.

"The committee felt that at stamp size it was just too busy," said Sheaff. "There was too much going on in the design."

For his second attempt, Hess went to a horizontal format, showing more ocean. As in his Grand Canyon design for the 25¢ America stamp, a solitary bird hovered over the scene. This island image, like its predecessor, was generic rather than specific.

"At that point the committee was wanting a specific place," Sheaff said. "But as Mark and I talked about it, we realized it had a lot of problems. On what specific place that's now part of the United States do we know for sure that Columbus's party set foot? Who knows? Maybe mainland Florida later on — if not Columbus, then someone after him; maybe one of the American Virgin Islands, or Puerto Rico. More likely, the places they actually touched down on are not under U.S. control.

"That isn't the point of it anyway; we're not trying to say, this is THE beach where Columbus landed, like Plymouth Rock. We're really trying to say, this is the kind of landscape that he found."

In the end, the committee approved the horizontal generic scene, and Hess made a finished painting for the American Bank Note Company to use in preparing its gravure printing cylinders.

Like the Grand Canyon design, the island design was devoid of any explanatory text. The selvage contained the PUAS logo, which was identified as representing the Postal Union of the Americas and Spain, and this message: "Natural surroundings seen by explorers: Tropical islands, American Caribbean."

First-Day Facts

For information on the first-day ceremony for both of the 1990 America commemoratives, see the chapter on the 25¢ America stamp.

$12.50 MIGRATORY BIRD HUNTING (DUCK) STAMP 1990-91

Date of Issue: June 30, 1990

Catalog Number: Scott RW57

Colors: magenta, yellow, gray, cyan, black (2) (offset); black (intaglio); black (flexographic back plate)

First-Day Cancel: June 30, 1990, Washington, D.C. (Smithsonian Institution)
July 1, 1990, Bloomington, Minnesota (Minnesota Valley National Wildlife Refuge visitor's center)

Format: Panes of 30, horizontal, 5 across, 6 down. Offset printing plates of 120 subjects (12 across, 10 down); intaglio printing sleeve of 240 subjects (12 across, 20 around); flexographic back plate of 120 subjects (12 across, 10 down)

Perf: 11.2 by 11.1 (Eureka off-line perforator)

Selvage Markings: sleeve number

Artist: Jim Hautman of Plymouth, Minnesota

Stamp Designer, Modeler and Typographer: Clarence Holbert (BEP)

Engravers: Gary M. Chaconas (BEP), vignette
Dennis Brown (BEP), lettering and numerals

Printing: 6-color offset, 3-color intaglio D press (902)

Quantity Ordered: 4,800,000
Quantity Distributed: 4,800,000

Sleeve Number Detail: one intaglio sleeve number at a pane corner

Tagging: untagged

The Stamp

The 1990-1991 Federal Migratory Bird Hunting and Conservation stamp, better known as the duck stamp, pictured a pair of black-bellied whistling ducks in flight. Its design was based on an original painting by Jim Hautman, a 25-year-old wildlife artist from Plymouth, Minnesota.

Five judges selected Hautman's painting in an open competition after examining the works of 603 artists during two days of judging at the Department of the Interior auditorium in Washington in November 1989. Hautman was the youngest winner in the 41-year history of the annual contest, which bestows on the victor prestige and more than $1 million in royalties from the sale of limited-edition prints to collectors.

Though young, Hautman was a veteran wildlife artist as well as a veteran of conservation stamp design contests. A self-taught painter, he began selling his works while still a senior in high school. He had entered four previous federal contests, beginning when he was 20, and had finished third in 1987 with an acrylic painting of a pair of bufflehead ducks flying over water.

He won competitions to design state duck stamps for Delaware (1988), Nevada (1988) and Minnesota (1989), and placed second in Minnesota pheasant stamp and Pennsylvania duck stamp contests. He was commissioned to design Australia's second federal duck stamp (1990-1991). Both of Hautman's parents are artists, and his brother, Robert, is also a wildlife painter who won the Minnesota duck stamp competition in 1988 — which meant that Jim's win the next year gave the family back-to-back victories.

On November 7, 1989, at home in Minnesota, Jim Hautman got a phone call from Secretary of the Interior Manuel Lujan with the

Jim Hautman's contest-winning original painting of two black-bellied whistling ducks in flight at sunrise.

good news that he had won that year's federal contest. "It was pretty shocking," he recalled. "I thought I had a chance, but I knew that it was a long shot." The next day he flew to Washington at Lujan's invitation to meet with President George Bush at the White House.

The 1990 duck stamp was officially placed on sale June 30 at the Smithsonian Institution's National Museum of American History in Washington. On July 1, the artist's home state was recognized when a second-day ceremony was held at the Minnesota Valley National Wildlife Refuge visitor's center in Bloomington, Minnesota. The stamp was available nationwide July 2.

The duck stamp is a revenue stamp. All waterfowl hunters aged 16 or older are required to carry a current one with their licenses. The face value of the 1990 stamp was $12.50, the same as in 1989. Since the first duck stamp was issued at $1 in 1934, there have been six price increases; a seventh, to $15, is scheduled for 1991.

In the 56 years of the program, more than $350 million raised from the sale of duck stamps has been spent to preserve nearly four million acres of wetlands. Many of the more than 440 national wildlife refuges in the United States have been paid for entirely or in part through duck stamp receipts. In fiscal year 1989, the U.S. Fish and Wildlife Service acquired 61,170 wetland acres by obligating $27.1 million from the Migratory Bird Conservation Fund, which includes revenues from duck stamp sales.

The contest for the 1990 duck stamp design, like the one before it, required competitors to choose their subjects from among five waterfowl species specified by the Fish and Wildlife Service from a list of North American species that hadn't previously been pictured on the stamps. Jim Hautman and his fellow artists were restricted to the black-bellied whistling duck, spectacled eider, red-breasted merganser, Barrow's goldeneye and black scoter.

For the 1991 stamp competition, which was judged in November 1990, the black-bellied whistling duck was dropped and the king eider added to the list. In the 1991 contest, the surf scoter was to be added, and, in 1992, the mottled duck. By 1997, through the process of elimination, duck stamps will have depicted all 42 species of waterfowl whose ranges include the contiguous United States and Alaska. (Hawaii's nene goose also has been shown, in 1964.)

Rick Kelley of Hudson, Wisconsin, placed second in the judging for the 1990 duck stamp design with an acrylic rendition of a lone red-breasted merganser. Third place went to Robert Leslie of Turnersville, New Jersey, for his painting of a pair of Barrow's goldeneyes.

Many of the waterfowl depicted on the stamps have been relatively familiar species that range over wide areas of the continental United States. That's not the case with the black-bellied whistling duck. This interesting bird is found in Mexico and Central America and South America as far south as Argentina, but in the United States it ventures only into extreme south Texas, in a strip along the Gulf of Mexico. Its most striking physical characteristics were all emphasized in Hautman's painting: red bill, pink feet and blackish underparts and underwing surfaces that contrast strongly with the predominantly white surfaces of the upper wings.

Whistling ducks constitute a group of nine species, primarily found in the tropics or subtropics, with clear, whistling voices that give them their name. Besides the black-bellied variety, only one other species, the fulvous whistling duck, visits North America. This bird was shown on the 1986 duck stamp. Male and female whistling ducks are indistinguishable by plumage; pairs are believed to mate for life, and males help incubate the eggs — a domestic virtue that is shared by no other North American waterfowl.

The judges for the contest won by Hautman were Kathy Foley, director of the Leigh Yawkey Woodson Art Museum of Wausau, Wisconsin; retired Lieutenant General David Grange, an art collector and conservationist from The Plains, Virginia; Fred Kindwill, Ducks Unlimited member and wildlife artist from Jackson, Wyoming; David Lank, wildlife art historian from Montreal, Canada, and Ron Schara, outdoor writer and broadcaster from Minneapolis, Minnesota. The alternate judge was Susan Bournique, photo editor for *The Nature Conservancy*.

The Design

"I picked the black-bellied whistling duck because it was one of the more attractive species on the list," Jim Hautman said. "Also, I had some good reference to work from. A guy about half an hour from my house has a game farm and raises some black-bellied whistling ducks, so I was able to see live specimens. I also had a couple of mounted birds and some photographs."

In preparing to do his final painting, Hautman made several preliminary color studies. All of these showed a pair of ducks in flight, which was the approach he had chosen from the outset, but with different color combinations and backgrounds.

"Normally on a stamp design I'll do several color studies and then choose the one I think is the most striking and has the best chance of winning," Hautman said. "Then I'll start fresh on the

Jim Hautman made this color study of two black-bellied whistling ducks in flight in preparation for his final painting. Note that in this picture the ducks are flying lower than the pair in the finished work, and the cypress trees are closer.

original, while looking at the preliminaries and taking some parts that I like from each of them."

Hautman's finished acrylic painting showed the two ducks flying against clouds that the sunrise had tinted in delicate golds and purples. Cypress trees draped with Spanish moss are seen in the background. Clarence Holbert of BEP, as designer-modeler, converted the painting into a finished stamp design. The stamp was printed on BEP's combination offset-intaglio D press.

The Interior Department, unlike USPS, doesn't try to limit stamp typography to a bare minimum. A duck stamp conveys a lot of information: the name of the sponsoring agency ("U.S. Department of the Interior"); the expiration date ("Void after June 30, 1991"); the denomination ("$12.50"); the line that identifies the stamp itself ("Migratory Bird Hunting and Conservation Stamp"), and the species identification ("Black-Bellied Whistling Duck").

In addition, there's information on the back. Turning bars on the D press turned the continuous web, after the stamp image had been printed, to allow the message to be applied to the gummed side by flexography. The 1990 message read: "Take Pride in America/Buy Duck Stamps/Save Wetlands/Send in all bird bands/Sign your Duck Stamps/It is unlawful to hunt waterfowl or use this stamp as a National Wildlife entrance pass unless you sign your name in ink on the face of this stamp." The reference to the entrance pass was a new addition to the inscription in 1990, and was a reminder that possession of a signed Duck Stamp admitted the bearer to certain wildlife refuges where entrance fees are charged.

Until 1977, duck stamps bore the inscription "Migratory Bird Hunting Stamp." Beginning that year, the words "and Conservation" were added after "Hunting." The early stamps in the series didn't name the species of waterfowl that was pictured, but beginning with 1952's harlequin ducks each species has been identified. Over the years the method of naming the species has been inconsistent; sometimes the plural form has been used and sometimes, as in 1990, it has been the singular.

First-Day Facts

The June 30 first-day ceremony was held in the Carmichael Auditorium at the National Museum of American History.

Joseph Harris, postmaster of Washington, D.C., sold the first 1990 duck stamp to Interior Secretary Manuel Lujan and the second one to artist Jim Hautman. He bought the third stamp himself and presented it to James H. Bruns, deputy executive director of the National Philatelic Collection, for the collection on behalf of the postal workers of Washington.

Among the speakers were Secretary Lujan, who gave the principal address; Bruns; Christopher D. Koss, president of the J.N. "Ding"

The federal duck stamp signing ceremony May 10 drew these participants: left to right, Fred Kindwill; Clarence Holbert of the BEP; Kathy Foley; Gary Chaconas; John Turner; Dennis Brown; Jim Hautman, 1990 duck stamp artist; Leonard Buckley; Senator Dave Durenberger of Minnesota; Sig Rogich; Catalina Vasquez Villalpando, U.S. treasurer; Peter H. Daly, BEP director, and Jim Range, National Fish and Wildlife Foundation director.

Darling Foundation, and Lonn W. Taylor, assistant director for public programs of the National Museum of American History. Each one paid tribute to the late "Ding" Darling, the Iowa editorial cartoonist who campaigned tirelessly in the 1920s and 1930s for waterfowl conservation programs, and whose drawing of mallards landing was used in the design of the first duck stamp in 1934.

Jim Hautman was also present at the July 1 ceremony in Bloomington, Minnesota. He signed programs, stamps and duck stamp souvenir cards (see separate chapter) at both events.

First-day cover service was provided, with collectors required to pay for first-class postage for their envelopes in addition to the $12.50 duck stamp. Two different pictorial cancellations were available, one at the Smithsonian's temporary "Duck Stamp Station," the other at the "Whistling Duck Station" in Bloomington.

STAMPED ENVELOPES

The movement away from old-fashioned embossing in U.S. stamped envelopes continued in 1990. For the second consecutive year, no new envelopes with embossed indicia were issued. USPS is increasingly confident that it has found other ways that are equally effective at protecting its envelopes against counterfeiting.

Four of the five new envelope varieties issued in 1990 had an inherent security factor, in that they were Official Mail types, intended for use only by federal agencies. The fifth envelope, saluting professional football, relied on a printing process that was even more challenging to counterfeiters than embossing: It incorporated a holographic image on a piece of metallic foil.

The Football envelope was USPS' second envelope of the hologram type. It was also the second in which a standard envelope was married to a high-quality printing surface through a simple adaptation of the old-fashioned window-making process. By exploiting this technique, USPS officials say, they will be able to bring not only 3-D but also high-quality color and detail to postal stationery, and be able to do it quickly and cost-effectively.

45¢ OFFICIAL MAIL STAMPED ENVELOPE

Date of Issue: March 17, 1990

Catalog Number: Scott U079

Colors: blue, black

First-Day Cancel: Springfield, Virginia

FDCs Canceled: 5,956

Size: 8⅞ by 4⅜ inches

Watermark: none

Markings: ©USPS 1988 under flap. Penalty notation in upper-left corner

Designer and Typographer: Bradbury Thompson (CSAC)

Art Director and Project Manager: Joe Brockert (USPS)

Printing: Westvaco-USEnvelope Division in two-color flexography on a VH machine

Quantity Ordered: 767,500
Quantity Distributed: 744,500

Tagging: Medium-sized square to left of denomination

The Envelope

In recent years USPS has issued stamped envelopes for an increasing variety of purposes and markets. For the general public, there have been a Christmas and a Love envelope, a double-window envelope, a philatelic return envelope and a security envelope. For government agencies, there have been Penalty Mail, or Official Mail, envelopes, including envelopes exclusively for mailing savings bonds. On March 17, 1990, USPS added two new Penalty Mail envelopes that it developed especially for the Department of State to use in transmitting passports.

Because envelopes containing passports normally weigh more than one ounce, the new envelopes bore denominations of 45¢ (two ounces) and 65¢ (three ounces). They were the highest-denomination U.S. postal stationery items of the 20th century to date. Their size (8⅞ inches by 4⅜ inches) and paper composition were also determined by passport mailing requirements. A heavier weight of paper was used to hold more securely contents weighing up to three ounces. The paper was unwatermarked.

The standard, all-purpose Penalty Mail envelope that was already in existence, bearing the 25¢ first-class rate, had an embossed indicium with the denomination printed at the side by flexography. However, these new specialized envelopes, like the Penalty Mail savings bond envelope of 1988, were printed by flexography exclusively. The Postal Service's envelope manufacturer, the Envelope Division of Westvaco in Williamsburg, Pennsylvania, uses a VH envelope-forming machine that can emboss only when the envelopes are to be formed in one of the two standard sizes, Number 6¾ and Number 10. And USPS has concluded that the anti-counterfeiting protection furnished by embossing isn't necessary in the case of envelopes that are to be used exclusively by government agencies in highly controlled settings.

"Mailing passports is a very labor-intensive operation," said Joe Brockert of USPS, art director for the project, "and the State Department came to us and asked us for any suggestions we might have on helping them expedite it. They thought that using a stamped envelope would be more efficient than affixing Penalty Mail stamps. But because of the weight of the passports, they would need envelopes in the higher denominations.

"Now, if a private customer told us he needed a two-ounce-rate stamped envelope, we would have to tell him no, because the rate-making authority for stamped envelopes rests with the Postal Rate Commission. However, that doesn't apply to government agencies. Under inter-agency agreements, we can respond to reasonable requests such as the one from State. So we worked with them to develop the necessary envelope size and weight of paper stock, and it was a fairly simple matter of responding to a customer's needs."

Collectors could obtain the envelopes only by mail order from the Philatelic Sales Division or in person at the Philatelic Center in the lobby of USPS headquarters in Washington. A 5¢ premium over face value was charged for each envelope.

The Design

The indicia printed by flexography on the two envelopes were the same as the one used on the 1988 envelope that was issued for mailing savings bonds, and were identical in basic design to the embossed indicium on the 25¢ Penalty Mail envelope of 1988.

The design, developed by Bradbury Thompson, CSAC design coordinator, featured the Great Seal of the United States in white on a blue background, with details of the seal in blue. The background was square, with rounded corners. To the left, in four lines of black type, was inscribed: "Official/Mail/ 45 (or 65)/USA."

In the upper-left corner of the envelopes was printed: "DEPARTMENT OF STATE / (space for return address) / OFFICIAL BUSINESS / PENALTY FOR PRIVATE USE, $300."

First-Day Facts

The two passport envelopes were first placed on sale at the Springpex 90 stamp show, held at the Robert E. Lee High School in Springfield, Virginia. Assistant Postmaster General Gordon C. Morison dedicated the envelopes. Peter Martin, chairman of Springpex, gave the welcome, and Arnold Petersen, vice president of the Retired Postal Management Association, introduced the guests.

Because the envelopes couldn't be purchased at post offices, and had to bear an official return address, customers weren't permitted to prepare their own first-day covers for cancellation. They were required to send a peelable return address label and 50¢ or 70¢ for each envelope desired to the postmaster at Springfield. USPS then added the official government return address, affixed the customer's labels and applied the first-day-of-issue cancellation.

65¢ OFFICIAL MAIL STAMPED ENVELOPE

Date of Issue: March 17, 1990

Catalog Number: Scott U080

Colors: blue, black

First-Day Cancel: Springfield, Virginia

FDCs Canceled: 6,922

Size: 8⅞ inches by 4⅜ inches

Watermark: none

Markings: ©USPS 1988 under flap. Penalty notation in upper-left corner.

Designer and Typographer: Bradbury Thompson (CSAC)

Art Director and Project Manager: Joe Brockert (USPS)

Printing: Westvaco-USEnvelope Division in two-color flexography on a VH machine.

Quantity Ordered: 387,500
Quantity Distributed: 375,000

Tagging: medium-sized square to left of denomination

The Envelope

The 65¢ Penalty Mail stamped envelope was created by USPS for use by the U.S. Department of State in passport mailings weighing between two and three ounces. It was issued with the 45¢ envelope on March 17 at Springpex 90 in Springfield, Virginia. Details on these two issues may be found in the preceding chapter.

45¢ OFFICIAL MAIL STAMPED ENVELOPE (SELF-SEALING)

Date of Issue: August 10, 1990

Catalog Number: Scott UO81

Colors: blue, black

First-Day Cancel: Washington, D.C.

FDCs Canceled: 7,160

Size: 8⅞ by 3⅜ inches

Watermark: none

Markings: ©USPS 1988 under flap. Penalty notation in upper-left corner. The word "Peel" appears in a repeat pattern on the release strip covering the grip-seal adhesive

Designer and Typographer: Bradbury Thompson (CSAC)

Art Director and Project Manager: Joe Brockert (USPS)

Printing: Westvaco-USEnvelope Division in two colors on a Jet offset press

Quantity Ordered: 287,000
Quantity Distributed: 287,000

Tagging: vertical bar to left of denomination

The Envelope

On August 10, in Washington, D.C., USPS issued its first self-sealing stamped envelopes. The envelopes were new versions of the

45¢ and 65¢ Official Mail stationery that had been issued March 17 for use by the U.S. Department of State in mailing passports. There was no first-day ceremony, but first-day cancellations were provided.

"The passport office asked us to conduct an experiment with them to see if self-seal technology would speed their mailing operation," said Joe Brockert of USPS, art director for the earlier versions of the two envelopes. "Passport mailing is very labor-intensive, and they thought it might speed things up and possibly enable them to automate. We agreed to provide the envelopes on a limited basis. The self-sealing envelopes are more expensive to produce."

At the end of the year the cost-effectiveness of the experiment was still being assessed, Brockert said.

Although the USPS announcement of the new varieties, dated July 3, gave the issue date as July 9, that day came and went with no sign of them. On August 3 USPS announced the revised issue date.

The envelopes featured a 1¼-inch wallet flap with grip-seal adhesive protected by a strip of silicone-coated release paper on which the word "Peel" was printed in a repeating pattern.

"Otherwise, they are identical to the previously issued envelopes," the USPS announcement said. However, this wasn't the case. Although the designs of the old and new indicia were the same, the indicia themselves were printed on different presses, and they looked quite different when laid side by side.

The reason was that USPS' envelope supplier, the Envelope Division of Westvaco, didn't have the equipment in its Williamsburg, Pennsylvania, plant to produce self-sealing envelopes. So the envelopes were manufactured at Westvaco's plant in Springfield, Massachusetts, where the copyright line was also applied on the reverse side beneath the flap. The envelopes were then sent to Williamsburg to have the indicia printed. This was done by the offset process on the company's Jet press rather than by flexography on its VH envelope-forming and printing machine, as had been the case with the earlier versions of the two envelopes.

The offset-printed images on the self-seal stationery were much clearer and crisper than the flexographic ones, which were printed directly from rubber plates. Whereas the stars were indistinct and the motto "E Pluribus Unum" was almost illegible on the first two envelope varieties, they were well-defined on the new ones. The typography was also different. The word "Official" measured 13 millimeters long on the first version, 14½mm long on the second. "USA" was 16mm long on the originals, 17mm long on the new envelopes. Also, the lettering and numerals on the original envelopes were slightly thicker than on the new ones.

The tagging on the earlier version was a medium-sized square, positioned to the left of the denomination. On the self-sealing version, the tagging was a long, vertical bar that appeared immediately to the left of the denomination.

The lettering in the return-address portion of the envelopes differed as well. On the earlier version, the letters were thicker and shorter than on the later version, making them appear boldface by comparison. The words "Department of State" measured 53mm on the first envelope varieties and 49½mm on the self-sealers. The remaining lettering on the later version was longer, however.

The Jet offset press used by Westvaco on the self-seal envelopes had previously been used to print the indicium on the Love envelope of 1989. The Love envelopes, like the self-sealers, were already formed when they received the stamped image; they had been cut, folded and sealed on the VH machine, which had also applied a background pattern of light blue diagonal lines by flexography.

First-Day Facts

The original announcement of the self-sealing envelopes gave collectors until August 8 to submit their requests for first-day covers. When the issue date was changed to August 10, the grace period was extended to September 9.

Like the earlier, conventionally sealed versions of the two envelopes, these could be obtained by collectors only by mail from the Philatelic Sales Division and at the Philatelic Center in the lobby of USPS headquarters in Washington. To obtain first-day covers, collectors were required to send a peelable return address label and 50¢ for each 45¢ envelope or 70¢ for each 65¢ envelope to the postmaster in Washington. USPS then added the official government return address, affixed the customer's labels and applied the cancellation.

65¢ OFFICIAL MAIL STAMPED ENVELOPE (SELF-SEALING)

Date of Issue: August 10, 1990

Catalog Number: Scott UO82

Colors: blue, black

First-Day Cancel: Washington, D.C.

FDCs Canceled: 6,759

Size: 8⅞ by 4⅜ inches

Watermark: none

Markings: ©USPS 1988 under flap. Penalty notation in upper-left corner. The word "Peel" appears in a repeat pattern on the release strip covering the grip-seal adhesive

Designer and Typographer: Bradbury Thompson (CSAC)

Art Director and Project Manager: Joe Brockert (USPS)

Printing: Westvaco-USEnvelope Division in two colors on a Jet offset press

Quantity Ordered: 262,500
Quantity Distributed: 262,500

Tagging: vertical bar to left of denomination

The Envelope

The 65¢ Penalty Mail self-sealing stamped envelope was created by USPS for use by the U.S. Department of State in passport mailings weighing between two and three ounces. It was issued with the 45¢ self-sealing envelope on August 10 in Washington, D.C. The two envelopes were printed by a different process from that used on the 45¢ and 65¢ envelopes issued earlier in the year. Details on the self-sealing varieties may be found in the preceding chapter.

25¢ FOOTBALL ENVELOPE

Date of Issue: September 9, 1990

Catalog Number: Scott U618

Colors: red; hologram

First-Day Cancel: Green Bay, Wisconsin (Green Bay Packer Hall of Fame)

FDCs Canceled: 54,589

Size: 10

Watermark: none

Markings: ©USPS 1990 under flap

Designer: Bruce Harman of Watsonville, California

Art Director and Project Manager: Joe Brockert

Typographer: John Boyd of Anagraphics Inc., New York City

Modeler: Light Impressions Inc., Santa Cruz, California

Printing: Holograms in rolls on foil by Light Impressions Inc. of Santa Cruz, California; Westvaco-USEnvelope Division printed in one-color flexography, affixed hologram and formed envelopes on a VH machine.

Quantity Ordered: 11,600,000
Quantity Distributed: 10,840,000

Tagging: vertical bar to right of hologram

The Envelope

The surprise entry of the year was a 25¢ hologram stamped envelope which was issued September 9 in Green Bay, Wisconsin, with only two days' advance notice. The envelope honored professional football, and its issuance coincided with the Green Bay Packers-Los Angeles Rams game on the first day of scheduled play in the National Football League's 1990-1991 season.

Unfortunately for the Postal Service, an elaborate plan to publicize the envelope nationally on the CBS television program *The NFL Today,* preceding live coverage of the day's games, fell through. Postmaster General Anthony M. Frank and NFL Commissioner Paul Tagliabue had been scheduled to deliver a videotaped message on the program, announcing the new envelope. "Television will bring more consumer attention to the envelope than all the other media combined," Dickey Rustin, manager of the USPS Stamp Product Development Branch, told *Linn's Stamp News* beforehand. But it didn't happen.

"We had a breakdown between the NFL and us, and as a result the taping was canceled," Rustin said afterward. "Someone failed to do what they were supposed to do."

Other events didn't go according to plan, either. For example, the USPS press release on the issue, dated September 7, said that "A first day pictorial postmark . . . will be available at the stadium," Green Bay's Lambeau Field. But this wasn't the case.

Postal employees, like the media, didn't get news of the envelope until a short time before the release date, and "it was too late to make available any retail facility at the stadium itself," Brian Holloway, director of marketing for USPS in Green Bay, told *Linn's* later. Instead, the postmark was applied at the Green Bay Packer Hall of Fame, which is located near the stadium.

The news release also said that "no first day of issue ceremony is planned." But on the morning of September 7, the local marketing department was given the go-ahead to conduct activities locally, and a brief ceremony was in fact held.

The envelope, issued in the Number 10 size, contained a holographic embossed image on a 1.23-inch by 1.25-inch square of metalized polyester that was attached to the envelope from the inside and showed through a die-cut opening. It was the second Postal Service product in less than a year to feature this kind of three-dimensional picture in the indicium.

The first, a Number 9 envelope depicting a futuristic Space Station, was issued December 3, 1989, at World Stamp Expo 89. The Space Station envelope proved to be extremely popular, postal officials said, and the initial print order of 20 million was followed by an order to print another 20 million. Postal customers who didn't normally buy stamped envelopes were asking for the holograms.

Pleased by the response, USPS decided to issue another hologram envelope before the anticipated 1991 rate change. Football was deemed an appropriate topic for autumn release and one that would offer some promising design possibilities, and officials of the NFL reacted positively to the idea.

Although the envelope that resulted wasn't billed as a commemorative, USPS in its announcement noted that the 1990-1991 NFL season would lead to the 25th anniversary Super Bowl game, to be played January 27, 1991, in Tampa, Florida. A reproduction of the Lombardi Trophy, which is presented annually to the winner of the Super Bowl, was featured prominently in the hologram.

The trophy, a silver football set at an angle on its base, is named for Vince Lombardi (1913-1970). Lombardi, coach and general manager of the Green Bay Packers from 1959 to 1968, is the man who coined the memorable, if inexplicable, slogan, "Winning isn't everything, it's the only thing." His Green Bay teams won NFL titles in 1961, 1962, 1965, 1966 and 1967, and won the first two Super Bowl games against the champions of the old American Football League following the 1966 and 1967 seasons.

Like all other stamped envelopes issued by USPS, this one was manufactured by Westvaco-US Envelope Division in Williamsburg, Pennsylvania. Westvaco assembled the envelopes and printed the "USA 25" and copyright line by flexography.

The holograms themselves were created by a firm called Light Impressions Inc. of Santa Cruz, California, and they were printed by

Bruce Harman painted two different foreground scenes, each featuring one offensive and two defensive players and the Lombardi Trophy. Note that the players' numbers, stockings, shoes and helmets differ in the two pictures.

a company called Spectratek. These were new suppliers for USPS; the Space Station holograms had been manufactured by American Bank Note Holographics Inc. of Elmsford, New York.

Joe Brockert, who served as art director and project manager for both the hologram envelopes, explained:

"Westvaco and the Postal Service decided mutually that American Bank Note Holographics simply would not be able to handle the quantity requirement of this envelope at the same time they were doing the Space Station envelope, which was still in production.

"We were already familiar with Light Impressions, and we agreed that this project should begin and end with an alternate manufacturer. Since Westvaco was actually the hologram buyer rather than the Postal Service, they made that recommendation to us.

"Westvaco was having some start-up problems with the Space Station; they were having some delivery delays on the hologram materials, and this was all just new to everybody. The hologram industry was being asked to manufacture things to specifications they had never manufactured before. They had never been asked to provide such a tight registration and repeat length. That was the critical part; the images had to be done to a precise repeat length to go into the window application in the envelopes.

"So Westvaco had to develop a system to accomplish this, and, once they had the system, the hologram industry had to meet the very exacting specifications to make it work. So everybody was doing something totally new.

"We were pleased with the results with the Space Station, but we knew we couldn't compound the question marks by throwing a second project into the same manufacturing cycle."

Brockert, along with technicians from USPS' Stamp Manufacturing Division and representatives of Westvaco, met early in the process with officials of Light Impressions. "We had less lead time on this one than on the Space Station, and we wanted to make sure that everybody was in on the ground floor," Brockert said.

"We decided that the quickest way to accomplish all this would be to have Light Impressions develop the artwork, with people who were familiar with their origination processes, with whom they could work closely. We probably could have developed the artwork ourselves, but we didn't want to take the chance that it wouldn't be compatible with their system. We knew they could originate art that would work for them, whereas we might be guessing."

The initial print order was for 10 million — half the number ordered of the Space Station hologram. With the rate change coming, USPS didn't want to run the risk of over-ordering and then having to shred large numbers of the envelopes.

"We thought we'd be conservative," Brockert said. "With this being the second hologram, it might attract less of the initial 'gee whiz' kind of attention. Also, larger mailers might be reluctant to order boxes of 500 that they might not use up in the next four or five months, before the new rates came in.

"So for those reasons we cut back to half the initial quantity of the Space Station, and we left the option available to reorder if the initial 10 million should sell out quickly."

The Football envelope, like other 25¢ envelopes, was sold at 30¢ each in quantities up to 500. Quantities of 500 or more were sold for $136, for a unit cost of 27.2¢. Custom-printed envelopes, bearing a return address, were offered at $15.20 per 50; before 1990, USPS had required a minimum order of 500 for this service.

The Design

While the design of the Space Station hologram was fairly self-explanatory, the new one may have puzzled some users. It combined a straightforward football scene — three players in action on a gridiron — with an out-of-context graphic element: the Lombardi Trophy (unidentified as such on the envelope) sitting on the turf in artificially enlarged form, towering over the players like an alien obstacle to the game.

The foreground plane of the hologram consisted of the trophy and the three players. Two of the players were defensive backs, one of whom appeared about to intercept a pass intended for the third player, an offensive receiver. The background plane included the lined turf beneath the players' feet, the sidelines, and a stadium tier full of spectators behind the players.

The general design concept for the hologram was worked out in the preliminary meeting between USPS staffers, Westvaco and Light

This stadium scene and lined playing field painted by Bruce Harman is similar to the artwork he provided for the hologram.

Impressions. Early in the talks, it was decided that the design would have to include both the Lombardi Trophy and two or three players.

"After talking with Light Impressions," Joe Brockert recalled, "we decided that the trophy should be a foreground object, on the same plane with the players. We couldn't have it fading into the background. Despite the fact that the trophy is all silver, and wouldn't give us a lot of color in the foreground, it had to have enough clarity and detail that it had to be a foreground image, even though we were going to have to sacrifice a little bit of color and excitement, if you will, to accomplish this."

Three West Coast artists were asked to submit sketches. They were given the basic requirements: the trophy and some football action in the foreground; a separate rendering of a stadium or stands that would provide the necessary depth in the finished product. Because time was short, USPS and Light Impressions quickly settled on one artist, Bruce Harman of Watsonville, California, whose work was well-known to the hologram maker. In addition to the pass-interception scene that was chosen for the final art, Harman did an alternative painting of a ball-carrier dodging two tacklers.

"The envelope hologram was the first widespread application of a new '2D/3D' process which Light Impressions developed," Brockert said. "It's the equivalent of a full-color hologram. If you look very closely at the image on the envelope, you can see that there are flesh tones on the players, that the jerseys actually change colors with the angle of vision: that sometimes they appear purple, sometimes they appear turquoise, sometimes they go orange. You can see the green

The differing sizes of lettering and denominations on these stamped envelopes look like die varieties, but are caused by wear on the flexographic plates.

grass reflected in the underside of the trophy. It's not your usual flat-color type of hologram image; there actually is the holographic equivalent of process colors going on in there."

The ever-changing nature of the uniform colors constituted insurance for USPS against any possible accusation that it was depicting identifiable football teams on the envelope. As a further precaution, however, Harman was directed to avoid placing any markings on jerseys or helmets that would closely resemble those of actual teams.

Brockert and John Boyd of Anagraphics Inc. worked out the typography, which was printed by flexography on the envelope next to the hologram's window. They decided they needed a "USA 25" with a sports look to it, and Boyd found a typeface resembling the letters and numbers found on football jerseys. Boyd added a thin outline around the numbers and letters after Westvaco officials gave assurances that the lines wouldn't break down as the rubber flexographic plates underwent wear.

(Actually, collectors did notice variations in the thickness of the lettering and numbers during the course of production, but there were no early reports of breakdown of the outlines themselves.)

For the ink to print the lettering and numerals, Brockert and Boyd chose a red that Brockert described as a little "warmer" than the red used for the denomination on the standard 25¢ Circle of Stars envelope that was issued in 1988.

First-Day Facts

A brief first-day ceremony was held at 9 a.m. Sunday, September 9, at the Green Bay Packer Hall of Fame, with Green Bay Postmaster Danny Jackson presiding. Those attending were given first-day postmarked envelopes free, but there was no first-day program.

The availability of the first-day cancellation was announced on

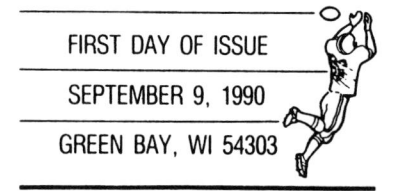

FIRST DAY OF ISSUE
SEPTEMBER 9, 1990
GREEN BAY, WI 54303

USPS used this pictorial postmark for first-day covers of the Football envelope.

the scoreboard of Lambeau Field during the Packers-Rams game. This announcement and other local publicity aided in the sale of an estimated 10,000 envelopes.

Because of the absence of any advance announcement, collectors were given 60 days to order first-day covers, until November 8, rather than the customary 30 days.

Green Bay had been the site of a previous first-day ceremony on July 7, 1934, when the 3¢ Wisconsin Tercentenary stamp, depicting explorer Jean Nicolet landing on the shores of the bay that gives the city its name, was dedicated there.

POSTAL CARDS

In 1990, USPS continued to use and explore the possibilities of the once-lowly postal card. Eight new varieties were issued, seven of them printed on the Government Printing Office's five-color Roland Man offset press. GPO installed that press in 1987 to enhance postal-card quality, and most observers would agree that it has done that job extremely well.

The Citizens' Stamp Advisory Committee continued to pursue its policy of using postal cards to commemorate anniversaries of institutions and events in categories that it had decreed to be inappropriate for postage stamps. Thus, there were cards for the centennials of Stanford University, the Chicago Symphony and the Daughters of the American Revolution. (The last of these was issued despite several years of vigorous campaigning by DAR officers for a postage stamp, reinforced by the promise of a previous postmaster general that they would have one.)

Two of the 1990 postal cards were picture postal cards, retailing at 50¢ each, which included the 15¢ postage. One was the DAR card; the other was what USPS called an "EXTRAordinary Art Card," a new subcategory in which paintings by U.S. artists would be reproduced on the picture side and in the indicium. Picture postal cards, of which four have now been issued, are an attractive new product, but USPS has been slow to find an effective way to market them, or even to make a convincing case that it will be able to do so.

The most unusual card of the year was the experimental Postal Buddy change-of-address card, designed by USPS but laser-printed on demand in special computer-equipped vending machines.

AMERICAN PAPERMAKING POSTAL CARD

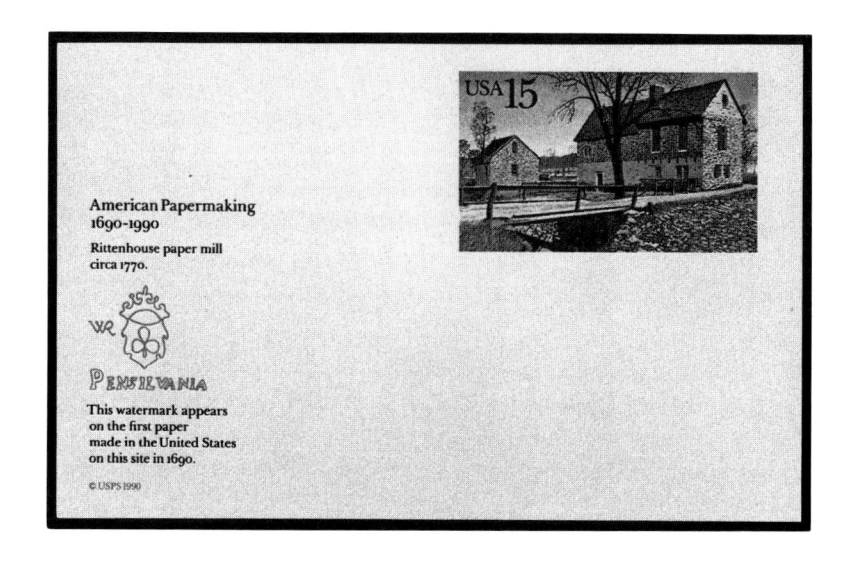

Date of Issue: March 13, 1990

Catalog Number: Scott UX145

Colors: magenta, yellow, cyan and black

First-Day Cancel: New York, New York

FDCs Canceled: 9,866

Format: Printed in 80-card sheets, but available only in single cards. Printing plates of 80 subjects 18 across, 10 around.

Size: 5½ by 3½ inches

Markings: ©USPS 1990

Designer: Harry Devlin of Mountainside, New Jersey

Art Director and Typographer: Bradbury Thompson (CSAC)

Project Manager: Joe Brockert (USPS)

Printing: U.S. Government Printing Office (GPO) on a five-color Roland Man 800 sheetfed offset press.

Quantity Ordered: 8,000,000
Quantity Distributed: 8,000,000

Tagging: vertical bar to right of stamp

The Postal Card

The American Paper Institute asked USPS for a commemorative stamp to be issued in 1990 to mark the 300th anniversary of papermaking in America, which began with the establishment of the Rittenhouse paper mill in Germantown, Pennsylvania, in 1690. The Citizens' Stamp Advisory Committee considered the subject an appropriate one, but, because a substantial number of stamps had already been scheduled for 1990, CSAC chose to recommend a postal card instead.

Finding an appropriate design was a problem. There was no picture of the original Rittenhouse mill, and "the 300th anniversary of papermaking didn't lend itself to a lot of visual images," said Joe Brockert of USPS, the project manager. Eventually it was decided to use a 19th-century photograph of the third and last Rittenhouse mill, a building that was erected around 1770.

CSAC briefly considered making the item a picture postal card, like the White House and Jefferson Memorial cards that had been issued in late 1989 for sale to visitors to Washington, D.C. Bradbury Thompson, design coordinator for CSAC, mocked up such a card, using the old photograph of the third mill for both the indicium and the picture side. But the building itself is gone; the site is now part of Philadelphia's Fairmount Park, near the intersection of Lincoln Drive and Rittenhouse Street, and isn't a significant tourist attraction. For that reason, the committee concluded that there would be no great demand for a picture card. A card in the Historic Preservation series would have been, by definition, inappropriate for a structure that no longer existed. So CSAC in the end opted simply for a commemorative postal card.

The item was a late addition to the USPS stamp and stationery program for 1990; it was announced on February 15, 1990, and issued March 13 at the annual meeting of the American Paper Institute in New York City.

In the earliest years of the American colonies, paper was a low-priority need. Newspapers didn't exist until after 1700. There were few books except those brought from abroad. Stephen Daye's press began printing in Cambridge, Massachusetts, in 1639 (an event that was commemorated by a stamp, Scott 857, in 1939), and other presses were set up in Boston, New York and Philadelphia, but the printed output was small. Correspondence wasn't extensive, and writing was largely left to the ministers and public officials. Imports took care of what demand for paper existed.

The opening of the first American paper mill wasn't inspired by any widespread public need, but rather from the combination of the small requirements of a single printer in Philadelphia, William Bradford, and the ambition of a newly arrived German papermaker, Wilhelm Rittinghuysen, who had anglicized his name to William

Rittenhouse. With three other investors they leased 20 acres on the banks of the Wissahickon Creek in September 1690 and built a mill in a little ravine on the banks of a stream, called Paper-Mill Run, that emptied into the Wissahickon.

William's son Claus was the principal papermaker at the mill, and over the next 15 years the Rittenhouses bought out the other partners and became sole owners. Bradford moved to New York in 1693, where he became the first well-known American printer and publisher, but he depended on the Rittenhouse mill — still the only source of paper in the colonies — to provide him with "printing paper, good writing paper and blue paper." Pennsylvanians found the mill an interesting addition, and one rhyming historian referred to it (and its need for raw materials) in this couplet:

"Kind friends when thy old shift is rent
Let it to th' paper mill be sent."

In 1700 or 1701 the original mill was destroyed by a flood, and a new mill was built below the site of the old one in 1702. William died in 1708, and Claus continued operations until his own death in 1734. The mill was left to Claus' son William. In later generations the building was reconstructed in whole or in part several times. Eventually a third mill was built farther down on Paper Mill Run by the third William Rittenhouse. This building, the one depicted on the postal card, survived nearly to the close of the 19th century.

Most of the paper made in the Rittenhouse mill was watermarked. The first watermark was the single word "Company." The second was a double; on one-half of the sheet was the monogram WR and on the other half was a shield, surmounted by a fleur-de-lis crest and bearing on its face a clover leaf — which was the town seal of Germantown — and beneath this device was the word "PENSILVANIA" in hollow capitals.

The Design

"Brad Thompson said to me, 'I've found this wonderful house painter for the card,' " Joe Brockert recalled with a smile, "and I had this instant vision of somebody who slaps paint on the sides of houses!" In fact, the person Thompson had in mind to design the papermaking postal card was Harry Devlin of Mountainside, New Jersey, one of the nation's leading architectural artists.

Devlin specializes in paintings of 19th-century homes of the eastern United States. His work captures the profuse details of the so-called Romantic era when domestic architecture was exuberant, expressive and diverse, with such indulgences as fanlights and sidelights, wrought-iron filigree, cupolas, pillars, octagonal rooms.

Seventy-two of his paintings, done over a 30-year period, were collected in a book with text by the artist, *Portraits of American Architecture,* that was published in the November 1989. Devlin sent a copy of the book to his old friend Stevan Dohanos, a former chairman and design coordinator for CSAC who had personally designed some 27 U.S. stamps. Dohanos, in turn, showed the book to Bradbury Thompson, and Thompson, as art director for the papermaking postal card, decided that he wanted Harry Devlin to translate the old photograph of the Rittenhouse mill into a painting for the card's indicium.

Devlin had done many different kinds of artwork in his 72 years. Among other things, he had been an editorial cartoonist for *Collier's* and *The New York Daily News,* and he and his wife Wende had collaborated on 21 children's books, with Harry providing the illustrations. This was his first postal design project, however. Some parts of the old photograph he used as his reference were obscure, particularly around the windows, and "I sort of reconstructed it," Devlin said. "It's quite accurate, though," he added. "There were only a few areas that I had to use my discretion on."

This is Bradbury Thompson's mock-up of both sides of a proposed picture postal card using a 19th-century photograph of the Rittenhouse mill in Germantown.

249

Converting the black and white of the photograph into color, Devlin painted the old stone building, with a smaller outbuilding and a wooden bridge over the stony-banked stream in the foreground. The bare branches of the trees, including a large one in front of the mill, indicated that the season was winter. Devlin did his painting in oil on gesso, and the committee asked for no changes. The finished work was 17 inches wide, which was as large as USPS would allow. "It's one of the smallest paintings I've done in years," the artist said.

As printed on the card, the image area was about 1¼ inches deep, making it slightly larger than most postal card indicia. It contained no typography other than "USA 15." All information about the theme of the card was contained in the cachet area.

The cachet offered a lot of facts in a limited space. "American Papermaking/1690-1990/Rittenhouse paper mill/circa 1770" appeared in four lines of black type. Beneath, in blue, was a replica of the second Rittenhouse watermark with the WR monogram and the shield with clover leaf. Below that, in four more lines of black, was "This watermark appears/on the first paper/made in the United States/on this site in 1690."

First-Day Facts

Postmaster General Anthony M. Frank dedicated the card March 13 as part of his address to the American Paper Institute at its annual meeting at New York's Waldorf-Astoria Hotel. Norma Pace of the USPS Board of Governors also took part in the ceremony.

15¢ LITERACY POSTAL CARD

Date of Issue: March 22, 1990

Catalog Number: Scott UX146

Colors: black, red, blue and gold

First-Day Cancel: Washington, D.C.

FDCs Canceled: 11,163

Format: Printed in 80-card sheets but available only in single cards. Printing plates of 80 subjects (8 across, 10 around).

Size: 5½ by 3½ inches

Markings: ©USPS 1990

Designer, Art Director and Project Manager: Joe Brockert (USPS)

Modeler: John Boyd of Anagraphics Inc. of New York

Typographer: Bradbury Thompson (CSAC)

Printing: U.S. Government Printing Office (GPO) on a five-color Roland Man 80 sheetfed offset press

Quantity Ordered: 15,000,000
Quantity Distributed: 14,200,000

Tagging: vertical bar to right of stamp

The Postal Card

For many years, U.S. stamps have been used to promote causes that are worthy and non-controversial. Called "message stamps" by the Postal Service and "propaganda stamps" by the irreverent, they have exhorted Americans to do such things as employ the handicapped, register and vote, stop traffic accidents, preserve the environment, prevent drug abuse, volunteer, be wise shoppers and take a bite out of crime.

A 1971 stamp proclaiming that "Giving blood saves lives" was credited by the Postal Service with bringing about a noticeable increase in blood donations. Less successful was the 1981 stamp with the inscription: "Alcoholism/You can beat it!" Not a few letter writers, afraid that the message would be taken personally, chose not to place it on their envelopes.

On March 22, 1990, an advocacy postal card was issued, its purpose to heighten public awareness of the importance of literacy. The card wasn't announced in advance, and all first-day and design information was released after it was placed on sale.

Although literacy was a cause enthusiastically embraced by First Lady Barbara Bush, and Mrs. Bush was present at the dedication ceremony for the postal card, she hadn't campaigned for a card or a stamp. The prime mover in this case was the Government Printing Office, which manufactures postal cards for USPS but doesn't normally suggest topics for them.

The customer service office of the GPO originated the idea of a card that would promote both literacy and printing; such a card, the office believed, could be issued in connection with a Literacy Week observance. The proposal was endorsed by Ralph E. Kennickell Jr., the public printer (which is the title of the presidentially appointed head of the GPO), and submitted to the Postal Service. To support

This is the original design idea for Literacy promotion that was proposed to USPS by the Government Printing Office.

the proposal, Kennickell sent over to USPS a design created by his typographic and design staff. It included the message: "Reading Opens The Door To Knowledge/Printing Opens the Door to Reading/Literacy Week."

USPS officials expressed interest, particularly in the literacy aspect. "At the time we knew that with the incoming (Bush) administration, there might be an interest in promoting literacy," said Joe Brockert of USPS, who would become the project manager-art director-designer of the postal card. "So we proceeded to see what we could develop and have available if, in fact, there was a request from the White House to do this."

As it happened, 1990 was International Literacy Year, and a few countries, including Canada, planned to issue appropriate stamps. Brockert worked with John Boyd of Anagraphics Inc., the New York firm that produces most of the lettering for U.S. stamp and postal stationery designs, to develop a design that the Citizens' Stamp Advisory Committee liked. The committee recommended the Literacy postal card for inclusion in the USPS 1990 program.

Assistant Postmaster General Gordon Morison told a reporter that issuing the item as a postal card instead of a stamp was appropriate because the two groups that most actively promote literacy — schools and libraries — are heavy users of postal cards. He said he hoped the Literacy card would be used by libraries to remind readers to return overdue books and by schools to remind parents to attend school meetings.

Illiteracy is a major problem in the United States, where between 20 million and 30 million adults can't decipher street signs or read help-wanted ads or simple instructions — in short, are shut out of the general day-to-day life that constantly employs the symbols of language. Barbara Bush, who had a lifelong interest in education and who was accustomed to instilling the joy of reading in her 10 grandchildren, decided while her husband was vice president to make the promotion of literacy her pet project.

For eight years Mrs. Bush seized every opportunity, speaking, visiting learning centers, schools, clinics and prisons, meeting new learners and volunteer tutors, encouraging, supporting and leading the way. She became, in the words of *The Saturday Evening Post,* "universally regarded as the most important national resource the literacy movement has." Among the many she converted to her cause was Harold W. McGraw Jr. of McGraw-Hill, who created the Business Council for Effective Literacy. Highlighting her crusade was the dramatic moment July 4, 1988, witnessed by millions of Americans on TV, when Mrs. Bush and J.T. Pace, a 63-year-old sharecropper's son who had learned to read only one year before, together read aloud the Preamble to the Constitution.

After she became First Lady, her efforts in this direction received even more public attention. In February 1990 Mrs. Bush enlisted her husband to preside over "To Be Free: The National Literacy Honors from the White House," at which presentations were made to eight successful new learners and contributors to the cause. "I believe if we can lick the problem of people being functionally illiterate — unable to read or write at the fifth-grade level — we will then go on to solve most of the other major problems besetting this country," she once told syndicated columnist Liz Smith.

The Design

The indicium displayed a blue Earth superimposed over the gold pages of an open book. In two lines of black below the image and to the left was the slogan: "The world/is an open book." "15 USA" was above and to the left, in red. Unlike most recent postal cards, this one was printed in four dedicated colors — black, red, blue and gold — rather than with a blend of process colors.

"These public-service things are always the hardest things to design," Joe Brockert said. "In this case, the slogan actually came first, and then the artwork."

Brockert told how he arrived at the slogan "The world is an open book," using the GPO's suggested "Reading opens the door to knowledge" as a jumping-off point. "I thought, an open book would seem to make sense — and then, books open the world to all kinds of things — and that's the way it went.

"After I had the slogan, I realized that we had some graphic images sitting around in various bits and pieces from other projects, and they would be ideal. For example, the book is from a piece of graphic art that had been prepared for the Federalist Papers postal card of 1988. The Earth, including the gridlines, was something we had available from a version of the non-denominated 'E' envelope that we had prepared in 1988 but never issued."

Brockert sketched his design idea in pencil, and John Boyd prepared an essay using the globe, book and pieces of type to show the members of CSAC. Following Brockert's sketch, he placed the slogan at the top and the denomination-USA logo at the bottom. But this caused the slogan to break awkwardly: "The world is an/open book." On the advice of Bradbury Thompson, USPS design coordinator and typography expert, the typographical elements were

The Literacy postal card design was based on this rough sketch by Joe Brockert.

switched, enabling the slogan to break in a more logical fashion: "The world/is an open book."

In the cachet area of the card, Brockert had Boyd place the secondary slogan: "Literacy:/a stronger future,/a better world." An earlier version had read: "Literacy: Learn and teach by reading."

"The idea of the 'learn and teach' slogan was to try to give both ends of the literacy issue, that it's important to teach literacy and also to acquire it if you needed to," Brockert said. "But it wasn't very effective. Also, obviously, an illiterate person wasn't going to get that message, so we decided that illiterate people constituted an audience we didn't particularly need to target; that what we needed to do was offer a more generic literacy message."

The "stronger future, better world" wording "probably came out of a brainstorming session that Don McDowell (director of the Stamps Division) and I had in his office," Brockert said.

As it turned out, the word "world" appeared in both the indicium and cachet messages on the completed card, but no one on the committee was bothered by that. In reviewing the artwork, however, CSAC members did suggest that because computer literacy was also worth promoting, the theme of the card could be extended to embrace that kind of skill as well.

"So we said, well, it would make sense then to make the inscription in the lower corner look as if it was reading off a computer screen," Brockert said. "So we came back to the committee with the computer image, and the design was approved at that point."

Brockert and Boyd, in consultation with the GPO, also experimented with the colors. They considered using a metallic gold for the open book, but when the gold was applied to a large area it "read" as brown, making the book look as if it was made of kraft paper. Canary yellow was tried, but that too was unsatisfactory; the

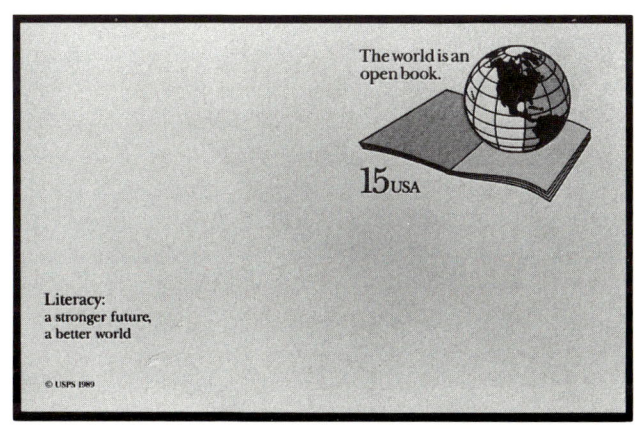

In this essay, the arrangement of the design elements is different from that of the finished card, the shading on the globe is different and no computer terminal is shown.

Postmaster General Frank and First Lady Barbara Bush unveil the Literacy postal card at the White House.

book looked too much like the Yellow Pages.

"We decided we needed something with a nice gold tone that wasn't too yellow and yet wasn't so dark as to be brown and cause us to lose the detailed lines of the pages," Brockert said. "So we had GPO give us proofs in different colors, and we eventually got to the right shade of orange."

Brockert had been listed previously as the designer of several stamped envelopes, but this was the first postal card for which he received design credit.

First-Day Facts

The brief lunchtime first-day ceremony on the White House grounds was closed to the public. After Postmaster General Frank unveiled the design of the postal card, Barbara Bush delivered a few remarks. Her husband, President Bush, "wants to wipe illiteracy out before the end of this century," she said. The first lady then answered a few questions from the approximately 20 members of the press who were present.

15¢ GEORGE CALEB BINGHAM
PICTURE POSTAL CARD

Date of Issue: May 4, 1990

Catalog Number: Scott UX147

Colors: magenta, cyan, yellow and black

First-Day Cancel: St. Louis, Missouri

FDCs Canceled: 13,632

Format: Printed on Krome Coat paper in 72-card sheets but available only in single cards. Printing plates of 72 subjects (8 across, 9 around).

Size: 5½ by 3½ inches

Markings: ©USPS 1990

Designer and Typographer: Bradbury Thompson (CSAC)

Art Director and Project Manager: Joe Brockert (USPS)

Printing: U.S. Government Printing Office (GPO) on a five-color Roland Man 800 sheetfed offset press.

Quantity Ordered: 6,000,000
Quantity Distributed: 2,771,000

Tagging: vertical bar to right of stamp

The Postal Card

The Postal Service announced on June 1, 1989, that its 1990 stamp and stationery program would include a stamp honoring the American artist George Caleb Bingham. Later, USPS switched signals and said Bingham would get a postal card instead. This surprised some collectors; many artists had been postally commemorated in the past, often with illustrations of their works, but always on stamps. Postal cards had never been used for this purpose.

All became clear on April 25, 1990, when USPS disclosed the details. The special qualities of the government-issued, prepaid postal card would be exploited to display a work of art more completely and faithfully than the Postal Service had been able to do before. The Bingham card would be a picture card, like the White House and Jefferson Memorial cards issued at World Stamp Expo 89 for the tourist trade. One full side would feature a glossy color reproduction of Bingham's well-known painting *Fur Traders Descending the Missouri.* On the address and message side, the same painting would be reproduced in miniature as an indicium.

The card was given the trademarked "EXTRAordinary" designation, which USPS reserves for unusual postal items — most of which are sold at a premium over face value. The Bingham "art card," as USPS called it, retailed at 50¢, representing a 35¢ markup over its 15¢ postage value. This was the same price that had been charged for the two Washington-scene picture postal cards. USPS said the 50¢ price was comparable to the price of commercial picture postcards when the cost of postage was included.

Like the two earlier cards, this one was offered to wholesalers at a discount for quantity purchases. But postal officials were reluctant to predict that the product would be a commercial success. The most logical market for art cards would be the retail shops run by art museums. However, USPS had no sales force available to push the cards to these potential customers, and it was unclear how the Postal Service expected to generate enough demand to make the cards a profitable item to produce.

The Bingham card was issued at the St. Louis Art Museum in St. Louis, Missouri, on May 4, near the end of a major exhibition of

George Caleb Bingham, in a self-portrait made while he was in his early 20s. The portrait is in the St. Louis Art Museum.

Bingham's two different versions of Jolly Flatboatmen in Port *were both considered for stamp designs. One version was privately owned and thus ineligible for reproduction on a stamp; the other showed a boatman swigging whiskey from a jug, a detail that some committee members feared would offend the public.*

Bingham's work, which the museum had organized. The exhibition consisted of 49 paintings from the museum's own and other collections (including *Fur Traders,* borrowed from the Metropolitan Museum of Art in New York City). Most of these works were what are known as genre paintings, meaning that they depicted commonplace events of everyday life. Also shown were a group of the detailed, finished drawings the artist had made in preparation for the paintings. The showing ended May 13, and most of the paintings then moved to the National Gallery in Washington, where they were exhibited from July 15 through September 30, while the National Museum of American Art in the capital showed the drawings.

The Citizens' Stamp Advisory Committee had discussed a stamp for Bingham for many years, and had examined a number of design proposals based on various paintings. However, some of these, when cropped to fit in a vertical or horizontal stamp frame, lost much of their effectiveness. Others presented other kinds of problems: For instance, committee members were afraid that some people might be offended at the glimpse of a boatman drinking liquor from a jug on *Jolly Flatboatmen in Port.* Still others were privately owned, and thus ineligible for reproduction on a U.S. stamp because of the likelihood that it would enhance the value of the original.

In 1981 the committee recommended a stamp depicting *Fur Traders Descending the Missouri,* and then-Postmaster General William F. Bolger approved it. The stamp never was issued, however. Bureau officials expressed their doubts that the dark-toned painting could be effectively reproduced in stamp size by any of the available methods — gravure, offset-intaglio or multicolor intaglio.

"It's the problem the committee has had for years in trying to put fine art on stamps," said Joe Brockert, project manager for the postal card. "The committee on the one hand wants to do it, and on the other hand realizes that trying to reduce a master painting down to postage stamp size is not always the most successful endeavor.

"But when CSAC began developing the two-sided picture postal card, it decided that this might be an appropriate avenue to consider for fine art. A lot of museums already publish little prints of some of their paintings, and so we did some proofs and tests, and we thought that this would probably be the best way to go."

The purchase by the Metropolitan Museum of *Fur Traders* in 1933 signaled a revival of interest in George Caleb Bingham. The interest continues to this day, and is reflected in prices: A 1987 auction of his 1846 painting *The Jolly Flatboatmen* brought $6 million.

Bingham (1811-1879) was born in Virginia, moved to Missouri with his family when he was 8, lived beside the Missouri River, taught himself to paint, resolved to earn money and fame as a portrait artist, and set out to find commissions. "If men refuse to have their faces transferred to canvas," he wrote in 1835 to his future wife, "I will look out for subjects among the dogs and cats." He did find willing human subjects, but none whose portraits would gain him the national acclaim he desired.

About half the sky in **Fur Traders Descending the Missouri** *had to be cropped to make the painting fit the rectangular dimensions of a picture postal card.*

In 1841 he moved to Washington and shared a studio in the Capitol basement, hoping to win portrait assignments from VIPs. He had little success, and after a few years he moved back to Missouri. Here he began a series of genre paintings that brought him national notice as "the Missouri Artist." They were welcome in a time when America was beginning to look to itself rather than to Europe for its culture. Today they are collectively considered his greatest achievement.

Gail King, in *The Wall Street Journal,* wrote that Bingham's genre art depicts "a settled, pastoral Missouri where there is time for play and song and dance and pets. His dogs form a Greek chorus: perky, sleeping, sniffing, cowering, snarling, staring. The genre paintings do not advertise the mud, floating bodies, mosquitoes or snakes that were a part of the Missouri River frontier."

In 1845 Bingham sent *Fur Traders,* which he first called *Fur Trader and his Half-Breed Son,* to the American Art-Union of New York, which bought paintings from artists, exhibited them and awarded them by lottery to its members, who paid $5 for memberships. The Art-Union paid him $75 for the painting and awarded it to Robert S. Bunker of Mobile, Alabama.

Verlyn Klinkenborg, writing in *Smithsonian,* described the work as Bingham's "masterpiece." It is the only painting, he wrote, in which Bingham allowed "an atmospheric mood, an emotion aroused by oblique sources, to supplant his customary directness." Klinkenborg developed the thought:

"The painting can of course be 'read,' as paintings of its kind were meant to be in the 19th century. It is a rising dawn, and this pair slips quietly down the widening Missouri toward St. Louis and its broadwater civilization in the Mississippi. The half-breed boy, the chained fox in the bow, the bundled furs, are all indications of wildness brought within the bounds of commerce, signs of America's ascending historical destiny.

"Such a reading, which emphasizes the downstream flow of this painting, is completely consistent with Bingham's beliefs, which, true to his time, were exuberantly expansionist. But it is not enough. The laconic figure of the fox hunched over its vertical shadow, the posture of the boy leaning back upstream, even the trader's upright paddle and the smoke drifting from his pipe counterbalance the flow

Bingham's **Boatmen on the Missouri** *of 1846 was tested in a horizontal stamp design.*

of the Missouri, while the boy's inscrutable gaze throws everything into question . . . *Fur Traders* can certainly be read as a painting in which the wilderness is brought into the frame of civilization, tending ever downriver. But it is more ambiguous than that, and ambiguity is an important source of its effect. Backlit by the diffuse light of the rising sun, offset by an island still in shadow, barely accented by a line of ducks wheeling over the far shore, these exotic figures are just as redolent of where they have been as of where they are going. And as time moves the viewer farther and farther downstream from the wilderness, it seems more and more as if this painting leads us upstream in imagination to the wilder country from which this man and boy have just descended."

Parenthetically, Klinkenborg's conclusion that the animal in the canoe is a fox is open to debate. It has been variously identified. The National Gallery, when it displayed the painting, called it a bear cub. Close examination of the painting itself shows the beast to have a sharp nose, thus eliminating a cat as a possibility. This facial feature is much less distinct on the postal card — particularly in the indicium — but it can be made out in the enlarged picture-side reproduction with the help of a magnifying glass.

The Design

Bradbury Thompson, design coordinator for CSAC, adapted the painting for the two sides of the postal card, and also designed the typography. On the picture side, about half the sky had to be cropped at the top to make the squarish original fit into postcard dimensions, and for the indicium the painting required an even tighter cropping that eliminated virtually all the sky along with a small amount of river at either end of the canoe.

In the upper left on the postage side, the words "Fur Traders Descending the Missouri/George Caleb Bingham, 1845/Metropolitan Museum of Art" appeared in three lines of light blue type.

This detail from The Wood-Boat *by George Caleb Bingham was fitted into a vertically arranged stamp design.*

First-Day Facts

Comer S. Coppie, senior assistant postmaster general, dedicated the card May 4 in the St. Louis Art Museum auditorium. He replaced Jerry K. Lee Sr., regional postmaster general, who had been named in the original announcement. Curator Michael Shapiro was the principal speaker, and James D. Burke, director of the museum, gave the welcome.

The late announcement by USPS of the first-day ceremony plans caused at least one St. Louis collector to miss a chance to attend the ceremony in his city. USPS' announcement, dated April 25, was published in the issue of *Stamp Collector* dated May 5 and the *Linn's Stamp News* dated May 7. "Doesn't the USPS realize that many collectors cannot take off from work on short notice to attend a ceremony?" the frustrated collector wrote to *Linn's. Linn's* commented on the letter with an editorial complaining that the Postal Service's traditional practice of providing first-day information in timely fashion had, in recent weeks, "unaccountably deteriorated into (an attitude) of foot-dragging indifference."

15¢ ISAAC ROYALL HOUSE POSTAL CARD
HISTORIC PRESERVATION SERIES

Date of Issue: June 16, 1990

Catalog Number: Scott UX148

Colors: magenta, yellow, cyan and black

First-Day Cancel: Medford, Massachusetts (Royall House)

FDCs Canceled: 21,708

Format: Printed in 80-card sheets but available only in single cards. Printing plates of 80 subjects (8 across, 10 around)

Size: 5½ by 3½ inches

Markings: ©USPS 1990

Designer: Frank Constantino of Winthrop, Massachusetts

Art Director and Typographer: Richard Sheaff (CSAC)

Project Manager: Joe Brockert (USPS)

Printing: U.S. Government Printing Office (GPO) on a five-color Roland Man 800 sheetfed offset press

Quantity Ordered: 12,000,000
Quantity Distributed: 12,000,000

Tagging: vertical bar to right of stamp

The Postal Card

The Isaac Royall House, considered one of the finest examples of Georgian design in Colonial America, was the subject of a 15¢ postal card in the Historic Preservation series that was issued June 16 in Medford, Massachusetts, a suburb of Boston.

The card was the 13th in a series that began in 1977, and the first in the set to depict a building in New England. A card for the Royall House was the idea of Dr. Mardges Bacon, professor of art and architecture at Northeastern University, and a director of the Society of Architectural Historians.

In the spring of 1988 the SAH was looking ahead to its 50th anniversary in 1990. The organization, made up of academics, architects and laypeople with a common interest in historic preservation, hoped to use the anniversary to help promote that interest. Dr. Bacon spoke with a member of the Citizens' Stamp Advisory Committee about the possibility of getting a commemorative stamp and was told that USPS already had a heavy schedule of stamps but that a Historic Preservation postal card might be a possibility.

"I discussed with my fellow board members an appropriate building for the subject," Dr. Bacon said. "Because the SAH was founded in Boston, and we were going to have our 50th anniversary celebration there, we thought that it would be nice to have something that would coincide with this. Our schedule and the Postal Service's didn't quite mesh and the card came out after our meeting.

"We wanted to show a property that represented a sustained commitment to preservation. The Isaac Royall House Association, which owns and operates the house, was an example of one such organization in the Boston area. Many buildings in New England are owned and operated by very large organizations with a large endowment. But Medford is a tiny town, and a lot of effort is done by a very small number of individuals at the Isaac Royall House Association. We were interested in honoring a smaller organization like this one that wouldn't normally get the recognition."

Also figuring in the choice, she said, was the fact that the Isaac Royall House had been among the buildings that SAH members had visited on the organization's first-ever field trip in July 1940.

In June of 1988, Dr. Bacon wrote a proposal for the postal card, describing the significance of the house as an unusually well-preserved example of Georgian architecture. As a professor, she was accustomed to writing proposals to accompany grant applications, but this time the purpose was a new one. The letter went to CSAC along with a letter of endorsement from William A. Slagle Jr., president of the Isaac Royall House Association. Also included were documentation of the historical importance of the house from published sources, and color transparencies of the front and back of the building, which the organization had hired a photographer to make.

Dr. Bacon learned in the summer of 1989 that USPS had commissioned artist Frank Constantino to make sketches of the house, and surmised, correctly, that the postal card had been approved.

The Isaac Royall House Association, which owns and maintains the building, was pleased with the publicity that attended the issuance of the postal card. Visitorship at the house more than doubled thereafter, according to Jay B. Griffin, the curator.

The house is a handsome 3½-story structure that began as a simple 2½-story building, one room deep, built by Governor John Winthrop in 1637. A later owner added a lean-to at the rear in 1692. Then, in 1732, Isaac Royall Sr. came to Medford after 33 years as a prosperous sugar planter in Antigua, West Indies, and bought a 500-acre estate that included the house. Over the next few years he transformed it into a mansion surrounded by quarters for the 27 slaves he brought from Antigua, farm outbuildings, orchards, gardens and a summer gazebo.

The structure's east, or main, facade is a clapboard wall, painted gray, with quoined corners simulating cornerstones, all applied over the original brick. The windows are connected vertically by spandrel panels. The west facade is altogether different; instead of clapboards, matched boards were cut to imitate stonemasonry, and above the windows on the first two floors are classical pediments. The end walls, in brick, rise to twin chimneys joined by parapets.

After Royall's death in 1739, his son and namesake inherited the estate. Born in Antigua in 1719, Isaac Jr. was schooled in Boston, served on the Governor's Council and was chairman of selectmen in

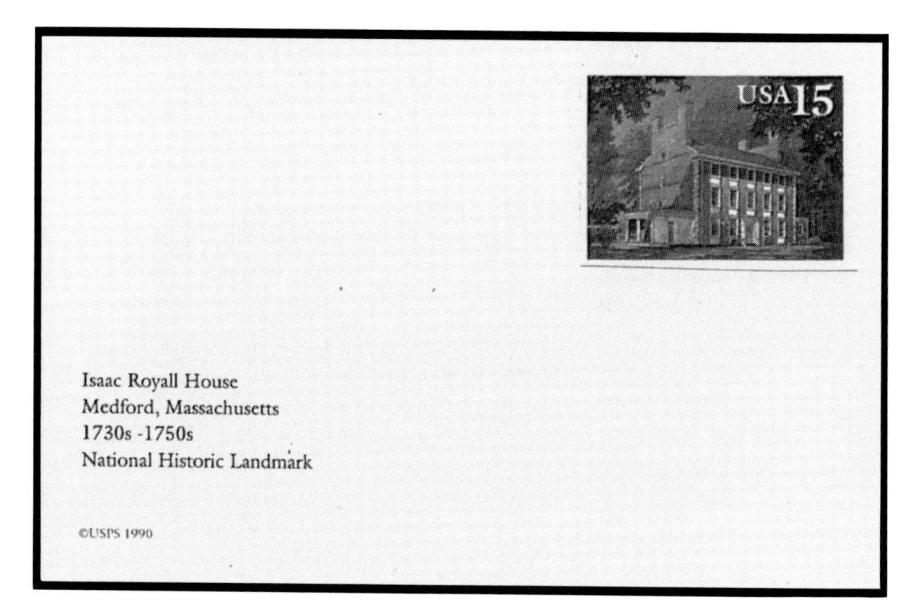

An early mock-up of the card with a preliminary draft of the cachet inscription.

266

both Charlestown and Medford. When the Revolution broke out, he remained loyal to the crown, and sailed for England after the British evacuated Boston in 1776. In his absence, the patriots confiscated the manor house and grounds. The house became the headquarters of General John Stark, who met there frequently with generals Washington, Sullivan and Lee. Mollie Stark, the general's wife, is

Two unused sketches by Constantino that focused on details rather than the entire house. Top, the rear (west) entrance; note the two pineapple posts, symbolizing hospitality. Bottom, a south side porch and entryway.

reported to have watched the movements of British troops camped along the Mystic River from a lookout on the roof.

Isaac Jr. died of smallpox in England in 1781. His will left property to Harvard, where the Royall professorship of law has become one of the university's venerable posts. The estate was returned to the Royall heirs in 1806, and it subsequently passed through several hands. Finally the Royall House Association bought the dwelling and opened it to the public in 1910. Its restoration was completed in 1946, and today its interior is rich with period furniture and decorations. Among those who helped in the project was architect Joseph Everett Chandler, whose restorations included the Paul Revere House and the House of Seven Gables.

In October 1989 *Colonial Homes* magazine featured the Royall House in an illustrated article along with several other historic dwellings along the route of Paul Revere's midnight ride of 1775. The house, a registered national historic landmark, is located at 15 George Street in Medford and is open to the public from May 1 to October 1 daily, except Monday and Friday, from 2 to 5 p.m.

The Design

Art director Richard Sheaff asked his architect friends and associates who they considered to be the leading architectural illustrators in the Boston area. One of the best, he was told, was Frank Constantino of Winthrop. Sheaff hired Constantino for the Royall House postal card project, and Constantino, working from reference materials supplied by Sheaff plus his own visits to the site, made several sketches in colored pencil or watercolor, including the front from at least two angles, a closeup of the west, or rear, entry, and a closeup of a porch on the south side.

"Eventually the committee decided the front was the side they liked," Sheaff said. "Then we decided to take some liberties with the scene. Frank was literally showing what was there now, and there were some trees kind of blocking the view, and sections of fencing. Look, we said, we want to show the house; we're not necessarily interested in showing what's there in 1990 on the street. Let's get rid of those trees and that fence, so we can see the building."

What emerged as Constantino's final art, dated December 22, 1989, was a painting of the front and south sides, with details such as individual boards and windowpanes carefully included and sun and shadow patterns superimposed, surrounded by greenery. Unfortunately, much of this detail was lost in the screening process when the offset plates were made, but even so, the postal card image itself, with its dropout white typography, was a handsome one.

The depth of the image area, 1.18 inches, was the same as that used on other Historic Preservation cards, but the length, 1.68 inches, wasn't as great, which gave the picture a more nearly square shape than was customary for the series. Sheaff cropped the painting in this fashion to give it an aspect ratio more similar to that of a stamp. "I didn't want it to be one of those stretched-out images such as we're using in the America the Beautiful series," he said.

Sheaff arranged to have the painting scanned and the color separations made by a private firm in Boston. The separations were then sent to the Government Printing Office, where the offset plates were made. In the past, GPO had received the original artwork and made

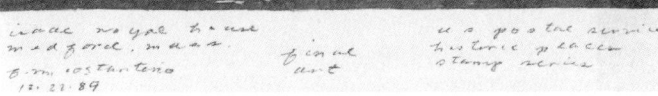

Top, Frank Constantino's finished painting for the Isaac Royall House postal card; bottom, an earlier sketch by Constantino, before trees, fence and wall were removed by the artist in order to show a full view of the building.

269

The first-day program for the Isaac Royall House postal card bore a frontal photograph of the historic building.

its own arrangements with outside firms to prepare the separations.

"That probably was the safest way for us to make sure we could get this dropout lettering," said Joe Brockert, project manager for the card. "This is the first time we've tried to drop out from process color. Every time we get the opportunity, we push the GPO a little bit further to see how far we can take that offset printing operation. They're very good printers, and we like to stretch our learning experience, to find out what we can get from the GPO press.

"Even dropping out these small letters from process color worked just fine. It's done by commercial printers all the time, but postal card stock is another matter, because it's a little more porous."

The cachet area of the card bears this inscription: "HISTORIC PRESERVATION SERIES/Isaac Royall House, 1700s/Medford, Massachusetts/National Historic Landmark." Some thought was given to adding a line drawing of the rear doorway of the house and the gate facing it. But it was decided that this would crowd the cachet area too much and the idea was abandoned.

First-Day Facts

William R. Cummings, regional postmaster general, dedicated the card in an elaborate ceremony at the Royall House attended by an estimated 1,000 persons. The principal speakers were Dr. Bacon of Northeastern University and Dr. Joseph V. Valeriani, president of the Medford Historical Society. Curator Jay Griffin introduced the distinguished guests. A proclamation was delivered by "Dr. Simon Tufts," played by Robert Hanson of the Massachusetts Lancers, and was read by "Isaac Royall" himself, played by William A. Slagle Jr., president of the Royall House Association.

15¢ POSTAL BUDDY POSTAL CARD

Date of Issue: July 5, 1990

Catalog Number: unassigned by Scott

Colors: black, red, blue

First-Day Cancel: Merrifield, Virginia

FDCs Canceled: 6,528

Format: sheets of four

Size: 5½ by 4¼ inches

Perf: extremely fine sawtooth

Markings: PATENTS PENDING, U.S. AND FOREIGN. ©1990 POSTAL BUDDY CORPORATION, SAN DIEGO, CA 92117-4328. Postal Buddy™ Authorized United States Postal Service change-of-address station (in repeat pattern)

Designer, Art Director and Project Manager: Joe Brockert (USPS)

Typographer: John Boyd of Anagraphics Inc., New York

Printing: Computerized printing by Postal Buddy vending machine.

Tagging: untagged

The Postal Card

One of 1990's major innovations was the Postal Buddy postal card, the first U.S. postal paper with a fixed denomination (in this case, 15¢) to be printed by a laser printer on demand. This method may some day be used for stamps as well, USPS officials have said.

The Postal Buddy card, machine-vended by a private corporation, was so novel that it wasn't listed in the Scott *1991 Specialized Catalogue of United States Stamps*. Its future catalog status was still uncertain as this was written.

Postal Buddy, a trademarked name, referred to a computerized change-of-address and instant printing terminal that was developed by entrepreneur Sidney R. Goodman, president of the Postal Buddy Corporation of San Diego, California. The terminals were used in a six-month experimental program authorized by USPS in 30 post offices and other sites in Northern Virginia, including supermarkets, shopping malls, and the U.S. Marine base at Quantico.

The cards that the machines printed were primarily intended to carry change-of-address information that the customer could input by using the computer keyboard. However, they could also contain such things as personal messages or meeting notices (touted by the company as a cost-effective alternative to commercial printing for small clubs), all generated in the same manner. The cards could be mailed at any time from any location.

They were 5½ inches long by 4¼ inches deep, three-fourths of an inch deeper than the standard postal card. Each card bore an indicium in black that depicted the USPS eagle logo alongside the wording "USA 15." Beneath the indicium was a line of small numbers indicating the terminal (five digits), date (two digits for the

A Postal Buddy machine.

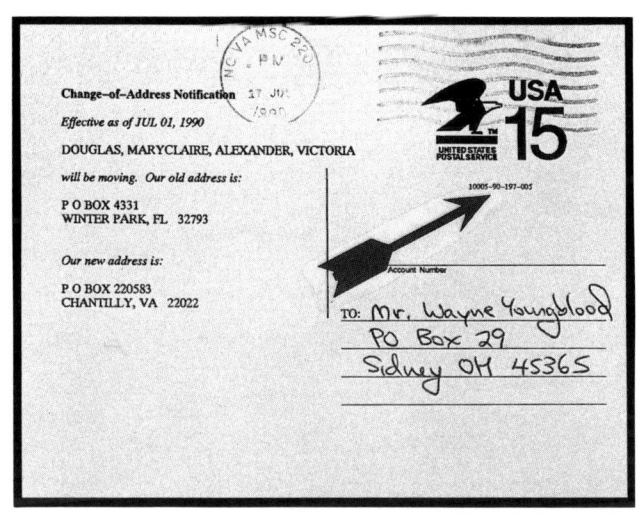

A Postal Buddy card bearing change-of-address information. The arrow points to the numbers containing machine identification, date and transaction number.

year, followed by digits representing the day's sequential number within the year) and that day's transaction number. On the same side were ruled lines on which the buyer could write an address.

The reverse side carried a border containing the USPS logo and the words "Postal Buddy (TM)" in blue and "Authorized United States Postal Service change-of-address station" in red, all of which was then repeated twice. The remainder of the side was blank and usable for a message if desired.

The cards were dispensed in sheets of four, separated by minuscule perforations, at a cost of 33¢ per 15¢ postal card. The sheets were 8½ inches by 11 inches, the same size as a standard sheet of typing paper and the same size as the only previous USPS postal card sheet-of-four, the se-tenant Cityscapes sheet of 1989. That sheet, however, included a disposable selvage strip at the bottom.

The cards, when loaded into a machine, were blank on the indicium side. However, the blue and red borders on the reverse were pre-printed by the company that supplied the stock to Postal Buddy. Postal Buddy considered the identity of this supplier to be proprietary information and declined to disclose it.

The postal cards were untagged during the experimental period. Dr. Douglas B. Quine, writing in *The United States Specialist,* reported that the dozen or so cards he had mailed generally had poorly positioned cancellations, possibly because they had been rejected by post-office facer/cancelers and then faced manually. If the decision eventually was made to put the program into regular operation, Tom Barry of USPS told *Linn's Stamp News,* the cards that would then be used would have tagging.

Why did Postal Buddy design the system so that the machine's laser printer printed the 15¢ indicia on the postal cards, rather than load the machines with cards with the indicia pre-printed?

It simplified things, according to Postal Buddy spokesman Marty Goodman. "We don't have to account for inventory, we don't have to buy the cards in advance, and we don't have to pay the Postal Service revenue until that stamp is generated," he said.

Furthermore, Goodman said, the use of pre-stamped cards would have required customers to buy the cards in multiples of four, rather than allow them to order as few or as many as they wanted. Finally, the same blank card stock, complete with scoring and with the blue-and-red borders on the reverse, was used for other kinds of product that the machine dispensed.

For example, the machine used one card to print a customer's receipt for each money transaction. It also printed, free on request, the USPS Change of Address Form 3575, which the customer could use to notify his postmaster of a pending address change.

The latter type of transaction used all four of the cards on a sheet. The two on the left side, which the customer detached and deposited in a slot on the machine, contained the address-change information he had keyboarded into the computer, along with the address of the postmaster-recipient and a non-denominated penalty indicium. The two on the right consisted of a card with the address-change information for the customer's own file, and a reminder to him to register to vote at his new address.

For change-of-address cards to be sent to friends, relatives and other correspondents, the machine entered the patron's name and names of family members, old and new addresses and an effective moving date. It could access a ZIP+4 database to provide the correct nine-digit ZIP code for the customer's new address.

Another customer option was a "philatelic" purchase of cards with no extraneous text, for collectors.

Because the cards were dispensed in multiples of four, one or more odd cards were sometimes left over once the ordered items and receipts had been printed. These bore the (self-contradictory) message: "This card intentionally left blank."

The machines also offered printed self-adhesive return-address labels, 45 to a sheet, at $2.29 per sheet, $1.39 for each additional sheet. Facsimile transmission (FAX) labels, which allow FAX users to dispense with a cover sheet in advance of the document of interest, were available at the same price. Sidney Goodman said he also planned to offer business cards, printed 10 to a sheet, if and when his machines were used nationally.

At no charge, the machine would also electronically provide address-change information to USPS and to any company that was on-line with the system. The 104 major mailers linked with Postal

Buddy during the experiment included *Time,* Amoco, Day-Timers, Riggs Bank, Sharper Image, Lands' End, Sears and J.C. Penney.

The machines accepted $1, $5, $10 and $20 bills, as well as credit cards for purchases over $5. They verified credit card purchases by dialing the credit card company for authorization just as some automated cash registers do. Sidney Goodman designed the system to be user-friendly, he told a reporter; the keyboard could withstand a coffee spill and was color-coded to match on-screen directions.

Both the inventor and USPS touted Postal Buddy as a potential money-saver for all concerned. USPS says there are more than 30 million residential address changes in the United States each year. The Postal Service believes that much of the mail it treats as undeliverable (more than 2.25 billion pieces annually, at a handling cost of $1.3 billion) is attributable to improper or late changes of address.

Since much of Postal Buddy's change-of-address system was electronic, changes would be immediate, which would result in a decrease in the amount of undeliverable mail, its supporters said. Publishers would find it advantageous to participate, since each forwarded magazine costs them around 30¢, plus the cost of processing duplicate changes of address.

A natural concern over a system such as Postal Buddy was security. USPS told *Linn's Stamp News* that pranksters would be deterred from randomly changing the addresses of potential victims by certain security features. These included a warning that appeared on the screen that tampering with the U.S. mail is a federal offense; a camera next to the computer screen that could record the faces of users, and a requirement that the user enter the last four digits of his Social Security number to validate a transaction.

The original mock-up of the Postal Buddy card bore a non-denominated penalty indicium.

In addition, the day after a customer used the machine, Postal Buddy automatically generated a change-of-address verification card that was mailed to the old mailing address. This provided a way to detect fraudulent change-of-address notification as well as giving patrons a second chance to spot any incorrect data they may have entered on the previous day.

Dr. Quine, in his *United States Specialist* article, questioned the security of the machine-generated postal cards themselves, which lacked the features commonly used to foil counterfeiters, such as difficult-to-reproduce printing techniques, embossing, tagging, perforating, watermarking and wraparound printing.

"Since these postal cards are produced on a laser printer, essentially the same process used in common office photocopiers and printers, it is natural to wonder whether security precautions have been employed in the design of these 'postage stamps' to prevent production by unscrupulous mailers," he wrote. "If these cards become widespread, such forgeries might be tempting both for the postage and the 18 cents surcharge that they would save . . .

"At this time it would appear that the only security feature is that the backs of the postal cards are printed with a red and blue border which would require a color press or photocopier to duplicate. This would present a barrier to a casual reproduction on the office copier, but would hardly pose a challenge to a commercial print shop."

Dr. Quine also discussed long-term problems which these cards might pose for collectors and suggested a way to deal with them.

"Laser printers use the same technology and toners as photocopying machines to print images," he wrote. "For this reason Postal

At one point officials considered using the new USPS logo, with Olympic rings and Olympic sponsorship information, in the indicium of the Postal Buddy card, but the width-to-depth ratio proved to be unsatisfactory.

Buddy products will likely exhibit the same storage characteristics as quality photocopies. While it is tempting to store these items in (non-vinyl) plastic sheet protectors, the black toner used in photocopiers easily sticks to plastic material (especially on hot days) and peels off the paper. A sheet of acid-free paper should probably be placed between Postal Buddy and any plastic material.

"The simplest approach may well be to photocopy both sides and then store the Postal Buddy pages between these copies with the copies facing out. In this way the originals are protected and they may be easily identified by the photocopies which will harmlessly deposit their toner on the plastic with time. The originals may be pulled out for examination at any time."

In December 1990, published reports quoted USPS spokesmen as saying the trial had been successful so far and that the Postal Service planned to seek bids in 1991 for a national network of Postal Buddy-type machines. Under one likely scenario, stores and other enterprises would invest in the machines and pay USPS the face value of the postage vended plus a percentage of sales.

The Design

"We wanted something simple, but something a little bit more interesting than just a penalty indicium," said Joe Brockert of USPS, project manager and art director for the Postal Buddy card. "It was a pretty basic graphic design project, to give the Postal Buddy people something on fairly short notice that they could use.

"Initially, they had thought about using penalty indicia, and we mocked up a sheet of four cards that way. Then it was decided that

This design was close to the one finally used, except that the information that ultimately was placed on the reverse of the issued postal card was stripped across the top of the indicium side on this design.

it would be better to turn it into live denominated postage — to put a value on it, rather than have it just say 'postage paid.' 'Postage paid' would have given us problems, come rate change time. At that point we decided that we had better make it look like postage.

"We thought of using the new Postal Service logo with the Olympic rings and the official sponsorship line on the left. On the mockup it proved to be a little big, and it didn't lend itself to the aspect ratio we needed for a postal card. So we decided to just use the Postal Service logo itself, and put a denomination beside it. It's not that different from our Official Mail postal card type of design."

Brockert worked with John Boyd of Anagraphics, Inc. in determining the size and location of the logo and the typography.

First-Day Facts

The test period began July 5 with the activation of the machine at the Merrifield, Virginia, post office. USPS provided Merrifield first-day cancellations bearing that date. On July 31, Postmaster General Anthony M. Frank attended a ceremony at the Merrifield post office formally inaugurating the Postal Buddy machine there.

Collectors wishing first-day cancellations on the Postal Buddy card could order their cards through the Philatelic Sales Division in Kansas City, Missouri, where the usual 50¢ handling fee and $10 minimum order applied. The cards, either mint or first-day canceled, were available only in sheets of four costing $1.32.

Ordering details weren't published until August 3, nearly a month after the date on the first-day postmarks, and collectors were given until September 3 to place their orders for the canceled specimens.

Those having access to Postal Buddy machines could submit their own cards to the postmaster at Merrifield for first-day cancellations, although the automatic dating information on the cards would make it obvious that the cancellations were backdated.

15¢ QUAD AT STANFORD POSTAL CARD
HISTORIC PRESERVATION SERIES

Date of Issue: September 30, 1990

Catalog Number: Scott UX150

Colors: magenta, yellow, cyan and black

First-Day Cancel: Stanford, California (Stanford University)

FDCs Canceled: 28,430

Format: Printed in 80-card sheets but available only in single cards. (Stanford University received a supply of 40-card half-sheets for its own use.) Printing plates of 80 subjects (8 across, 10 around).

Size: 5½ by 3½ inches

Markings: ©USPS 1990

Designer: Jim M'Guinness of Los Altos, California

Art Director and Project Manager: Joe Brockert (USPS)

Typographer: Bradbury Thompson (CSAC)

Printing: U.S. Government Printing Office (GPO) on a five-color Roland Man 800 sheetfed offset press.

Quantity Ordered: 10,000,000
Quantity Distributed: 10,000,000

Tagging: vertical bar to right of stamp

The Postal Card

Stanford University in Palo Alto, California, launched its centennial year celebration September 30, 1990. USPS marked the occasion by issuing a postal card in the Historic Preservation series that depicted a scene at the heart of the Stanford campus: the ornate arches of Memorial Court as viewed from the Inner Quadrangle.

As with most Historic Preservation cards, the project began with a request for a stamp. In 1986 the committee planning Stanford's centennial took note of the 56¢ Great Americans stamp portraying John Harvard, which USPS had issued that year in connection with Harvard University's 350th anniversary. The committee, headed by Professor Gerald J. Lieberman, decided that an appropriate recognition of Stanford's forthcoming celebration would be a stamp carrying portraits of the couple who founded the university: Leland Stanford, Western pioneer, railroad magnate and former governor of California, and his wife Jane.

In June 1987 a letter went to USPS from John Gardner, a Stanford alumnus and founder of Common Cause, the self-styled citizens' lobby. With it was information on what Gardner called the Stanfords' "extraordinary legacy as early American philanthropists."

"Given the nature and scale of their benefaction, it is surprising that the Stanfords are not more often acknowledged in the same breath as the Carnegies, Rockefellers and Vanderbilts, who have

Jane Stanford and the couple's only son, Leland Jr., whose death led his parents to found the university that would bear his name.

Leland Stanford: Western pioneer, transcontinental railroad builder, governor of California, U.S. senator and co-founder of a university.

since come to personify this nation's distinctive commitment to public charity," Gardner wrote. "The year 1991 will mark the 100th anniversary of Stanford University's opening. I can think of no better occasion to accord Jane and Leland Stanford the distinction they have so long merited . . ."

Other letters of support went to USPS from California's U.S. senators, Alan Cranston and Pete Wilson, and Donald Kennedy, the university president. In December 1988, representatives of the Stanford University Centennial met in Washington with Don McDowell, general manager of the USPS Stamps Division, and were told that a stamp had been turned down, but that a postal card in the Historic Preservation series had been approved. A similar card was in the works for Georgetown University; its 200th anniversary would be marked in January 1989 with a Historic Preservation card depicting Georgetown's Healy Hall.

Possibly none of the participants in the negotiations was aware that Leland Stanford in fact had once been pictured on a U.S. stamp, although he wasn't identified thereon. A 1944 commemorative (Scott 922) reproduced a mural in the Salt Lake City railroad

Leland Stanford wields the sledge in the "golden spike" ceremony at Promontory Point, Utah, depicted on this 1944 commemorative stamp (Scott 922).

281

station depicting the driving of the golden spike at nearby Promontory Point in 1869 to complete the building of the first transcontinental railroad. The man wielding the silver sledge in the picture was Stanford, who was president of one of the two railroads that were linked that day, the Central Pacific.

The artwork for the Stanford University postal card was unveiled on May 20, 1990, by the university's president, Donald Kennedy, and Postmaster General Anthony M. Frank in Newport Beach, California, during a Stanford centennial celebration event.

"People here were quite pleased with the postal card alternative that was offered to us," said Sandi Risser, associate director of the Centennial Year. "It was something that was very usable internally and would also be marketed and used around the country, and it didn't isolate us on a stamp that might have an odd denomination and thus see only limited use."

Stanford University came about because of a family tragedy. In 1884, 15-year-old Leland Stanford Jr., the only child of Leland and Jane Stanford, died of typhoid fever. The grieving parents decided to found and endow a university at their horse farm in Palo Alto in his memory. "The children of California shall be our children," the father said to the mother on the morning of their son's death.

Leland Stanford Junior university was six years in the planning and building. Ex-Governor Stanford hired Frederick Law Olmsted, the landscape architect who had created New York City's Central Park, to develop the general plan — long, low buildings connected by arcades to form a double quadrangle. A young Boston architect, Charles A. Coolidge, designed the buildings themselves.

The architectural style was called Richardsonian Romanesque, after Coolidge's mentor, Henry Hobbs Richardson. Reminiscent of the California missions, it featured rectilinear stone buildings joined by covered arcades formed of successive half-circle arches supported by short columns with decorated capitals. The building material was a buff sandstone from a quarry south of nearby San Jose. Red tile roofs completed the picture. It was, wrote Olmsted, "for the first time an architecture distinctly Californian in character."

On October 1, 1891, the Inner Quadrangle of 12 classroom buildings, with its central place reserved for the future Memorial Church, was ready, along with three engineering buildings and residence halls for men and women. The man whom Stanford — by now a U.S. senator — had picked only a few months earlier to be his president, David Starr Jordan, welcomed 465 students to the brand-new institution. "These long corridors with their stately pillars, these circles of waving palms, will have their part in the student's training as surely as the chemical laboratory or the seminary room," Jordan predicted that day. "Each stone in the quadrangle shall teach its lesson of grace and genuineness."

Stanford has gone on to become one of the nation's great private universities, alma mater of many distinguished Americans (including Herbert Hoover, a member of the first graduating class).

Twice the university has been damaged by earthquakes. The worst of these was the great 'quake of April 18, 1906, the same one that destroyed San Francisco, 30 miles to the north. It struck during Easter vacation, and, miraculously, only two lives were lost at Stanford. The spire-topped clock tower on Memorial Church, built by Jane Stanford in memory of her husband and dedicated in 1903, crashed into the building's chancel. The 100-foot-high Memorial Arch with its frieze by Augustus Saint-Gaudens, central structure of the Outer Quad, was wrecked beyond repair. Damage to walls and arches was widespread. Reconstruction cost $2 million.

Then, on October 17, 1989, in the university's 99th year, another earthquake ripped along the same fault line. The Memorial Church was damaged again, so badly that it had to be closed to the public. On the same day the postal card was issued the university launched a $10 million fund drive to repair the structure. Some of the arches in the Quad were also damaged, and hairline cracks developed in unreinforced sandstone walls all across the campus.

Because the university's actual centennial would occur in 1991, that was the year that appeared on the postal card, although the year of issue was 1990 and so was the copyright year (which also was printed on the card). The fact that 1991 was shaping up as a rate-change year influenced the decision to issue the card in 1990, said Joe Brockert of USPS, the project manager and art director.

"We didn't know how far into the year we'd be before we could put a new rate on a card," Brockert said. "We knew that the rate change would occur fairly early in the year. Faced with the prospect of having something that would be useful for a few months before a rate change or a few months after a rate change, the university preferred that the card be issued beforehand. And since we had no particular preference, and that's what the folks who were celebrating wanted, there was no reason for us to overrule it."

The Design

The indicium of the card was the work of Jim M'Guinness, a graphic designer, illustrator and cartoonist from Los Altos, California. M'Guinness was recommended to USPS by Stanford University, where he had worked from 1960 to 1979 as staff artist and art director at the Publications Service, designing note cards, posters, book covers and brochures — even faculty club menus — for the institution. This was his first USPS assignment (although as a young artist, he recalled, he had sold cartoons for $5 apiece to a philatelic publication, *The Stamp Wholesaler).*

M'Guinness submitted four concept sketches, done in colored

These concept sketches by Jim M'Guinness showed the entrance to the Quad, as seen from Palm Drive, and two views of Hoover Tower, one from inside the Quad, the other from outside.

pencil. One was a frontal view of the Quad, with the Memorial Church behind it, as seen from Palm Drive, the long avenue that leads into the campus. Two others featured Hoover Tower, the 280-foot carillon tower, built in 1940, that is the university's most prominent landmark.

The sketch selected by CSAC depicted Memorial Court, a memorial to the Stanford family, which connects the Inner and Outer Quads. The view looks north from the Inner Quad through two of the three ornate arches that constitute its main entance; from this vantage point, Memorial Church is at the viewer's back. M'Guinness executed the finished work in ink in what he calls his "sketch style" and colored it with watercolor.

Several years ago USPS began placing wording and/or design elements in the lower left corner of postal cards — the "cachet area" — to explain the purpose of the card. This enabled the designers to produce clean, colorful indicia, free of all typography except "USA" and the denomination. But the presence of wording in the lower left created "infrequent but occasional mail processing problems," said Joe Brockert, who has been USPS project manager and art director for most recent postal cards.

Even though designers were increasingly careful not to include city names or two-letter state abbreviations on the bottom lines of the cachet-area inscriptions, the automated address readers sometimes were thrown off by the presence of typography where an address might normally be found, Brockert said.

With the Stanford card, typographer Bradbury Thompson experimented with placing the informational wording just to the left of the indicium. "But then we thought, no, as soon as you get a cancellation up there, it will become a jumbled mess," Brockert said. "So that wouldn't work, even though it wouldn't affect automation."

So the inscription went in the cachet area after all. In five lines of

This mock-up used a smaller indicium than appeared on the issued card, with different wording, differently placed.

blue type it read: "Stanford/Centennial/1891-1991/Memorial Court/ The Quadrangle." The same placement was used for the last postal card that was issued in 1990, for Chicago Symphony Hall.

"But these will probably be the last postal cards with inscriptions below," Brockert said. "We're probably going to take those lines of wording off entirely. We don't want to do anything to have a negative impact on our automation programs."

The exception, he said, would be picture postal cards, on which the necessary information would probably be put in the upper left-hand corner of the address side. Users of picture postcards are accustomed to having only a portion of one half of the address side to write on anyhow, and they would find nothing unusual about having the normal return-address area occupied by printing.

First-Day Facts

Postmaster General Anthony M. Frank dedicated the card in the Sunday afternoon public ceremony held in the Inner Quad at Stanford, with the audience facing Memorial Court. The principal speakers were California's Republican U.S. senator, Pete Wilson, who some five weeks later would be elected governor of the state, and Robert Setrakian, chairman of the USPS Board of Governors and a 1949 graduate of Stanford.

The welcome was given by Stanford President Donald Kennedy. Joseph Caraveo, regional postmaster general for the Western region, presided, and Rosemary C. Hornby, president of the Stanford Historical Society, introduced the honored guests, who included James C. Gaither, president of the university's board of trustees, and Ira D. Hall, a USPS Board of Governors member.

285

15¢ CONSTITUTION HALL-MEMORIAL CONTINENTAL HALL PICTURE POSTAL CARD

Date of Issue: October 11, 1990

Catalog Number: Scott UX151

Colors: magenta, yellow, cyan and black

First-Day Cancel: Washington, D.C.

FDCs Canceled: 33,254

Format: Printed on Krome Coat paper in 72-card sheets but available only in single cards. Printing plates of 72 subjects (8 across, 9 around).

Size: 5½ by 3½ inches

Markings: ©USPS 1990

Designer: Pierre Mion of Lovettsville, Virginia

Art Director: Derry Noyes (CSAC)

Project Manager: Joe Brockert (USPS)

Typographer: Bradbury Thompson (CSAC)

Modeler: John Boyd (Anagraphics Inc., New York, New York)

Printing: U.S. Government Printing Office (GPO) on a 5-color Roland Man 800 sheetfed offset press.

Quantity Ordered: 3,000,000
Quantity Distributed: 2,519,000

Tagging: vertical bar to right of stamp

The Postal Card

On October 11, 1990, USPS issued a picture postal card depicting, on its opposite sides, the two principal buildings in the Washington, D.C., headquarters complex of the National Society Daughters of the American Revolution (DAR). The date was the 100th anniversary of the DAR's founding.

The indicium showed the great auditorium known as Constitution Hall; the glossy picture side depicted Memorial Continental Hall. Both are designated Registered National Historic Landmarks.

The card was the third in a series that USPS calls EXTRAordinary View Cards. The first two were issued during World Stamp Expo in 1989, with one depicting the White House and the other the Jefferson Memorial. Like those cards, the Constitution Hall-Continental Hall card had a face value of 15¢ and retailed at 50¢ each, a price USPS considers to be competitive with privately produced picture postcards when the value of the postage is included. USPS also makes its EXTRAordinary View Cards available in quantity, at a negotiated discount, for resale.

The DAR card was originally intended to be a standard postal card in the Historic Preservation series, picturing only Constitution Hall, the better known of the two buildings. How it came to be turned into a picture postal card — how, in fact, it came to be issued at all — is an involved story involving DAR pressure and persistence and Postal Service diplomacy, ingenuity and a bit of fancy footwork.

The story emerges from a file of correspondence between the two parties, which was made available to this writer by Mrs. Eldred Martin Yochim, the current president general of the DAR. It began in February 1983, when Mrs. Richard Denny Shelby, who was then the DAR president general, wrote to then-Postmaster General Wil-

When this model was made, the card was planned as a conventional card in the Historic Preservation series.

287

liam F. Bolger informing him that the DAR's 100th anniversary would fall in October of 1990. "I want to start early to request a commemorative stamp during 1990," she wrote.

Bolger was well aware that the DAR was not only an important service organization that deserved to be considered for postal recognition, but was also an influential group made up of influential people. A year later, in January 1984, he told Mrs. Shelby in confidence that CSAC had recommended, and he had approved, a DAR stamp for 1990. The following June, Bolger put his commitment to issue a stamp in writing, in a letter to Mrs. William Henry Sullivan Jr. of the DAR's Centennial Jubilee Committee.

The years passed, postmasters general and DAR presidents general came and went, and on June 30, 1989, the newest president general, Mrs. Yochim, wrote to Postmaster General Anthony M. Frank. "Since 1990 is approaching rapidly," she told him, "the members are asking when the stamp commemorating (our 100th) anniversary will be available for purchase. We would appreciate receiving this information from you."

In the intervening time, however, Citizens' Stamp Advisory Committee and USPS officials had had a change of mind.

They had found the Historic Preservation postal card series to be a useful alternative to commemorative stamps when it came to marking the anniversaries of such things as organizations, colleges and universities. They had decided to honor the DAR centennial with such a card, just as they were planning to do for two other American institutions approaching their 100th birthdays, Stanford University and the Chicago Symphony Orchestra. And for the design subject, they had chosen Constitution Hall, as the DAR-owned building best known to the American public. In fact, when Mrs. Yochim wrote her letter, the Constitution Hall card had already been announced to the philatelic press in the Postal Service's first listing of the stamps and stationery that it would issue in 1990.

The postmaster general answered Mrs. Yochim's letter carefully. "Thank you for your June 30 letter concerning a philatelic tribute for the Daughters of the American Revolution Constitution Hall," he wrote. "I am pleased to inform you that the (CSAC) . . . has announced that the Daughters of the American Revolution Constitution Hall will be honored next year on a Historic Preservation series postal card. I am sure you will agree that the issuance of this postal card will be a most meaningful complement to your centennial celebration."

In her answering letter, Mrs. Yochim made it clear that this wouldn't do. "We asked for a stamp using Memorial Continental Hall, which was our first building," she wrote. "Your recent letter mentions Constitution Hall. This was the third and last building built. It is Memorial Continental Hall that we want."

The postmaster general next tried some salesmanship. "I am sure you can appreciate that the Citizens' Stamp Advisory Committee, the group responsible for the selection of all United States philatelic issues, has many considerations to face when selecting the subjects for stamps and postal stationery," he wrote. "Primary among the committee's concerns is selecting subjects which will be most popular with the American public as a whole. Also, every effort is made to fit the selected subjects into our established series . . .

"One of our most popular and long-running series is our Historic Preservation postal cards . . . It is our fervent belief that Constitution Hall is a most fitting addition . . . as it is well-known by the American public and is generally identified with the Daughters of the American Revolution. In response to your latest letter, however, I am requesting that the committee review your proposal that Memorial Continental Hall be commemorated, rather than Constitution Hall . . ."

Mrs. Yochim gave no ground. "While we are most appreciative of a Historic Series Post Card, it is a DAR Centennial Stamp we have been requesting since 1983. Please refer to the enclosed correspondence," she wrote. "With a membership of over 200,000, the overall usage of a stamp, and the pride of having a stamp, would create an overwhelming purchase. If you still wish to have the post card, it could be in addition to the stamp."

Postmaster General Frank, in his next reply, dated October 13, 1989, took refuge in semantics — and followed that with still another fervent sales pitch for postal cards.

"The Postal Service issues a variety of stamps and stationery items each year, including definitives, commemoratives, airmail issues, specials, postal cards, stamped envelopes and aerogrammes," he explained. "We refer to all the issues collectively as the 'stamp program' and 'stamp' can be used interchangeably for the various items. Hence, when a proposal is approved by CSAC, the term 'stamp' may be applied until the committee has decided on the exact nature of the philatelic tribute . . .

"Many organizations honored on Historic Preservation series postal cards have found the cards to be a convenient and meaningful way to communicate their goals, inform their membership of upcoming events and generally increase public awareness. Postal cards enable the organization to produce an attractive, self-contained souvenir that can be customized with original artwork. For instance, I have enclosed a copy of the Hull House Historic Preservation series postal card the Hull House Association prepared with their design printed on the card. This limited edition card was produced as a souvenir and to assist in fund raising activities."

"The DAR's card," he went on, "will feature a beautiful color rendition of the Hall and, in the lower left, the words 'Washington:

Constitution Hall Daughters of the American Revolution Centennial" in four lines of type. In this way, the postal card will communicate a greater amount of information than what could be included in the design of a stamp in sheet format, a design the committee did not recommend for the DAR centennial.

"I should point out that the Postal Service has recently experienced an enormous increase in the sale of postal cards. The attractive designs and affordable 15-cent rate have made them a popular way for businesses, organizations and individuals to communicate and keep in touch. This . . . card will share your centennial with millions of people across America."

At this point Mrs. Shelby, the past president general, who had been briefed by Mrs. Yochim, weighed in with a letter to Frank. For her part, she was still insisting on what she termed a "genuine stamp" — and one that would depict Memorial Continental Hall. "We want total cooperation with you," Mrs. Shelby wrote, "as you plan to implement what the late Bill Bolger confirmed to me . . ."

On November 15, Postmaster General Frank proposed a new solution to President General Yochim. USPS was about to issue its first two "view" postal cards, Frank wrote. "I believe the view card format would be ideal for honoring the centennial of the DAR," he went on hopefully. "One side of the card could feature Memorial Continental Hall, and the other, Constitution Hall. It also would be possible to offer quantities of this card to your group at less than the 50 percent per card price, so that they could be made available to your members and other interested individuals and organizations."

As late as January 25, 1990, Mrs. Yochim was still striving to persuade the postmaster general to change his mind and issue a Memorial Continental Hall stamp ("We feel this could be possible if you would give it your personal approval"). On February 27, however, she gracefully threw in the towel. "We would like to make plans for a first day issue of the postal card on October 11, 1990 — our 100th birthday," she wrote to Frank Thomas of the Stamp Support Branch. "The view card in color of Memorial Continental Hall on the front and Constitution Hall in the indicium area on the reverse is our choice."

After the card was finally issued, Mrs. Yochim told this writer that it was "beautiful" and that the members were "very pleased" with it. Her office had obtained a supply of both mint cards and first-day covers and was filling orders from members, she said. However, curiously enough, the DAR Museum's gift shop, located in the administration building that links Memorial Continental Hall and Constitution Hall, didn't carry the postal card in stock.

That highlighted the fact that, with three picture postal cards and one picture art card under its belt, USPS late in 1990 was still looking for an effective way to market these cards — and to determine what the future of this kind of product might be. Moreover, some observers wondered whether a Constitution Hall-Memorial Continental Hall card, depicting buildings that are off the beaten path for tourists, would sell at all to the general public.

"It's sort of like a live test," said Joe Brockert, the project manager for all the picture postal cards issued to date. "This will give us some more information by the end of the year as to the kinds of things we might be able to put on our picture postal card series. It also gives us a fair comparison, because these (DAR) buildings are also in Washington, and we can do some direct comparisons of sales with the White House and Jefferson Memorial cards.

"Should we stick with nationally recognized landmarks, or can we consider doing more local-interest things, things that have less of a national profile? It's all part of an effort to give us a little more data to see where we want to go with the picture postal card program."

The National Society Daughters of the American Revolution was organized on October 11, 1890, for "historic, educational and patriotic purposes." It was incorporated by an Act of Congress in 1896, and since then has reported annually to Congress.

A prospective member must be able to prove her lineage back to an ancestor who served the American cause during the American Revolution. More than 725,000 women have been admitted to membership in its 100 years, and present enrollment totals some 203,000 members in chapters in each of the 50 states, the District of Columbia and several foreign countries.

The organization's headquarters complex, which includes the buildings shown on the postal card, is a short distance from the White House and fills the city block bounded by 17th, 18th, C and D streets. Just across C Street is the Pan-American Union building, depicted on a U.S. airmail stamp of 1947 (Scott C34).

Memorial Continental Hall, facing 17th Street, was the first building erected by the DAR. It was designed by Edward Pearce Casey and built in 1910 at a cost of more than $500,000. It is of white marble, with two colonnaded porticos and corner pavilions. The larger portico or porte-cochere forms the central feature of the east facade. The 13 Ionic columns of the semicircular south portico symbolize the 13 original states and were donated by state DAR chapters and legislatures. Triple bronze doors at the main entrance memorialize the founders, charter members, and heroes of Connecticut and Massachusetts.

The building was the site of the historic conference on the Limitation of Armament, held from November 11, 1921, to February 6, 1922. Today it houses the organization's genealogical library, museum galleries and individual state chapter rooms, which are furnished in a manner typical of early American homes. It was designated a National Historic Landmark in 1973.

Constitution Hall, facing 18th Street, was built in 1928 to house the DAR's annual Continental Congress. It was designed by John Russell Pope and constructed of Alabama limestone at a cost of nearly $1.7 million. Its 4,000-seat auditorium is the largest in Washington. An Ionic entrance portico, surmounted by a pediment bearing a sculptured American eagle, accents the west facade. A carriage entrance with drive ramp extends along the north side, and on the south front is an entrance with a promenade terrace. The building was designated a National Historic Landmark in 1985.

Constitution Hall's history is marked by an extraordinary event that, although unfortunate in itself, provided the occasion for one of the few great affirmations of civil rights in America before World War II. The event centered on singer Marian Anderson, a contralto of whom Arturo Toscanini had said: "A voice like hers comes once in a century." She was black, and in 1939 the DAR refused to allow her to sing in Constitution Hall — then the only large concert auditorium in the nation's capital — because of her race.

This incident sparked widespread indignation, even in a largely segregated country that was still more than 20 years away from its civil-rights revolution. First Lady Eleanor Roosevelt resigned from the DAR in protest, and Interior Secretary Harold Ickes offered the singer the use of the Lincoln Memorial for an outdoor recital that would be free to the public. Here, on Easter Sunday, Marian Anderson stood at the base of the memorial to the "Great Emancipator" and sang for an audience estimated at 75,000.

Thus rebuked by public opinion, the DAR ultimately changed its policy for Constitution Hall. Anderson first appeared there in a concert for the benefit of wartime China relief and thereafter in several regular performances. In her 1956 autobiography, *My Lord, What a Morning,* she wrote: "When I finally walked into Constitution Hall and sang from its stage I had no feeling different from what I have in other halls. There was no sense of triumph. I felt that it was a beautiful concert hall, and I was happy to sing in it."

The Design

Pierre Mion of Lovettsville, Virginia, was chosen to do the artwork for the postal card. Among Mion's previous design projects for USPS had been the White House and Jefferson Memorial picture postal cards, and a 1988 Historic Preservation postal card for Blair

Mion offered CSAC this head-on view of Constitution Hall, but the committee members preferred a view as seen from an angle.

This was Pierre Mion's watercolor concept sketch for the picture side of the card, showing Memorial Continental Hall as seen from the corner of 17th and D streets. The DAR flag flies from the pole in the foreground. The committee asked him to paint his finished picture from the other front corner (C Street), to show the semicircular portico on the south of the building.

House, also in the capital.

Mion's original instructions were to do concept sketches of Constitution Hall for an indicium design for the Historic Preservation card that USPS, at that time, intended to issue. Mion visited the building, took photographs and prepared sketches of two views of the 18th Street entrance: a head-on view, in pencil, and an angled view from the D Street side, in watercolor.

The committee chose the angled view, and Mion was commissioned to do final art. Working at four times stamp size, he made a gouache painting based on his color sketch. He changed only one detail: At the committee's request, he left out three human figures that he had originally placed in front of the entrance.

Mion delivered the painting, was paid — and then learned that there was still work to be done. Because of the DAR's preference for Memorial Continental Hall, he was told, USPS might make a switch in which Constitution Hall would be dropped and a picture of the other building would be used for the indicium. The artist was asked for concept sketches of Memorial Continental Hall. It was while he was at this stage of his work that USPS made the final decision to show both buildings on a picture postal card.

Mion submitted a watercolor sketch of Memorial Continental Hall from a corner that showed the D Street side as well as the main entrance on 17th Street. He preferred this angle, he said, because to his eye the rounded portico on the south, or C Street, side made an unattractive contrast to the rectangular front portico on 17th Street. Mion also made a pencil sketch from the other corner, however, and it was this view that the committee members called for in finished form. The corner they chose happened to be the one on which the American flag is flown; the DAR's own flag flies from the other flagpole, on the D Street corner.

In critiquing the postal card afterward, Mion said: "I'm not real thrilled with the fact that both paintings, of Constitution Hall and Memorial Continental Hall, have the same vanishing point. They both taper off to the right. If I had designed the whole card from the beginning I would have done one building from one direction and one from the other."

When USPS still was planning the card as a conventional Historic Preservation item, John Boyd of Anagraphics, Inc., prepared a

Pierre Mion's watercolor concept sketch of Constitution Hall. In his finished painting, which was used for the card's indicium, he removed the people from the scene.

mockup using the Constitution Hall indicium and, in four lines in the lower-left corner, the words: "Washington:/Constitution Hall/ Daughters of the American/Revolution Centennial." On the card as issued, the wording, in three lines on the address side, read: "Washington: Constitution Hall (at right)/Memorial Continental Hall (reverse side)/Centennial, Daughters of the American Revolution."

First-Day Facts

Senior Assistant Postmaster General Comer S. Coppie dedicated the card on October 11 in the DAR Museum Gallery. Welcoming remarks were given by Mrs. Yochim, the president general of the DAR, and the invocation and benediction were offered by Mrs. Harold William Roberts, the organization's chaplain general.

The picture side of the DAR postal card.

15¢ CHICAGO ORCHESTRA HALL POSTAL CARD
HISTORIC PRESERVATION SERIES

Date of Issue: October 19, 1990

Catalog Number: Scott UX152

Colors: magenta, yellow, cyan and black

First-Day Cancel: Chicago, Illinois (Orchestra Hall)

FDCs Canceled: 28,546

Format: Printed in 80-card sheets, but available only in single cards. Printing plates of 80 subjects (8 across, 10 around)

Size: 5½ by 3½ inches

Markings: ©USPS 1990

Designer: Michael Hagel of Arlington Heights, Illinois

Art Director and Project Manager: Joe Brockert (USPS)

Typographer: Bradbury Thompson (CSAC)

Printing: U.S. Government Printing Office (GPO) on a 5-color Roland Man 800 sheetfed offset press

Quantity Ordered: 10,000,000
Quantity Distributed: 9,141,000

Tagging: vertical bar to right of stamp

The Postal Card

The centennial performance season of the Chicago Symphony Orchestra, 1990-1991, was commemorated October 19, 1990, with a postal card that paid tribute to Orchestra Hall, the building where the ensemble performs. The card, issued as part of the Historic Preservation series, depicted in its stamp area an interior view of Orchestra Hall's auditorium. It was the first card in the series to show the inside of a building.

Two previous Historic Preservation cards had also featured the homes of American orchestras. They were Cincinnati Symphony's Music Hall in 1978 (Scott UX73) and the Philadelphia Orchestra's Academy of Music in 1982 (Scott UX96).

As was the case with the Constitution Hall-Memorial Continental Hall card and the Quad at Stanford card (see preceding chapters) and many other Historic Preservation cards, this one began with a request for a commemorative stamp. The request was made in 1988 by Zane Knauss, director of the orchestra's special projects office for the centennial year, and Evelyn Meine, associate director. The Citizens' Stamp Advisory Committee guidelines preclude stamps for the anniversaries of institutions, but Historic Preservation postal cards have frequently been used for this purpose. Orchestra Hall had been on the National Register of Historic Places since 1978. The Chic-

Chicago's Orchestra Hall on South Michigan Avenue, designed by Daniel H. Burnham and completed in 1904.

agoans were invited to pursue the postal card route.

Richard Thomas, chairman of the Chicago Symphony Orchestra's trustees, and others wrote in support of the proposal. Information was supplied on the history of the orchestra and the building's credentials. CSAC voted its approval, and the card was publicly added to USPS' 1990 schedule in a February 15, 1990, news release.

(The release erroneously referred to the building to be honored as "Chicago Symphony Hall." This prompted one Michael S. Wehling to write a letter to *The American Philatelist* noting that the correct name was "Orchestra Hall." USPS subsequently got it right in an August 3 press release announcing the first-day date and city.)

The "Chicago Orchestra" gave its first concerts on October 16 and 17, 1891, in the Chicago Auditorium Theatre. Its founder, German-born Theodore Thomas, served as music director for 13 years, giving the first hearing in America to composers then known only to Europeans, among them Richard Strauss, Bruckner, Brahms and Sibelius. Thomas died in January 1905, only three weeks after the dedication of the orchestra's permanent home, Orchestra Hall. For eight years thereafter the ensemble was formally known as the Theodore Thomas Orchestra; it received its present name in 1913.

Among the orchestra's other distinguished conductors have been Frederick Stock, who succeeded the founder and served for 37 years; Rafael Kubelik, Fritz Reiner, and, since 1965, Sir Georg Solti. Sir Georg was scheduled to step down as music director at the end of the 1990-91 season, to be succeeded by Daniel Barenboim.

The Chicago Symphony Orchestra is recognized as one of the world's great orchestras. It tours the globe, and its full-length concerts are broadcast over more than 400 U.S and foreign radio

The Chicago Symphony Orchestra under Sir Georg Solti, music director, on the stage of Orchestra Hall.

stations. Since 1916, when it became the first American symphony orchestra to record under its regular conductor, it has made more than 500 recordings and has received more than 40 Grammy awards from the National Academy of Recording Arts and Sciences.

Orchestra Hall was designed by Daniel Hudson Burnham, who was one of the chief architects of Chicago's World's Columbian Exposition in 1893, and was completed in 1904 at a cost of $750,000. The nine-story structure at 220 South Michigan Avenue overlooks Grant Park and Lake Michigan. Its facade, in brick and stone, typifies Burnham's classic revival style. The hall houses a 2,574-seat auditorium on four levels, a ballroom, music library and the offices of The Orchestral Association.

Its years as the home of the orchestra may be numbered, however. *Chicago Magazine* reported in October 1990 that the hall "is outdated because of its inadequate backstage facilities, cramped public spaces, and unexceptional acoustics; there is now talk of a new performing arts center."

The Design

"This was a toughie," said Joe Brockert, art director for the card.

The exterior of Orchestra Hall, shown here in Michael Hagel's pencil and acrylic sketches, wasn't considered interesting enough to be shown in the card's indicium.

"There just wasn't a whole lot for us to look at."

The Chicago Symphony supplied exterior and interior photographs of Orchestra Hall for use by Brockert and Michael Hagel, the Arlington Heights, Illinois, commercial artist who was signed to do concept sketches. Their first thought was of an exterior view, like those used on all the previous Historic Preservation postal cards. But the outside of Orchestra Hall wasn't very promising, despite its high arched windows and the composers' names — Bach, Mozart, Beethoven, Schubert, Wagner — carved along the facade.

"The problem," said Hagel, "was that it's not really a distinctive looking building. There are buildings built right next to it, connected onto it. So it's just really one 'storefront,' you might say, on Michigan Avenue. I tried as many angles for rough sketches as I could, coming in close on the front, going back, and we finally decided it wasn't going to be distinctive enough to warrant an exterior view."

At one point Brockert even suggested that they might consider

These are Michael Hagel's pencil and acrylic sketches of the Orchestra Hall auditorium from the gallery level. They differ in some details because the artist based his pencil drawing on a photograph taken before the 1981 renovation, when a Moeller pipe organ was installed. The acrylic sketch, and the finished postal card, showed how the interior looked at the time the card was issued in 1990.

abandoning Orchestra Hall as a subject in favor of the Auditorium Theater, a Louis Sullivan-designed building where the Symphony had performed in its early years. Hagel did a sketch of this building, located at 430 South Michigan Avenue. Ultimately, they decided to stick with Orchestra Hall, but to try an interior view.

Hagel worked at first from old photographs supplied by the Symphony, particularly one that had been taken from deep in the far corner of the gallery (the fourth and last level of seats), looking down on the lower levels and the stage, with the balcony railing curving along to the left. He did a pencil sketch from this picture, full of detail, with each seat and floorboard carefully defined.

Later Hagel went to the building and took his own photographs, shooting from the same point from which the older pictures had been taken. He found that many changes had been made during the auditorium's $3.4 million renovation in 1981 that accompanied the installation of a Moeller pipe organ. In his finished acrylic painting, Hagel showed the auditorium as it is today.

"I had to take a little bit of liberty as far as the angle went," Hagel said. He tried to show in his picture what a human eye, with its peripheral vision, would see, which was more than a camera would take in, even with a wide-angle lens. "I took a series of photographs and then built from that," he said.

CSAC members agreed that the interior view was the best solution to the design problem. The prevailing opinion, Brockert admitted, was that "the interior isn't that much more interesting either, but at least it's more colorful."

Back in 1982, however, USPS officials hadn't been reluctant to depict the exterior of a downtown auditorium on a postal card. The design of the Philadelphia Academy of Music card, by Melbourne Brindle, showed a straightaway view of the exterior of the Academy, whose facade and windows are quite similar to those of Orchestra Hall.

First-Day Facts

The public first-day ceremony was held at 11:30 a.m. in Orchestra Hall and was followed a short time later by one of the orchestra's scheduled Saturday matinee performances. Tickets were required for those staying for the music.

Michael J. Shinay, executive assistant to the postmaster general, dedicated the card. The principal speaker was Daniel H. Burnham IV, great grandson of Daniel H. Burnham, the architect of Orchestra Hall. John C. Stetson, chairman of the Centennial Committee of the Orchestral Association, gave the welcome.

ARIPEX 1990
SOUVENIR CARD (BEP)

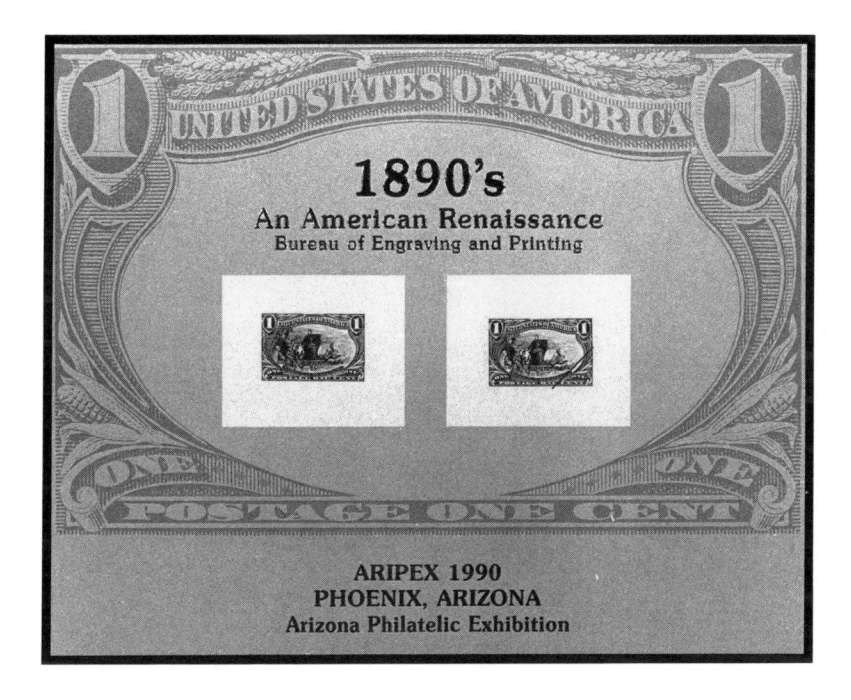

Date of Issue: April 20, 1990

Catalog Number: Scott 128

First-Day Release: Phoenix, Arizona (Aripex 90) and Washington, D.C. (BEP Visitor's Center)

Colors: gray, light green, green (offset); green, black (intaglio); silver foil (letterpress); gray (offset back plate)

Size: 10 by 8 inches

Conceptual Design: Steve Manset, BEP

Designer and Modeler: Clarence Holbert, BEP

Paper Stock: White Poseidon Perfect

Printing: 6-color Miller offset sheetfed press; foil stamping on Kluge letterpress; intaglio die stamper

Quantity: 9,500

The Card

The Bureau of Engraving and Printing issued two souvenir cards in 1990 to honor philatelic exhibitions. Both of them had as their theme one of U.S. philately's most intriguing "might-have-beens."

This was the set of bicolored stamps the U.S. Post Office Department had originally planned to issue for the Trans-Mississippi and International Exposition, held in Omaha in 1898. The plan was scrapped after the coming of the Spanish-American War placed extra demands for revenue stamp production on the Bureau of Engraving and Printing, and the Trans-Mississippis were printed in conventional single colors. Even in that form the set is considered one of the most handsome groups of stamps the United States has ever produced. But, collectors agree, with black vignettes and colored frames they would have been truly spectacular.

Each of the two BEP philatelic souvenir cards of 1990 featured two intaglio die imprints, one of a Trans-Mississippi stamp as issued, the other of a two-color essay of a stamp of the same denomination. The first of these was issued April 20 for Aripex 1990, the Arizona Philatelic Exhibition, in Phoenix, Arizona.

The Aripex card had on its right side a die imprint of the 1¢ green stamp of the series (Scott 285), depicting Father Jacques Marquette preaching to Indians on the upper Mississippi River. On the left was an imprint of an essay of the same design, but with the center in black and the frame in green. Both die impressions were shown on white rectangles surrounded by a green offset-produced enlargement of the frame design of the 1¢ stamp. Above, in three lines of gold embossed lettering, were the words: "1890's/An American Renaissance/Bureau of Engraving and Printing."

The imprint of the issued version of the stamp had a black diagonal line across the lower right corner to prevent its use as postage, although, as many collectors have pointed out, it would be a strangely motivated individual indeed who would cut a stamp image from a card selling for $5.50 and try to use it to cheat the Postal Service out of a penny.

On the reverse side of the card was a text block describing the stamp images on the front and giving the background of the Trans-Mississippi stamp series. Although the text said that the William Lamprecht painting, *Marquette on the Mississippi,* was "loaned from Marquette University . . . to create the central scene on this stamp," the late George Sloane, an expert on the Trans-Mississippi stamps, has written that in actuality the Post Office Department hired a commercial photographer to go to the university and take a picture of the painting, for which he charged the department $3.

The 1¢ stamp was designed by BEP's R. Ostrander Smith. The vignette was engraved by G.F.C. Smillie, and the frame was engraved by Douglas S. Ronaldson.

The card was available by mail order from BEP for $5.50 mint or $5.75 with show cancellation.

On several previous occasions, stamps of the Trans-Mississippi series had been featured on souvenir cards. The $1 value (Scott 292), showing *Western Cattle in a Storm,* was reproduced in enlarged form on a Post Office Department card for Efimex in Mexico City in 1968. In 1983, for National Stamp Collecting Month, USPS issued a card depicting the $2 Bridge at St. Louis stamp (Scott 293), enlarged and bicolored. The next year the 10¢ Hardships of Emigration stamp (Scott 290) was reproduced, enlarged, on a USPS card for Ausipex 84 in Melbourne, and in 1986 BEP honored Lobex 86 in Long Beach, California, with a card that contained a block of four die impressions of the 50¢ Western Mining Prospector stamp (Scott 291) with the postage and denomination references removed.

STAMP WORLD LONDON 90 SOUVENIR CARD (USPS)

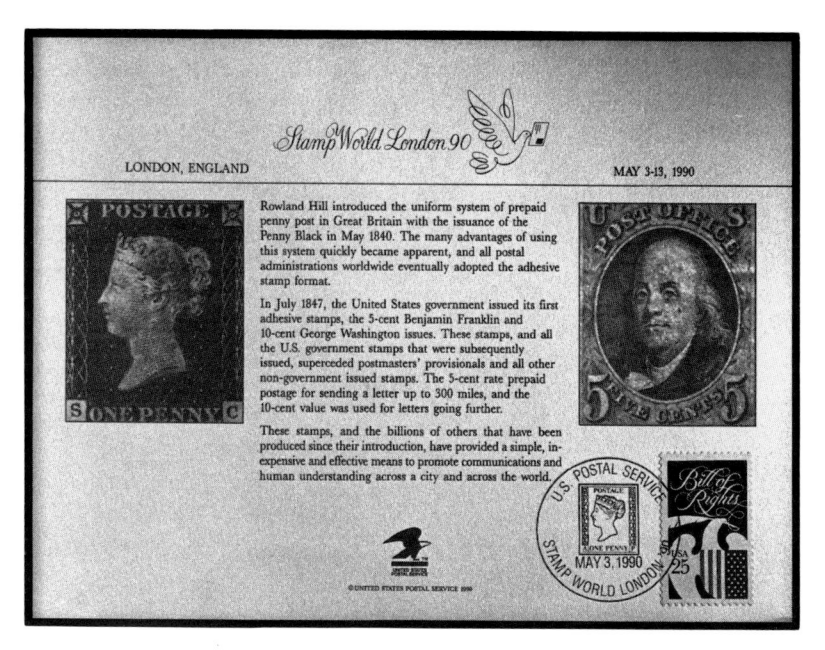

Date of Issue: May 3, 1990

Catalog Number: unassigned by Scott

Colors: black, red brown (PMS 1685)

Size: 8 by 6 inches

Project Manager and Designer: John Spiehs (USPS)

Paper Stock: Strathmore-Fairfield acid-free 120 lb. white stock

Printing: Offset litho by Associated Printers Inc., Baltimore, Maryland

Quantity: 70,000

The Card

On May 3 USPS issued a souvenir card for the Stamp World London 90 international philatelic exhibition that was held in Alexandra Palace in London, England, from May 3 to May 13. It was the only souvenir card produced by the Postal Service in 1990.

The card marked the 150th anniversary of the introduction by Sir Rowland Hill of the first adhesive postage stamp, the Penny Black. This was also the theme of the exhibition. The occasion would seem

304

to have been a natural for a commemorative stamp, and several other countries, including the Soviet Union, did observe the anniversary in that way. But USPS never seriously considered the idea.

"We didn't get an invitation to do so," said Don McDowell, director of the Postal Service's Office of Stamp and Philatelic Marketing. "The Citizens' Stamp Advisory Committee always basically looks at stamps with foreign themes from the standpoint of whether this country would be responding to the expressed wish of another one."

"The committee did discuss the Penny Black at one point," added Joe Brockert. "The members said, 'We don't think we should unilaterally issue a stamp, but if Great Britain asks us, we'll certainly consider it.'" No such request ever came.

Fifty years earlier, however, at the time of the centennial of the Penny Black, many U.S. stamp collectors and organizations actively supported the idea of a stamp or souvenir sheet for the occasion, and President Franklin D. Roosevelt wrote to Postmaster General James Farley that he thought that "participation in the centennial anniversary of the first adhesive postage stamp is excellent." A model of a souvenir sheet showing the first U.S. stamp — the 5¢ Franklin of 1847 (Scott 1) — was prepared for FDR's consideration.

But no stamp or sheet was ever issued. In the spring of 1940 Great Britain was at war with Nazi Germany, but the United States was officially neutral, and although FDR openly wished to aid the British war effort, he faced heavy domestic opposition to such a policy. So, when the president suddenly and unexpectedly told Farley to forget about a Penny Black commemorative, some persons believed it was because he wanted to avoid any kind of trivial controversy that might interfere with his larger goal.

Both the Penny Black and the 1847 U.S. Franklin stamp were depicted, in enlargement, on the USPS souvenir card that was issued for Stamp World London 90. The card bore the exhibition logo, a stylized dove carrying a letter, and carried textual information about the introduction of the two countries' first stamps.

The card was designed by John Spiehs of USPS and offset-printed by Associated Printers Inc. of Baltimore, Maryland. USPS lent the printer an unused copy of the U.S. stamp from its vault so the

This pictorial cancellation was offered by U.S. Postal Service at Stamp World London 90.

stamp's reddish-brown color could be matched on the souvenir card; for the Penny Black, the Postal Service furnished a transparency. USPS sold the card in two versions: mint ($2), and bearing a 25¢ Bill of Rights commemorative stamp of 1989 with the May 3 pictorial cancellation that USPS offered at London 90 ($2.25).

On two previous occasions the 5¢ 1847 stamp had been reproduced on souvenir cards, but both times it was paired with the 10¢ Washington stamp (Scott 2), which had been issued simultaneously. The first of these was a BEP card issued in 1971 for Anphilex 71 in New York City; it bore engraved images of the two stamps, with postage and denomination references removed. The second was a USPS card honoring San Marino 77, an international stamp exhibition held in that tiny country. It displayed reproductions of the first two U.S. stamps, along with San Marino's first issue.

STAMPSHOW 90
SOUVENIR CARD (BEP)

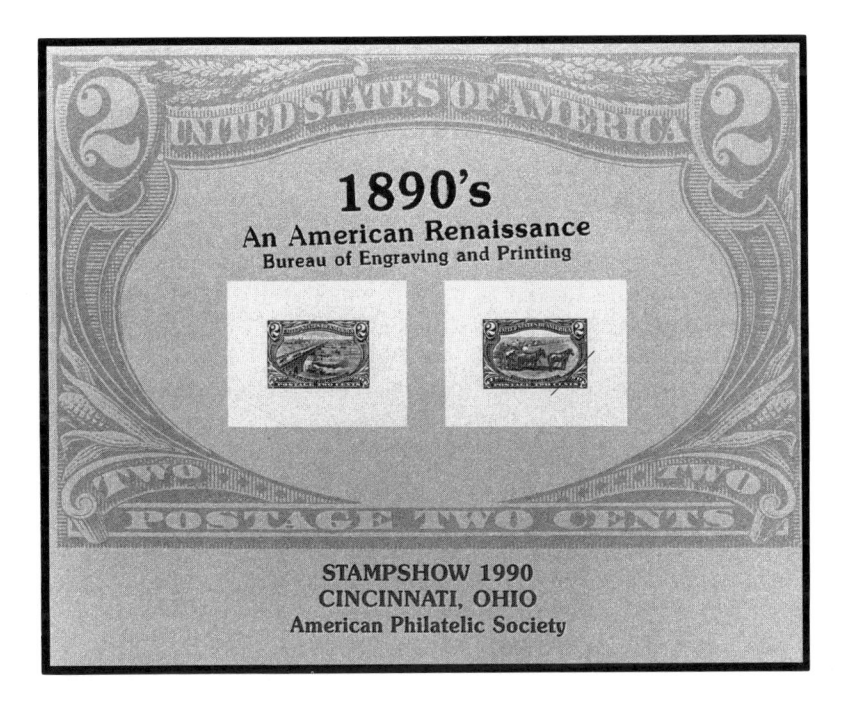

Date of Issue: August 23, 1990

Catalog Number: Scott 129

First-Day Release: Cincinnati, Ohio (Stampshow 90) and Washington, D.C. (BEP Visitor's Center)

Colors: gray, red, light red (offset); maroon, black (intaglio); silver foil (letterpress); gray (offset back plate)

Size: 10 by 8 inches

Conceptual Design: Steve Manset, BEP

Designer and Modeler: Clarence Holbert, BEP

Paper Stock: White Poseidon Perfect

Printing: 6-color Miller offset sheetfed press; foil stamping on Kluge letterpress; intaglio die stamper

Quantity: 9,500

The Card

The second and final 1990 Bureau of Engraving and Printing souvenir card was released August 23 at the American Philatelic Society's annual Stampshow, held this year at the Cincinnati Convention Center in Cincinnati, Ohio.

Like the Aripex 90 card issued earlier, this one featured two intaglio die impressions related to the Trans-Mississippi Exposition commemorative stamp series of 1898: one of a stamp actually issued in the series, and the other of a bicolored essay that wasn't actually put into production.

The nine Trans-Mississippi stamps were originally planned as bicolors, with frames of various colors around black vignettes. But the outbreak of the Spanish-American War in April 1898 created a sudden and large need — in those days before the income tax — for proprietary and documentary stamps to finance the U.S. war effort. The BEP had made dies and plates for printing the Trans-Mississippis in two colors, and die proofs exist of the set in that form, but in the end the decision was made to manufacture the commemoratives in single colors, a faster and less costly process.

On the right side of the Stampshow 1990 card was a die impression of the 2¢ Trans-Mississippi stamp as issued, in copper red color, with a vignette labeled "Farming in the West." This print was "canceled" with a diagonal black line across the lower right corner. On the left was a die-printed essay of the 2¢ denomination as it was originally intended to look. Not only was it a bicolor, with the frame in copper red and the center in black, but the vignette was different: It was titled "Mississippi River Bridge" and showed the triple-arched bridge at St. Louis that was designed and built by James Buchanan Eads and completed in 1874.

The Post Office Department's plan had been to depict the bridge on the 2¢ denomination and the farming scene on the $2 stamp, the highest value of the series. George B. Sloane, writing on the Trans-Mississippis in the 1943 *Stamp Specialist,* explained what happened:

"The transposition of the two pictures on the stamps, as eventually issued, is said to have occurred when the proofs were exhibited and discussed with the congressional postal committee. It was suggested that inasmuch as the 2¢ stamp was in wider circulation than the $2 value, the lower denomination should be more representative of the West and typify one of the purposes for which the Trans-Mississippi Exposition was being held, that is, to advertise and emphasize the natural advantages of the western part of the country. The farming element in the committee membership advanced the argument that the message carried by the 2¢ stamp should be an invitation, by suggestion, that 'the harvest awaits the reaper.' " Accordingly, the switch was made; it was the only such change made in the Trans-Mississippi set.

BEP's decision to place on the souvenir card the 2¢ essay showing the bridge offered most stamp collectors their first opportunity to study and appreciate the exquisitely detailed work that had been done on that particular vignette by the BEP's great engraver, Marcus W. Baldwin. Before that, the engraved image was generally accessible only on the rare $2 value in the stamp series.

The farming scene on the 2¢ denomination was from a photograph taken on one of the farms of the Amenia & Sharon Land Company near Amenia, North Dakota, and used as a lithograph on the company's stationery. It depicted several teamsters who were very much alive at the time and identifiable, despite U.S. policy forbidding the portrayal of living persons on stamps.

R. Ostrander Smith designed the 2¢ stamp, and the engravers were Marcus Baldwin (vignette) and Douglas S. Ronaldson (frame). The same BEP team also produced the $2 stamp. The source of that stamp's bridge vignette was an engraving on an admission ticket to the 1896 Republican National Convention in St. Louis.

On the Stampshow 1990 souvenir card, the two die impressions were set on white rectangles against a gray offset-printed background that reproduced in enlarged form, in red, the frame of the 2¢ Trans-Mississippi stamp. Above the die prints, in embossed gold lettering, was the inscription: "1890's/An American Renaissance/Bureau of Engraving and Printing." A block of type on the reverse side described the stamp images on the front and gave a brief account of the Trans-Mississippi stamp series.

The card was available by mail from BEP for $5.50 (mint) and $5.75 (canceled).

1990-91 DUCK STAMP SOUVENIR CARD (FISH AND WILDLIFE SERVICE)

Date of Issue: June 30, 1990

Catalog Number: none

First-Day Release: June 30, 1990, Washington, D.C. (Smithsonian Institution)
July 1, 1990, Plymouth, Minnesota

Colors: yellow, magenta, cyan, gray, black, black (offset); gold foil (letterpress); black (offset) text on back of card

Size: 10 by 8 inches

Designer, Typographer and Modeler: Clarence Holbert, BEP

Paper Stock: White Poseidon Perfect

Printing: 6-color Miller offset sheetfed press (4-subject plates); Kluge letterpress for gold foil stamping

Quantity: 10,000

The Card

For the fourth consecutive year, the National Fish and Wildlife Foundation, a non-profit organization chartered by Congress to support wildlife conservation projects, sponsored a duck stamp souvenir card to help fund its programs.

The card, offset-printed by the Bureau of Engraving and Printing, bore an enlarged replica of the 1990 duck stamp in full color, with simulated perforations around the edges, against a gray background. The card carried the signatures and the agency seals or logos of Manuel Lujan, secretary of the Interior; John Turner, director, U.S. Fish and Wildlife Service, and James Range, chairman, National Fish and Wildlife Foundation, plus the signature of duck stamp artist Jim Hautman of Plymouth, Minnesota.

Ten thousand cards were printed. These cards, with a specimen of the $12.50 stamp itself attached, were sold for varying prices. The least expensive were 8,250 cards without serial numbers or cancellations. Their price was $18 each.

The remaining 1,750 cards had "first-day" cancellations from Washington, D.C., where the cards went on sale June 30, and Bloomington, Minnesota, where they were first sold on July 1. Of these canceled cards, 1,000 bore no serial numbers and sold for $25 each, and 750 were numbered in gold and sold for $150 each (numbers 1 through 10), $75 each (11 through 100) or $50 each (101 through 750). The gold numbers were applied by letterpress.

The $12.50 cost of the stamp was deducted from the proceeds of each card, and the Washington-based Foundation retained the balance. After paying BEP for the printing costs, the Foundation used the funds for its conservation programs.

THE YEAR IN REVIEW

Plans announced for National Postal History and Philatelic Museum

Robert C. McAdams, secretary of the Smithsonian Institution, and Postmaster General Anthony M. Frank signed an agreement November 6 to relocate the National Philatelic Collection, now at the Smithsonian, to a new facility in Washington, D.C.

The National Postal History and Philatelic Museum will house and display the nation's philatelic and postal history collection, the largest and most comprehensive of its kind in the world. It consists of more than 12 million stamps and four million postal documents and artifacts, including a stagecoach, a 1921 Model T Ford equipped with skis, two airplanes and other vintage mail-carrying vehicles.

The new museum will be located in a section of the City Post Office Building on Massachusetts Avenue, next door to Union Station, and is expected to open in 1993. Renovation and construction costs for the new museum, estimated at $15.4 million, will be provided by USPS.

USPS will raise the money, Frank said, from a philatelic exposition similar to the 1989 World Stamp Expo, and "through the release of assorted philatelic materials." World Stamp Expo brought in revenues of approximately $20 million, which USPS used to defray the costs of hosting the 20th Universal Postal Congress.

The annual operating budget of the new museum calls for $3 million. Of this total, $2 million will be guaranteed by USPS and $1 million paid by the Smithsonian in direct and indirect costs. The latter sum is the same amount now being spent on the philatelic collection at the Museum of American History.

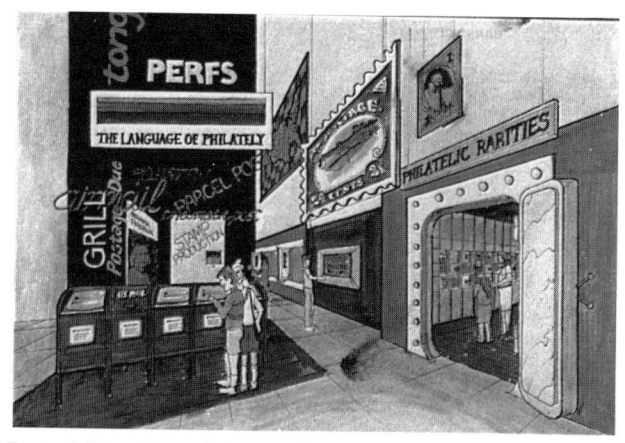

Part of the planned layout for the National Postal History and Philatelic Museum, including a vault exhibit of rarities.

The museum will occupy 76,000 square feet, including 34,700 square feet for exhibition space and 7,000 square feet for a research library. At present, only 8,600 square feet is devoted to these uses.

James H. Bruns was named acting director of the new museum. For the past three years, Bruns had served as deputy executive director of the National Philatelic Collection. He continues to hold the title of curator of postal history, as he has done since 1984.

CIA gives four inverts to Smithsonian

Four single copies of the so-called "CIA invert," the $1 Rush Lamp stamp of the Americana series (Scott 1610c) with the candle and holder inverted in relation to the flame, were transferred from the Central Intelligence Agency to the National Philatelic Collection at the Smithsonian Institution during the week of October 29.

At the same time, the CIA commented on the case for the first time. It was disclosed that the four copies sent to the Smithsonian had been returned to the CIA by four of the nine employees of that agency who sold a partial sheet of 86 stamps to error dealer Jacques Schiff in 1986. Four other employees involved in the sale had chosen to give up their jobs rather than return their four specimens of the invert, the CIA said. The ninth employee told the CIA the stamp he kept for himself was lost. The agency apparently believed him, and he was kept on the payroll.

The partial upper-right pane of 95 stamps, which was missing five stamps from the top horizontal row, including the plate number single, was originally purchased with CIA funds at a McLean, Virginia, post office substation on March 27, 1986. The error pane was later replaced by the employees with a pane of normal $1 stamps.

Each employee shared the profits of the sale and kept one invert for himself. The group had originally told a Bureau of Engraving and Printing investigator that nine of the stamps had been used for postage. It was later discovered that the employees had each kept a stamp.

The transfer of the four stamps brought to five the number of CIA inverts in the National Philatelic Collection. Another single had been donated by Donald Sundman, president of Mystic Stamp Company of Camden, New York, who purchased, with two partners, a total of 50 of the 86 stamps sold to Schiff.

USPS, BEP sign agreement on stamp production

For the first time in nearly a century of association, the U.S. Postal Service and the Bureau of Engraving and Printing signed a formal agreement specifying the terms under which BEP would provide postage stamps for USPS.

The five-year agreement was signed June 11 after more than three months of negotiations. It followed a December 1989 report to

Congress by the General Accounting Office that reviewed a decade of strained relations and misunderstandings between the two agencies and urged them to negotiate a settlement of their differences and a plan for the future.

"The purpose of this agreement," the preamble stated, "is to provide USPS with a reliable source for stamp production and to provide BEP with a commitment by which it can project long-term planning of capital investment, research and development, inventory of supplies and personnel needs."

BEP agreed to provide a specified but diminishing proportion of the USPS requirement for conventionally gummed stamps, excluding rate-change items, during the period. The percentages were: 80 percent for Fiscal Year 1991; 75 percent for FY 1992 and FY 1993, and 70 percent for FY 1994 and FY 1995. The FY 1991 percentage was based on a 40 billion stamp program. The product mix was defined as follows: Sheets (15 percent of the total program): commemoratives, 20 percent; aerogrammes, 1 percent; airmail sheets, 7 percent; prime rate, 25 percent; ordinary sheets and reprints, 47 percent. Booklets (30 percent of the total): commemoratives, 16 percent; prime rate, 84 percent. Coils (50 percent of the total): coils of 100, 66 percent; coils of 500, 14 percent; coils of 3,000, 20 percent.

The issue of rush jobs ordered by USPS was addressed in an article entitled "Leadtimes." The leadtimes for artwork and type mechanicals were listed as follows: single-color intaglio, 70 days before first-day sale (FDS); multicolor intaglio, 120 days before FDS; offset/intaglio (single image), 120 days before FDS; offset/intaglio (multiple image), 180 days before FDS; offset or gravure (up to five subjects), 120 days before printing; offset or gravure (more than five subjects), 270 days before printing; gravure/intaglio, to be determined on a case-by-case basis, "but no stamp will be accepted that requires tight registration."

Select (philatelic) stock was defined and the terms of its selection agreed upon. BEP agreed to provide select stock for the first year on a trial basis, and to inform USPS of its intent to continue to supply (or to cease to supply) such stock by January 1 preceding the start of the fiscal year to be affected. The quality of select stock had been a bone of contention; Carl V. D'Alessandro, BEP assistant director of operations, told *Linn's Stamp News* that "philatelic stamps are probably 15 percent of our stamp work, but they account for 90 percent of all the difficulties we have with the Postal Service."

BEP and USPS agreed to jointly evaluate a report commissioned by USPS from the consulting firm of Deloitte & Touche called "Study of Stamp Production via the Private Sector." This would include a preliminary assessment of a single-level, modern postage stamp printing and processing plant for BEP.

Procedures were established for billing, communications, meetings, quality standards and assurance, research and special projects, extensions of the agreement and other details. The signatories were Peter H. Daly, director of BEP, and Gordon C. Morison, assistant postmaster general, Philatelic and Retail Services Department.

New booklet producer signed

USPS announced September 25 that it had entered into a five-year contract with Banta Corporation of Menasha, Wisconsin, under which Banta would produce postage stamp booklets for the Postal Service. Banta was described as one of the nation's leading graphic arts companies, offering diverse printing and graphic/video services. USPS said its account would be serviced by two Banta Corporation subsidiaries, KCS Industries Inc. of Milwaukee, Wisconsin, which assumed overall responsibility for the account, and The Press Inc. of Chanhassen, Minnesota.

USPS hosts private-vendor conference

On June 18, USPS played host to a conference on stamp production attended by nearly 100 individuals representing 44 different printers and paper suppliers, including some from abroad.

The Postal Service held the conference and distributed solicitations for stamp printing contracts in order to open a dialogue with the private sector, officials said. They stressed to those attending that USPS will rely increasingly on private printers for stamp production as a result of its June 11 agreement with the Bureau of Engraving and Printing (see above).

All current stamp printing methods — intaglio, gravure, offset and offset/intaglio — were contained in the solicitations. A specification common to all solicitations was that the winning firm must be able to furnish select (or philatelic) stock for USPS to provide to collectors. August 3 was the date set for receipt of final proposals.

The solicitations gave collectors their first glimpse of what USPS had in mind for two major commemorative issues in the future. One was for a series of souvenir sheets for the 50th anniversary of World War II, to be issued at a rate of one each year from 1991 through 1995. Each sheet would contain 10 stamps surrounding a central map. The other was for a set of six souvenir sheets marking the 500th anniversary of Columbus' arrival in the New World in 1492. The sheets would exactly reproduce stamps of the 1893 Columbian Exposition issue; they would appear three to a sheet with the exception of the $5 value, which would occupy a sheet all its own. Plans for both issues were subject to change, USPS said.

CSAC changes

Jack Rosenthal, a broadcasting corporation executive and stamp collector of Casper, Wyoming, became chairman of the Citizens' Stamp Advisory Committee in July. He succeeded Belmont Faries, who retired as chairman after 15 years in that post but remained a committee member. Rosenthal was appointed to CSAC in 1985.

Postmaster General Frank announced the appointment of five new members to the committee October 2. They were: David Lewis Eynon, executive vice president of Amichetti, Lewis & Associates Inc., Bryn Mawr, Pennsylvania; Bernard Hennig Sr., attorney and international philatelic judge, Chicago; Karl Malden, actor and president of the Academy of Motion Picture Arts and Sciences, Beverly Hills, California; Stephen T. McLin, president, American First Financial Corporation, San Francisco, California, and Robert H. Power, general partner, Nut Tree Restaurant, Nut Tree, California.

Free franking for the troops

U.S. troops participating in Operation Desert Shield, the military deployment in the Persian Gulf area, were granted the franking privilege on September 12 by Postmaster General Frank.

The order allowed military personnel in the area to mail letters and audio cassettes free, without stamps, to destinations in the United States by merely writing the word "Free" on the envelopes where the stamps would normally go. The privilege didn't apply to parcels or to mail to foreign destinations. Under legislation passed by Congress and signed by President Bush, all costs for free-franked mail were reimbursed to USPS by the Department of Defense.

In the early days of Operation Desert Shield, service personnel complained that stamps were hard to come by in Saudi Arabia and those that were available tended to stick together because of heat, humidity and perspiration. On September 7 USPS announced it was shipping more than 400,000 Eagle and Shield self-adhesive stamps to U.S. forces in the Gulf area and would sell them for face value ($4.50 for a booklet of 18 25¢ stamps), waiving the 50¢ surcharge assessed for the stamps in the United States. However, Postmaster General Frank's September 12 announcement meant the need for stamps by the troops would be sharply reduced.

Autopost experiment discontinued

The four experimental Autopost machines in the Washington, D.C., area were removed from service May 7. These dispensers of computer-printed self-adhesive postage strips, in denominations specified by the purchaser, had been used in an experimental program at two locations — the White Flint Mall in Kensington, Maryland, and the Martin Luther King station in Washington. The experimental program began August 23, 1989. Two additional machines had been set up at the 20th Universal Postal Congress that met at the Washington Arena in November and December 1989. The machines were inaccessible to the public and were taken out of service at the end of the congress.

USPS said the experiment was highly successful as a learning experience. However, the machines were not of a type that could be mass-produced for USPS, officials explained.

The Autopost strips became popular with collectors. A limited number of first-day-dated strips were created and sold by the Philatelic Sales Division, although they were never listed in the division's *Philatelic Catalog.* Speculation as to whether the items would be recognized by Scott was ended when the *1991 Specialized Catalogue of United States Stamps* came out containing a section devoted to "Computer Vended Postage" that listed 26 basic Autopost varieties, representing various denominations/classes of postage from the four machines, in the two basic design types that were sold.

BEP runs out of paper

At one point in 1990, the Bureau of Engraving and Printing ran out of LP40 paper, an intaglio paper used to print a number of current definitive stamps. BEP said that 92.5 percent of the 1990 production of LP40 paper stamps had been completed prior to the shortage. The Bureau had enough forewarning of the impending shortage that USPS could advise postmasters, in the September 6 issue of *Postal Bulletin,* that they might experience shortages of certain stamps, including numerous Great Americans sheet and booklet stamps and Transportation coils. During the shortage, postmasters were authorized to accept false frankings (bulk-rate stamps of the "wrong" denominations, with the mailer later charged for or credited with the difference).

USPS sponsors stamp art contest

USPS invited artists to submit designs for a 1992 Olympic Games stamp, to be issued as part of a unified Olympic sponsorship program in which USPS and 30 other postal administrations around the world would participate. Each country would conduct its own stamp art contest and select a single design to be developed as a finished stamp and issued in its nation, USPS said. The stamps would commemorate the Olympic Games and be jointly issued during worldwide dedication ceremonies held between the 1992 Winter and Summer Olympics.

Artists were told that their designs must represent Olympic baseball and be in color. An entry fee of $100 was required. Entries would be screened by a panel of experts in philately, art and printing, USPS said, and the top 100 designs would go to the Citizens' Stamp Advisory Committee, which would select a single winner.

The winning artist would receive $3,000 and be sent by USPS to the 1992 Summer Games in Barcelona, Spain.

Classic Mail Transportation block tops *Linn's* stamp poll

The perforated block of four commemorative stamps showing forms of classic mail transportation was voted the most popular U.S. stamp issue of 1989 by *Linn's Stamp News* readers. Voter participation was the heaviest in the annual poll's 41-year history.

The Classic Mail Transportation stamps were designed by Mark Hess of Katonah, New York. They were printed by BEP on its combination offset/intaglio D press.

The winning block received 690 of the more than 4,900 votes cast in the poll. The runner-up was the $2.40 Priority Mail stamp marking the 20th anniversary of the first manned moon landing, which received 573 votes. The Prehistoric Animals block of four was third, with 451. At the other end of the scale, the Hull House postal card, 25¢ security mailing envelope and sheet of four Cityscape postal cards tied for least popular issue with two votes apiece.

Results in other categories included:

Definitives, best design: $2.40 Priority Mail, 2,613; 25¢ Eagle and Shield self-adhesive, 497; 28¢ Sitting Bull, 397. Definitives, worst design: Eagle and Shield, 1,407; 1¢ Official Mail, 862; Sitting Bull, 538. Definitives, most important: Priority Mail, 2,046; Eagle and Shield, 561; Sitting Bull, 513. Definitives, least necessary: Eagle and Shield, 1,350; 1¢ Official Mail, 1,262; Sitting Bull, 456.

Postal Stationery, best design: Space Station hologram stamped envelope, 917; Jefferson Memorial postal card, 694; Oklahoma Land Run postal card, 359. Postal Stationery, worst design: Love envelope, 975; Space Station, 604; Security envelope, 449. Postal Stationery, most important: Space Station, 727; Montgomery Blair aerogram, 404; White House postal card, 364. Postal Stationery, least necessary: Love envelope, 1,067; Space Station, 474; Philatelic Mail envelope, 461.

Commemoratives, most important: Bill of Rights bicentennial, 1,480; World Stamp Expo, 408; French Revolution bicentennial (45¢ airmail), 386. Commemoratives, least important: Letter Carriers, 919; Prehistoric Animals block of four, 711; America (45¢ airmail), 492. Commemoratives, best design: Classic Mail block of four, 1,043; Steamboats booklet, 540; Prehistoric Animals block, 466. Commemoratives, worst design: Letter Carriers, 1,435; Bill of Rights, 491; U.S. Senate bicentennial, 272.

Another poll, conducted by *Stamp Collector,* found the $2.40 Priority Mail stamp to be the overall favorite for 1989. No figures were given, but *Stamp Collector* said the Priority Mail stamp "squeaked by" the Classic Mail Transportation block. Third was the

Prehistoric Animals block, fourth was the Steamboats booklet and fifth was the Space Station envelope.

USPS bulletin informs clerks that imperf items are valid

USPS took action March 22 to inform its employees that a group of imperforate stamps issued in 1989 — the souvenir sheets commemorating World Stamp Expo and the self-adhesive Eagle and Shield definitive — were good for postage.

The *Postal Bulletin* for that date contained a full-page pull-out poster picturing each of the souvenir sheets and the Eagle and Shield stamp. "Some offices are incorrectly returning letters and packages bearing stamps from these souvenir sheets," the poster said. "Please advise all employees who verify postage that these souvenir sheets, whether used entirely or separately, are acceptable as postage."

The poster bore a similar message for the Eagle and Shield stamp,

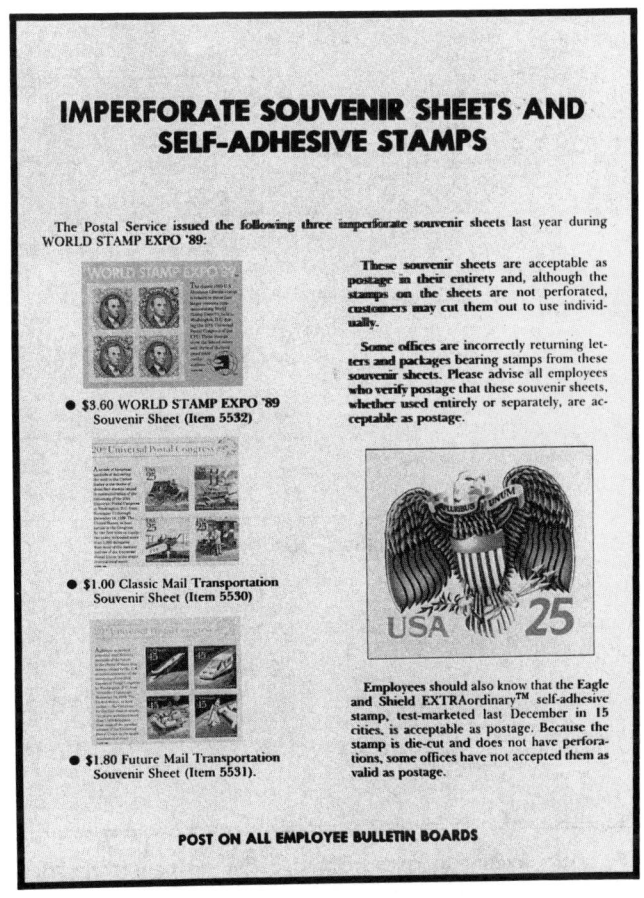

This pull-out poster was included in the March 22 issue of the U.S. Postal Service's Postal Bulletin.

which "some offices have not accepted . . . as valid as postage."

Inverted Jenny arrow block sold at auction

The unique left arrow block of the U.S. 24¢ inverted Jenny airmail stamp (Scott C3a) was auctioned for $297,000, which included the 10-percent buyer's premium, by Christie's, New York, on October 25. The block was part of the stock built up by Raymond and Roger Weill, stamp dealers of New Orleans, and sold to a London bank. In 1989, from the same stock, Christie's had sold the inverted Jenny plate number block of four for $1.1 million and a line block of four for $528,000, both figures including the premium.

VARIETIES

Block tagging ends

Several stamps that previously were block tagged appeared with overall tagging in 1990 as a result of a Bureau of Engraving and Printing production decision.

A BEP spokesman told *Linn's Stamp News* in December that all future stamps produced by the Bureau would have "full-coverage tagging." That meant that all printings of new and existing stamps would either have overall tagging or would be printed on pre-phosphored or phosphor-coated paper. By the end of the year, the following stamps that originally were produced with block tagging had been discovered with overall tagging: 20¢ Harry Truman (Scott 1862), 4¢ Stagecoach coil (Scott 1898A), 10¢ Red Cloud (Scott 2176), 15¢ Buffalo Bill Cody (Scott 2178), 25¢ Jack London (Scott 2183), 45¢ Harvey Cushing (Scott 2188), $1 Johns Hopkins (Scott 2194A), 15¢ Tugboat (Scott 2260) and 20¢ Cable Car (Scott 2263). In each case the new variety appeared with no advance notice from USPS or BEP.

For years, BEP had avoided overall tagging because the taggant wore out perforating pins and other processing equipment. But

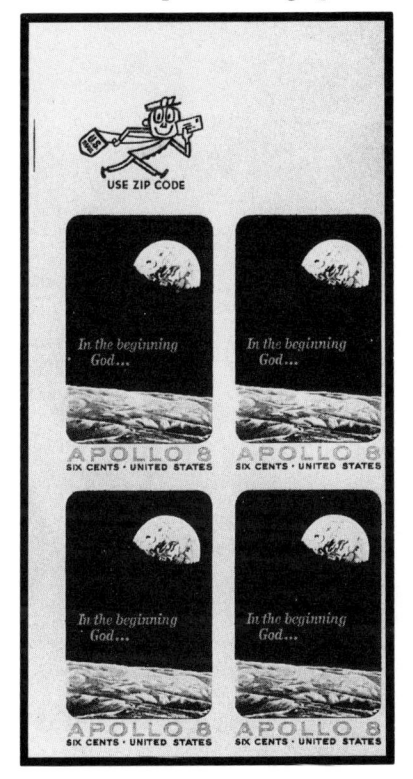

An imperforate block of four from an imperforate pane of 50 Apollo 8 commemoratives that remained hidden for 21 years.

321

This is the ZIP block from a complete pane of Antarctic Explorers stamps that was found horizontally imperforate.

block tagging presented registration problems, and BEP's eventual finding that the taggant had only minimal effect on its high-speed equipment cleared the way for the change.

Possibly as a result of the conversion, two untagged errors were reported by collectors late in the year. Rolls of untagged Tugboat coils were found in California, and untagged Johns Hopkins sheet stamps turned up in Indiana. In addition, an older untagged error came to light: It was on an 11¢ Stutz Bearcat coil (Scott 2131).

Imperforate Apollo 8 pane surfaces

An imperforate pair of the 6¢ Apollo 8 commemorative of 1969 (Scott 1371a) was auctioned by Jacques C. Schiff Jr. during the American Stamp Dealers Association's national show November 1-4 at New York's Madison Square Garden. The block sold for $1,900,

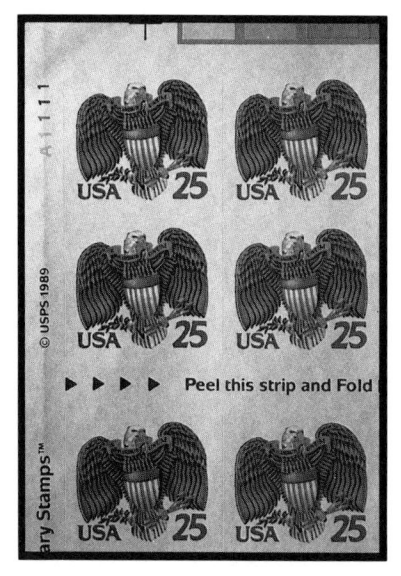

A horizontally uncut error, discovered on a single pane of the Eagle and Shield self-adhesive, is the first of its kind on a U.S. stamp. The pane's upper-right pair was sold at auction. Other collectible positions from the error pane could include vertical pairs or strips with a gutter between.

plus a 10-percent buyer's commission.

The Apollo 8 stamp was printed on the Giori press by BEP. The pair sold at auction was from a full upper-right pane of 50, completely imperforate, that a collector in eastern Pennsylvania bought at a local post office in June 1969. He put the pane in storage for 21 years. In 1990 Schiff handled the sale of the pane to an unidentified buyer for an undisclosed price. The new owner later consigned the imperforate pair to be auctioned by Schiff.

Antarctic Explorers found imperforate between

A full pane of 50 of the 1988 Antarctic Explorers stamps was discovered horizontally imperforate (Scott 2389c). The stamps, which consisted of four se-tenant designs, were produced by the American Bank Note Company and perforated on an L perforator, which perforates in only one direction at a time. The ZIP block was

Shown here is the plate block from a pane of Classic Mail Transportation stamps of 1989 completely missing the blue intaglio ink ("USA 25"), the only line-engraved design elements on the stamps.

323

sold by Jacques Schiff at a September 13-14 auction for $1,900, plus a 10-percent buyer's commission.

Eagle and Shield die-cutting error found

A single pane of 18 of the 25¢ Eagle and Shield self-adhesive stamp of 1989, which was die-cut rather than perforated, was found without horizontal die-cutting (Scott 2431b). The error was the first of its kind on a U.S. stamp. The pane showed faint vertical die-cutting. There was speculation that the pane had stuck to another pane as it passed through the die-cutting equipment.

The Eagle and Shield stamps were die-cut by Label Systems Inc. after being printed by Sennett Enterprises for the American Bank Note Company on a leased gravure press at J.W. Fergusson and Sons. Jacques Schiff sold the pane's upper right vertical pair for $360, plus a 10-percent buyer's fee, at his December 7 auction.

Classic Mail Transportation pane lacks intaglio blue

A collector in Oregon found a pane of 40 Classic Mail Trans-

A used single 1986 Christmas Madonna stamp was discovered with the brown "Christmas" completely omitted. A normal stamp is shown in the inset.

Prehistoric Animals stamps with the black engraved portion completely missing turned up in California and Ohio.

portation commemoratives of 1989 completely missing the blue intaglio ink (USA 25). This typography was the only line-engraved design element on the stamps (Scott 2437b), which consisted of four se-tenant designs and were printed by the offset/intaglio D press at BEP. The complete error pane was sold in a private transaction through dealer Jacques Schiff.

Christmas stamp found with color omitted

The first major error to be found on the 1986 traditional Christmas stamp (Scott 2244) was a used single, still on piece, completely missing the special brown used only to print the word "Christmas" across the top of the stamp. The stamp was printed by the gravure process by BEP, and although other brown tones appeared in the design, they were printed by mixing color dots of the magenta, yellow and cyan process inks.

The error copy received a May 9, 1990, American Philatelic Society expertizing certificate stating that the stamp was genuine. The stamp was sold in the July 18-19 Jacques Schiff auction for $850, plus a 10-percent buyer's commission.

Prehistoric Animals stamps lose their typography

Sixty copies of the se-tenant Prehistoric Animals stamps of 1989 surfaced with the intaglio black portion of the design omitted (Scott 2425b). This comprised all the lettering and numerals on the stamps, leaving the error copies with their offset images looking much like dinosaur labels.

Jacques Schiff told *Linn's Stamp News* that 20 stamps with the color-missing error were bought from a USPS vending machine in

California. The stamps were folded into a small glassine $5 vending pack envelope, making the perforations quite fragile. Schiff sold a block of the error stamps, separated into two pairs, for $1,100, plus a 10-percent buyer's premium, at his September 13-14 sale.

Bill Langs, another U.S. error specialist dealer, reported the discovery of two more $5 vending packs, each with 20 error stamps. One was discovered in California and the other in Cleveland, Ohio.

CARE stamps, black omitted, turn up 19 years later

A portion of a pane of the 1971 8¢ CARE commemorative with black omitted (Scott 1439a) was found by a Texas collector late in 1989. It was the first discovery of an error in this issue in the 19 years since its release.

The stamp was printed by BEP on the Andreotti gravure press. A total of 10 copies on the pane of 50 have the color-missing error. Other stamps on the same pane have partially missing black.

According to Jacques Schiff, the finder was breaking down the pane for postage when he noticed the color omission. Schiff auctioned the plate block of eight, containing four error stamps, for $15,000, plus a 10-percent buyers' commission, in his March 30-31 sale.

This is the plate block of eight CARE stamps that was sold at auction. Ten stamps (two vertical strips of five) from a pane of 50 were discovered with the black completely missing, including the black cylinder number.

Two major errors found on Priority Mail stamp

The $2.40 Priority Mail stamp of 1989, issued to commemorate the 20th anniversary of the first U.S. moon landing and printed in intaglio and offset on BEP's combination D press, was found in 1990 with not one but two major errors.

The first to be reported consisted of two full 20-stamp panes that completely lacked the black intaglio ink that provided details of the two astronauts' space suits and the lunar surface. Also missing was the single-digit intaglio sleeve number that normally would appear in the selvage adjacent to the four corner stamps. Small spots of black and blue appeared in the design portion on the white "dropout" images where the intaglio black should have been, but they appeared to be spatters of offset ink.

The error stamps were discovered by an unidentified collector who bought 10 Priority Mail panes at the Oak Forest station of the Houston, Texas, post office. Upon examination, the collector found the two error panes in the middle of the group. Bob Dumaine of Sam Houston Philatelics of Houston bought both panes from the finder. The error was given the Scott catalog designation 2419a.

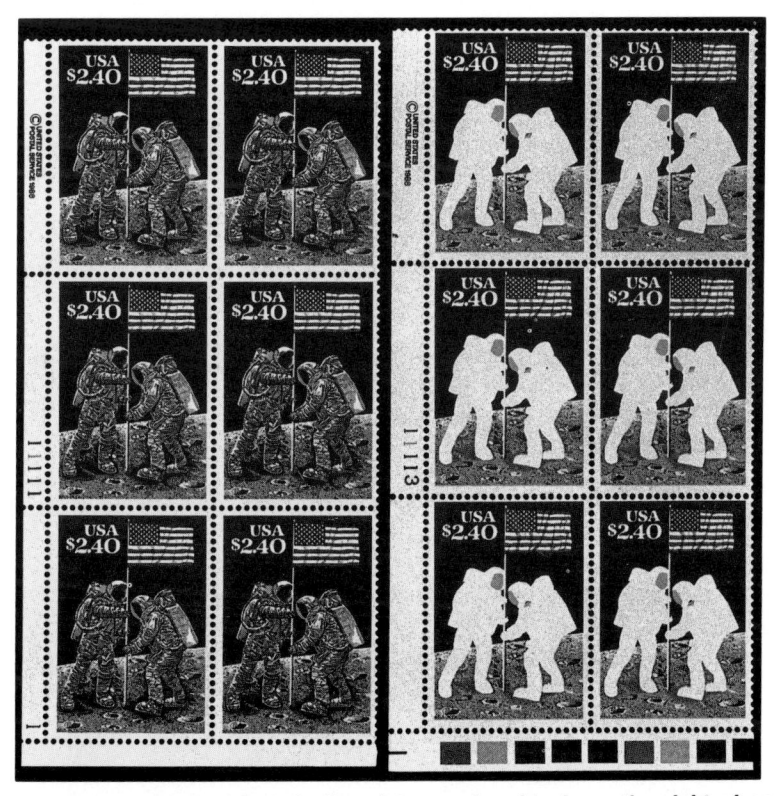

The missing intaglio black in the plate number block on the right gives the white images a ghostly appearance. A normal block is on the left.

Later in the year, collectors learned of the discovery in California of two full panes and one partial pane of imperforate Priority Mail stamps (Scott 2419b). Merle Spencer, owner of The Stamp Gallery in Walnut Creek, California, purchased the error stamps from a collector who manages a company in the area on the east side of San Francisco Bay. Five stamps from one pane had already been cut and used for postage. Spencer declined to identify the company, and the individual who bought the stamps wouldn't identify the post office where they were obtained.

'Loveless' Love envelope found in box of 500

A New Jersey office worker discovered a single copy of the 1989 Love envelope missing the offset red and dark blue colors. It was the last envelope in a box of 500 that had been purchased for business use.

The variety came about as the result of the two-press operation used to produce the envelope by Westvaco-USEnvelope Division of Williamsburg, Pennsylvania. Westvaco's VH machine flex-

A corner block from an imperforate Priority Mail pane.

The Love stamped envelope with the indicium missing contrasts with the normal copy that is overlapped at the top of this illustration.

ographically printed an overall pattern of narrow, light blue diagonal lines on the front of the web, and a copyright inscription on the reverse. After the envelopes were formed, the red and dark blue "love!/USA 25" indicium was applied by a two-color offset Jet press. The accidental omission of the second step created the error.

The envelope was sold for $500, plus a 10-percent buyer's premium, in the July 18-19 sale of William A. Fox Auctions, Springfield, New Jersey.

Oil Wagon 'second' precancel also found imperforate

The 10.1¢ Oil Wagon coil stamp of the Transportation series was issued in 1985 in two forms: tagged-unprecanceled, and untagged and bearing the overprint "Bulk Rate" in black. In 1988, after a rate change, it was reissued in the untagged-precanceled form, but with a new imprint in red: "Bulk Rate/Carrier Route Sort." The first overprinted version had previously been found imperforate, and in 1990 the second version turned up with the same kind of error.

The 10.1¢ Oil Wagon coil stamp with Bulk Rate/Carrier Route Sort precancel was found imperforate, just as its predecessor had been.

The pair of stamps shows a transition from a stamp with the black color partially missing (left) to one with the black completely missing. A normal stamp is shown at right for comparison.

(Scott, following its policy of not differentiating among precancels, acknowledged the existence of two distinct overprints but assigned both errors the same catalog number, 2130b.)

A single roll containing an undisclosed number of the imperforate second-version precancels was found by New Jersey dealer William S. Langs. Dale Hendricks, proprietor of Dale Enterprises Inc. of Emmaus, Pennsylvania, offered imperforate pairs for $14.95, which was believed to be the lowest price at which a newly found U.S. error had ever been initially offered to the collecting public. Plate number strips of six were advertised for $199.

Color-omitted error found on New Jersey stamp

A major color-omitted error on the gravure-printed 22¢ New Jersey Statehood stamp (Scott 2338) was found, slightly more than three years after the stamp's September 11, 1987, release. The error stamps were missing the black color, which on a normal stamp provided the statehood date, "USA 22," a flock of birds flying across the sun in the stamp design, and some shading in the picture.

According to dealer Jacques Schiff, five affected stamps were found by an individual in the Syracuse, New York, area who was breaking up the pane for use on mail. All were from the bottom row of the pane. Four of the stamps were complete color-omitted errors, and the fifth was a transition freak showing some of the black coloring. A pair, with the transition stamp on the left and a color-omitted stamp on the right, was sold by Schiff in his February 8-9, 1991, sale for $5,060, including the 10-percent buyer's premium.

The 22¢ New Jersey Statehood stamp was printed by the American Bank Note Company.

PLATE NUMBERS

All reported plate numbers for Transportation coil stamps.

Prior Transportation Coils (not precanceled)

1¢ Omnibus (1983) 1,2,3,4,5,6
1¢ Omnibus (1986) 1,2
2¢ Locomotive (1982) 2,3,4,6,8,10
2¢ Locomotive (1987) 1
3¢ Handcar (1983) 1,2,3,4
3¢ Conestoga Wagon (1988) 1
3.4¢ School Bus (1985) 1,2
4¢ Stagecoach (1982) 1,2,3,4,5,6
4¢ Stagecoach (1986) 1
4.9¢ Buckboard (1985) 3,4
5¢ Motorcycle (1983) 1,2,3,4
5¢ Milk Wagon (1987) 1
5.2¢ Sleigh (1983) 1,2,3,5
5.5¢ Star Route Truck (1986) 1
5.9¢ Bicycle (1982) 3,4
6¢ Tricycle (1985) 1
7.1¢ Tractor (1987) 1
7.4¢ Baby Buggy (1984) 2
8.3¢ Ambulance (1985) 1,2
8.5¢ Tow Truck (1987) 1
9.3¢ Mail Wagon (1981) 1,2,3,4,5,6
10¢ Canal Boat (1987) 1
10.1¢ Oil Wagon (1985) 1
10.9¢ Hansom Cab (1982) 1,2
11¢ Caboose (1984) 1
11¢ Stutz Bearcat (1985) 1,2,3,4
12¢ Stanley Steamer (1985) 1,2
12.5¢ Pushcart (1985) 1,2
14¢ Iceboat (1985) 1,2,3,4
14¢ Iceboat (1986) 2
15¢ Tugboat (1988) 1,2
17¢ Electric Auto (1981) 1,2,3,4,5,6,7
17¢ Dog Sled (1986) 2
17.5¢ Racing Car (1987) 1
18¢ Surrey (1981) 1 through 18 complete
20¢ Fire Pumper (1981) 1 through 16 complete
20¢ Cable Car (1988) 1,2
25¢ Bread Wagon (1986) 1 through 5 complete

1990 Transportation Coils (not precanceled)

5¢ Circus Wagon 1
$1 Seaplane 1

Prior Transportation Coils (precanceled)

3.4¢ School Bus (1985) 1,2
4¢ Stagecoach (1982) 3,4,5,6
4.9¢ Buckboard (1985) 1,2,3,4,5,6
5.2¢ Sleigh (1983) 1,2,3,4,5,6
5.3¢ Elevator (1988) 1
5.5¢ Star Route Truck (1986) 1,2
5.9¢ Bicycle (1982) 3,4,5,6
6¢ Tricycle (1985) 1,2
7.1¢ Tractor (1987) 1
7.1¢ Tractor (1989) 1
7.4¢ Buggy (1984) 2
7.6¢ Carreta (1988) 1,2,3
8.3¢ Ambulance (1985) 1,2,3,4
8.3¢ Ambulance (1986) 1,2
8.4¢ Wheel Chair (1988) 1,2,3
8.5¢ Tow Truck (1987) 1,2
9.3¢ Mail Wagon (1981) 1,2,3,4,5,6,8
10.1¢ Oil Wagon (1985) 1,2
10.1¢ Oil Wagon (1988) 2,3
10.9¢ Hansom Cab (1982) 1,2,3,4
11¢ Caboose (1984) 1
12¢ Stanley Steamer (1985) 1,2
12¢ Stanley Steamer (1987) 1
12.5¢ Pushcart (1985) 1,2
13¢ Patrol Wagon (1988) 1
13.2¢ Coal Car (1988) 1,2
16.7¢ Popcorn Wagon (1988) 1,2
17¢ Electric Auto (1981) 1,2,3,4,5,6,7
17.5¢ Racing Car (1987) 1
20.5¢ Fire Engine (1988) 1
21¢ Railroad Mail Car (1988) 1,2
24.1¢ Tandem Bicycle (1988) 1

ITEMS WITHDRAWN FROM SALE IN 1990

Commemoratives: 1988 $5 25¢ Classic Cars booklet, (10/31)
1989 25¢ Montana Statehood, (2/28)
1989 25¢ A. Philip Randolph, (2/28)
1989 25¢ Washington Statehood, (4/30)
1989 25¢ North Dakota Statehood, (4/30)
1989 25¢ Arturo Toscanini, (4/30)
1989 25¢ World Stamp Expo '89, (4/30)
1989 25¢ U.S. House of Representatives, (6/30)
1989 25¢ U.S. Senate, (6/30)
1989 25¢ U.S. Executive Branch, (6/30)
1989 $3.60 World Stamp Expo 89 souvenir sheet, (8/30)
1989 $1.00 UPU Classic Mail Transportation souvenir sheet, (8/30)
1989 25¢ South Dakota Statehood, (10/31)
1989 25¢ Lou Gehrig, (10/31)
1989 25¢ North Carolina Statehood, (10/31)
1989 25¢ Ernest Hemingway, (10/31)
1989 25¢ UPU Classic Mail Transportation (4 designs), (11/20)

Definitives: 1973 $1 Eugene O'Neill coil, (6/30)
1985 22¢ John James Audubon, Eureka perforator, (12/31)
1986 5¢ Hugo Black, (sold out as of 3/1)
1987 22¢ Flag over Capitol, prephosphored, (2/28)
1988 $5 25¢ Pheasant booklet, (2/28)
1988 $5 25¢ Jack London booklet (12/31)

Airmails: 1989 $1.80 UPU Future Mail Transportation souvenir sheet, (8/30)
1989 45¢ French Revolution, (10/31)
1989 45¢ UPU Future Mail Transportation (4 designs), (11/20)

Postal Cards: 1988 15¢ Iowa Territory, (10/31)
1988 15¢ Hearst Castle, (10/31)
1988 15¢ Federalist Papers, (12/31)
1989 15¢ New York Cityscape, (10/31)
1989 15¢ Hull House, (12/31)
1989 15¢ Healy Hall, (12/31)
1989 15¢ Settling of Oklahoma, (12/31)

Duck Stamps: 1987 $10 Redheads, (8/30)

Souvenir Cards: 1987 Hafnia 1987, mint, (11/20)
1987 Hafnia 1987, canceled, (11/20)
1987 Monte Carlo 1987, mint, (11/20)
1987 Monte Carlo 1987, canceled, (11/20)
1989 World Stamp Expo 89, mint, (11/20)
1989 World Stamp Expo 89, canceled, (11/20)

Maximum Cards: 1987 Locomotives, canceled on reverse, (2/28)
1987 Locomotives, canceled on front, (2/28)
1987 Locomotives, mint, (4/30)
1988 Classic Cars, mint, (11/20)
1988 Classic Cars, canceled, (11/20)
1989 UPU, mint, (11/20)
1989 UPU, canceled, (11/20)

1989 FIRST-DAY CANCELLATION TOTALS

The following are first-day cancellations for 1989 issues unreported in the 1989 *Yearbook*.

25¢ Eagle and Shield pressure-sensitive stamp (108,225)
$3.60 World Stamp Expo 89 souvenir sheet (281,725)
25¢ Classic Mail Transportation block of four (916,389)
$1 Classic Mail Transportation souvenir sheet (241,634)
45¢ Future Mail Transportation block of four (765,479)
$1.80 Future Mail Transportation souvenir sheet (257,826)
45¢ Montgomery Blair aerogram (48,529)
15¢ Washington, D.C., Cityscape postal card (47,146)
15¢ The White House picture postal card (52,090)
15¢ Jefferson Memorial picture postal card (59,568)
60¢ Cityscapes postal cards sheet of four (38,439)
25¢ Space Station hologram envelope (131,245)

ERRATA

We are grateful to Richard C. Sennett, president of Sennett Enterprises Inc. for correcting the record in the 1989 *Linn's U.S. Stamp Yearbook* as follows:

1. The gravure printing cylinders for the Lou Gehrig and Ernest Hemingway commemorative stamps (pages 75, 84) were manufactured by McKay/Gravure Systems, Florence, Kentucky, rather than by Roto Cylinder of Palmyra, New Jersey.

2. The Christmas Greetings sheet stamp (page 154) and commemoratives furnished by the American Bank Note Company were printed by ABNC's subcontractor, Sennett Enterprises, rather than by ABNC itself, although ABNC provided security for the printing operations. "The difference between the commemorative issues and all other gravure issues furnished by ABNC is the fine distinction between Sennett Enterprises' role as a consultant/printing manager for ABNC and its role as a subcontractor," Sennett wrote.

3. "The exact role of all the players in the (Eagle and Shield) pressure-sensitive stamp issue becomes confusing," Sennett continued (pages 180-181). "ABNC was the prime contractor for this issue. Sennett Enterprises modeled the stamp, prepared the layouts and completed all other pre-press work, printed the issue, arranged for and supervised other operations except for security, examination, packaging and forming into final 5,004-stamp coils. These finishing operations were carried out by ABNC at its Chicago plant.

"The web was printed on both sides in one pass through a seven-station gravure press at J.W. Fergusson and Sons in Richmond, Virginia. Press rolls were slit and rewound into three rolls, two of which were two booklets wide and one of coil stamp width. The slit rewound work was shipped to Label Systems Inc. for die-cutting and sheeting in multiple booklet sheets or, in the case of coil stamps, die-cut, matrix-stripped and rewound into large rolls. ABNC shipped all material to the Chicago plant for examination, packaging and delivery to USPS. ABNC provided security for all activities, with security officers present at each operation."

Also: In the chapter on the Stampshow 89 souvenir card (page 324), the intaglio colors listed should include blue, the color of the stamp die imprint on the card.